THE ART AND MIND OF SHAW

THE ART AND MIND OF SHAW

Essays in Criticism

A. M. Gibbs

St. Martin's Press   New York

All rights reserved. For information, write:
St. Martin's Press, Inc., 175 Fifth Avenue, New York, NY 10010
Printed in Hong Kong
First published in the United States of America in 1983

ISBN 0-312-04992-7

Library of Congress Cataloging in Publication Data

Gibbs, A. M. (Anthony Matthew), 1933–
    The art and mind of Shaw.

    Includes index.
    1. Shaw, Bernard, 1856–1950 — Criticism and
interpretation.   I. Title.
PR5367.G48   1983   822'.912   82-19158
ISBN 0-312-04992-7

Contents

Preface

This study presents an exploration of Shaw's dramatic art, which takes into account his masterly use of all the various 'languages' of the theatre in the creation of meaning. Eighteen of the plays are studied in depth and some consideration is given, where appropriate, to other dramatic and non-dramatic writings of Shaw. A close study is made of his use of key thematic images and allusions in the plays, and of his manipulation of source material derived from opera, drama and prose fiction. The play texts themselves are the central subject of discussion, but in some cases they also provide a focal point for more general analysis of Shaw's treatment of such topics as the relations of the sexes, politics and economics, religion and race.

The biographical introduction in Chapter 1 is concerned with Shaw's formative years in Ireland and London. His family background and upbringing in Ireland, his childhood reading and self-education in the arts, his tangled love affairs and early political associations in London, are examined in this chapter as shaping influences on his mind and art. The critical introduction (Chapter 2) provides a survey of the salient characteristics of Shaw's art, and traces the main outlines of his development as a dramatist. This chapter presents an account of the ways in which Shaw's free-ranging and fertile comic invention and his ideological stances combined to influence structural form in his plays, and shows how the Shavian forms differ from those of early contemporary dramatists in England, such as Pinero and Jones.

The plays selected for study in this book are drawn from all periods of Shaw's career as a dramatist, though the main emphasis falls on the plays of the early and middle periods, up to and including *Heartbreak House*. The chapters on *Man and Superman* and *Heartbreak House* are revised and expanded versions of essays which appeared, respectively, in *Modern Drama* (June 1976) and in my study of Shaw in the *Writers and Critics* series

(1969). Chapter 10 is partly based on my article 'Yeats, Shaw and Unity of Culture', in *Southern Review* (Australia, September 1973).

Except where otherwise indicated, all references to the plays and prefaces of Shaw are to *The Bodley Head Bernard Shaw: Collected Plays with their Prefaces*, ed. Dan H. Laurence (London: Max Reinhardt, The Bodley Head, 1970–4) 7 vols. Shaw's system of spelling and punctuation, which in some respects is unconventional (as in the omission of the apostrophe from words such as 'don't'), has been followed throughout in quotations from his writings.

Acknowledgements

Research for this book was carried out with the aid of grants from the Australian Research Grants Committee and the Macquarie University Research Fund, for which grateful acknowledgement is made here. I am also glad to acknowledge the kindness and help of members of staff in the British Library; Department of Rare Books, Cornell University Library; the Houghton Library, Harvard University; the Humanities Research Centre, University of Texas, Austin; the Southern Historical Collection and Manuscripts Department, University of North Carolina, Chapel Hill; and the New York Public Library.

Permission to quote from published and unpublished works of Shaw was granted by the Society of Authors, on behalf of the Bernard Shaw Estate; previously unpublished Shaw texts © 1983 the Trustees of the British Museum, the Governors and Guardians of the National Gallery of Ireland and Royal Academy of Dramatic Art. The editor of *Modern Drama* has kindly allowed me to reprint (with minor revisions) the essay on *Man and Superman* which forms Chapter 9 of this study.

For assistance with the preparation of the typescript I wish to thank Mrs Judy Faulkner and Miss Mary Feely, and for preparation of the index and other editorial assistance, Dr Jeremy Steele.

1 The View from Dalkey Hill: Shaw's Formative Years

> If a man is a deep writer all his works are confessions.
>
> (*Sixteen Self Sketches*)

> What was the Romantic movement? I dont know, though I was under its spell in my youth.
>
> (*Our Theatres in The Nineties*)

On Dalkey Hill, outside Dublin, the family into which Bernard Shaw was born in 1856 shared a summer residence, Torca Cottage, with the enterprising and eccentric conductor and music teacher, George Vandaleur Lee, with whose career as a musical entrepreneur in Dublin the Shaws had become associated. The cottage commanded views of vast expanses of sea and sky. All Dublin Bay was in view from the garden, and from the hall could be seen Killiney Bay, with the Wicklow mountains in the background. Shaw delighted especially in the skies, which he declared unequalled for beauty even in Italy: 'and I always look at the sky', he added.[1] Perhaps their memory is recalled in the '*great breadths of silken green in the Irish sky*' which are called for in the stage setting of *John Bull's Other Island*.

Dalkey Hill provided the young Shaw with one escape from various prisons of the soul in Dublin: from Sunday church-going in a Protestant congregation of 'set faces, pale with the malignant rigidity produced by the suppression of all expression';[2] from a series of schools, beginning with the Wesleyan Connexional (later Wesley College) and ending, in Shaw's fifteenth year, with the Dublin English Scientific and Commercial Day School, all of which Shaw hated. Dalkey was one of what Shaw called the three

1

colleges of his university. The other two were the National Gallery of Ireland – Shaw believed himself to be the only Irishman who had ever been in it, except for the officials – and Vandaleur Lee's Amateur Musical Society. No other university was open to Shaw, because of his father's impecuniousness. Though not a dull pupil, he found the narrowly academic curricula of his schools distasteful, and considered himself lucky in having his youthful mind well stocked by 'Michael Angelo and Handel, Beethoven and Mozart, Shakespear and Dickens and their like, and not by Latin versemongers and cricketers'.[3] The vigour and independence, as well as some of the brashness, perhaps, of Shaw's mind are partly attributable to the fact that he was largely a self-educated man.

Shaw described himself as a social downstart.[4] His father's family included a baronet in its living ranks, and the Shaws traced their lineage back to Macduff, the Thane of Fife and slayer of Macbeth. George Carr Shaw, Bernard's father, however, ex-civil servant and partner in an unsuccessful corn merchant business, was one of the family's poor relations. He was a weak and ineffectual man, but good-natured and affectionate, with a keen sense of humour and a fondness for comic anti-climax. The scraps of letters written in 1857 by his father to his mother, which Shaw published as Part I of Sixteen Self Sketches, show a man of gentleness and warmth:

> 6.8 I was home in the middle of the day and had a good ½ hour's fun with Yup [Shaw's sister, Agnes] and Bob [Bernard Shaw, aged one].

> 8.8 I delivered your kisses to Yup and Bob but contrary to your instructions I fobbed a few for myself – you know how sweet a stolen kiss is!

But overshadowing all Shaw's memories of his father were the recollections of his besetting weakness, an addiction to drink. The young Shaw responded to this in a way which provides a forecast of some essential characteristics of his mature outlook. There was only one way in which the pain and humiliation caused by his father's drunkenness could be tolerated, and that was in laughter:

the drunkenness was so humiliating that it would have been unendurable if we had not taken refuge in laughter. . . . A boy who has seen 'the governor' with an imperfectly wrapped-up goose under one arm and a ham in the same condition under the other (both purchased under heaven knows what delusion of festivity), butting at the garden wall in the belief that he was pushing open the gate, and transforming his tall hat to a concertina in the process, and who, instead of being over-whelmed with shame and anxiety at the spectacle, has been so disabled by merriment (uproariously shared by the maternal uncle) that he has hardly been able to rush to the rescue of the hat and pilot its wearer to safety, is clearly not a boy who will make tragedies of trifles instead of making trifles of tragedies.[5]

Shaw's mother, Lucinda Elizabeth Shaw, presents an image of dour, though not unattractive, plainness and strength. She had, Shaw tells us, 'no comedic impulses'.[6] Inhibited by a strict upbringing and embittered by her husband's addiction to alcohol and the social ostracism it created, she appears, at least from Shaw's account, to have been severely limited in her capacity for affection. Shaw told one of his biographers that she spoke with disgust about her husband's attempt to kiss her in the carriage on the way back from their wedding.[7] To the young Shaw she was an idolized but remote figure:

She did not hate anybody, nor love anybody. The specific maternal passion awoke in her a little for my younger sister, who died at 20; but it did not move her until she lost her, nor then noticeably. She did not concern herself much about us.[8]

In the bitterness of her unhappy marriage Mrs Shaw's solace was music: she was an accomplished singer, with a fine mezzo-soprano voice. She took lessons in singing from Lee, and thus began an association with him in which she became 'not only prima donna and chorus leader but general musical factotum in the whirlpool of Lee's activity'.[9] The infiltration into the Shaw household of the magnetic and energetic Lee, with his gypsy background and unorthodox opinions, became complete after the death of his brother, when he and the Shaw family left their respective houses and took up residence together in Hatch Street.

Shaw's early adolescence was thus spent in the presence of a curious *ménage à trois*, a domestic arrangement reluctantly endured by George Carr Shaw for some five years. By the time Shaw was fifteen his parents' marriage had broken up. Mrs Shaw followed Lee to London to join him in a new music teaching venture there, later taking along her attractive daughter, Lucy, and leaving husband and son behind in Dublin.

Shaw denies suggestions that his mother's association with Lee was anything other than platonic. He declared that his mother was the type of woman who could act as matron in a cavalry barracks from the age of eighteen to forty without acquiring the slightest stain on her character, and described her as 'a Bohemian anarchist with ladylike habits'.[10] It is conceivable, but unlikely, that Shaw mis-judged his mother: certainly she communicated to him the feeling that she disliked sex. She reacted strongly against openly passionate characters in Shaw's plays, such as Julia in *The Philanderer* and Hypatia in *Misalliance*, and thought of them as the outcome of 'the Shaw taint' in her son.[11] Shaw recalls, in a memorable phrase, that Lee developed 'a certain sexual sentimentality' in London which offended the young Lucy and led to the breaking off of the Shaw ladies' relations with him.[12] Whatever the precise nature of the relationship between Lee and Mrs Shaw, it seems likely that the existence of an alien 'father' in the household must have had an unsettling effect on Shaw's boyhood. Later he was to trumpet the advantages of his having had three fathers: his natural one, Lee and a Rabelaisian uncle Walter who, in spells of leave from his employment as a ship's surgeon, enlivened the household with his humour, bawdy limericks and uproarious blasphemies. But one misses the note of any liking for Lee in Shaw's remarks about him. After Lee's death Shaw suppressed his own knowledge of the actual cause of death, a heart disease, and announced that the autopsy revealed a long-standing disease of the brain.[13] Altogether, Shaw's recollections of his childhood leave little to the imagination as to the reasons for that frequently revealed uneasiness about sexual relations, which he never quite overcame, despite having tried what he called 'all the experiments'.[14]

The imprint of Shaw's childhood experiences on his dramatic art can be traced in several different ways, and the ingredient of autobiography is significant because it can often be seen to relate to primary sources of emotional energy in the plays. Two plays, of the early and middle period of Shaw's development, *You Never Can Tell* and *Major Barbara*, are built around an initial situation of marital estrangement. In neither play does the action lead to a reuniting of the parents. But in both cases a kind of *entente* is reached, a neutral accord based on agreement about the future destiny of the younger generation. In both plays the broken marriage in the older generation is, as it were, repaired by a new marriage in the younger generation.

In *You Never Can Tell* Mrs Clandon has been living apart from her husband, Crampton, for eighteen years, in company with her two daughters and one son. The lonely, rather regal, figure of the estranged wife in this play is one of the finest of Shaw's early dramatic portraits. Mrs Clandon is an intelligent, graceful woman, full of humanitarian causes, but vulnerable and dis-illusioned, and repelled by sexuality through her experiences with her husband. Her story, as she relates it in Act III, one guesses to be very close to that of Lucinda Elizabeth Shaw:

> I married before I was old enough to know what I was doing. As you have seen for yourself, the result was a bitter disappointment for both my husband and myself. So you see, though I am a married woman, I have never been in love; I have never had a love affair.

Unable to reach her children at any deep emotional level, she remains an occasionally affectionate and concerned, but nervous and reproving, centre in the dance of their irrepressible vitality. Her husband has been driven into a shell of rejection and bitterness, and takes to drink for consolation. Before meeting him, the children have found a surrogate father in the genial waiter, William, whose paternal perfection has something of the quality of a wish-fulfilment.

Other recollections of Shaw's own experience can be seen in this early comedy. The young dentist, Valentine, is one of several early Shavian protagonists who are fairly obviously in some respects self-portraits. Like Marlowe's Leander, Valentine is a 'bold sharp sophister' when he is engaged in the verbal encounters of the duel of sex. But at crucial moments in the struggle of passion and will in which he is involved with Gloria

Clandon he becomes like a child out of depth in water. Shaw described a similar sensation in an entertaining letter to Mrs Patrick Campbell about his experiences with her:

> But to be gathered like a flower and stuck in your bosom frankly! . . . to draw the sword for the duel of sex with cunning confidence in practised skill and a brass breastplate, and suddenly find myself in the arms of a mother – a young mother, and with a child in my own arms who is yet a woman; all this plunges me into the wildest terror as if I were suddenly in the air thousands of feet above the rocks or sea.[15]

Gloria Clandon, the elder daughter of the family in *You Never Can Tell*, also seems close to the young Shaw in the way in which her priggish superiority incompletely masks a lack of vital knowledge and experience.

In *Major Barbara*, the marital estrangement, though less discussed, again occupies a central position in the dramatic situation, and forms an essential part of the play's emotional and intellectual patterns. Again in this play we have a glimpse into the past, of the wife as the resisting sexual partner, when Lady Britomart refers to Undershaft's attempts to overcome her objections to his opinions with 'affectionate nonsense'. Undershaft's dynamic, successful character obviously sets him at a far remove in some ways from George Carr Shaw. But the Shaw family situation is recalled when even this most powerful of Shavian fathers quails before the domestic authority of the wife. *Major Barbara* is, in part, a dramatization of a power struggle between two parents, with the moral direction of the children as the chief issue at stake. At the end of Act I Undershaft has a victorious exit with the children, leaving the deserted Lady Britomart on stage overcome by '*a little gust of tears*'. But the situation is almost reversed at the end of the play, when the children flock to the mother for support and comfort.

Shaw continually returns to the figure of the father in his plays, often in ways which seem either obliquely to mirror or, as in the case of William the waiter, to correct his childhood experience. In *Mrs Warren's Profession*, a play which links incest with corrupt or failed patriarchal authority in the capitalist society, the father, the Rev. Samuel Gardner, is a figure of ridicule, ironically referred to as 'gov'nor' and 'the Roman father' by his facetious son, Frank. Gardner is a father without authority, a man *'clamorously asserting himself as father and clergyman without being able to command respect in either capacity'*. In *Man and Superman* the defeat of paternal authority implicit in the development of the play's action is associated with ideas of revolution and change in society at large.

In some cases, male characters who appear to be closely linked with Shaw's own viewpoint in the plays themselves have, or assume, a paternal or mentor role, rather than being opponents of paternal authority.[16] This applies to Caesar in *Caesar and Cleopatra*, Undershaft in *Major Barbara*, Higgins in *Pygmalion*, Shotover in *Heartbreak House* and, to some extent, Magnus in his relation with Orinthia in *The Apple Cart*. A common function of the master–pupil relation is to expose the idols of the tribe to a new consciousness, to what the mentor perceives to be more highly developed ethical values, or more truthful ways of looking at the world. But if the mentor is a critic of conventional ideologies, he himself may also be seen in a critical light. Caesar and Magnus are the more or less flawless Shavians of their plays, but Undershaft, Higgins and Shotover can each be seen to suffer from a serious lack of understanding and sympathy.

Early in 1876, at the age of twenty, Shaw left Dublin and a job with an estate agent to join his mother and Lucy at Ventnor on the Isle of Wight, where, four days before his departure from Ireland, his sister Agnes had died of consumption.[17] From 1876 until his marriage to Charlotte Payne Townshend twenty-two years later Shaw lived, in some discomfort as regards his physical surroundings, but harmoniously, with his mother in London: for the first years in a state of financial dependence which gave rise to his celebrated remark, 'I did not throw myself into the struggle for life: I threw my mother into it.'[18] In an early letter from London to his childhood friend, Matthew Edward McNulty, he wrote: 'I have a notion hazy that mother thinks me crazy and Lucy thinks me lazy.'[19] From a photograph taken at Ventnor a beardless young man with a slightly pained and self-conscious expression gazes wonderingly into the future.

In his early London days Shaw suffered from acute shyness and a lack of social ease. He agonized over the prospect of social evenings at the Lawsons', an artistic family who lived at Cheyne

Walk, the scene of Eliza Doolittle's sensational début in London society at one of Mrs Higgins's at-home days.[20] He studied books of etiquette with titles such as *The Manners and Tone of Good Society*. He forced himself to speak at meetings of a discussion group called the Zetetical Society, eventually overcoming his initial condition of 'heartbreaking nervousness',[21] and laying the foundation for his later fame as one of the most able and impressive public speakers of his day.

But however shy he may have been in public, the correspondence which has survived from this period of his career already reveals some marks of the intellectual decisiveness and wit of Shaw's maturity. In the earliest surviving letter of Shaw's, written in bantering spirit to his sister Lucy early in 1874, the 'arrant prig' that Shaw described himself to be (in *Sixteen Self Sketches*) in his young manhood and the budding comedist vie with one another for supremacy:

> Cara Lucia
>
> I am sorry to say that I have read your letter. I shall take especial care not to do so again for you really are worthy of your parent in the matter of verbosity and far more personal. Your remarks are most offensive. Let my nose alone, better a bottle than a peony. Did the Mar mention that the cat has got mange as well as Paddy. It has no hair at all on its head which adds to its already prepossessing appearance. Mamma on arriving sat down in the cab with such violence that she burst open the door which I had to hold shut during the rest of the journey. . . . I have found in the house a great bundle of stuff and whether it is red worsted or Agnes' hair I don't know.[22]

But the Shaw correspondence – one of the richest and liveliest collections of letters in the language – begins to acquire its proper sparkle and depth of insight a little later, in the letters written in the early 1880s to one of his first loves, Alice Lockett.

Shaw was very attractive to women, and was in turn much attracted towards them. In the early 1880s three of his closest female friends were Alice Lockett, Elinor Huddart and Jenny Patterson. With the 'tyrannical but irresistible'[23] Alice, Shaw had a stormy, quarrelsome, unconsummated love affair lasting for about three years. Alice Lockett was not unintelligent, and she was certainly handsome, but she was clearly unable to keep pace with Shaw's rapidly expanding artistic and intellectual interests. She had, it seems, a rather prim, conventional self which Shaw addressed as 'Miss Lockett', and another more natural and generous self he addressed as 'Alice'.

Shaw's letters to Elinor Huddart have not survived, but her letters to him reveal a person of considerable maturity of mind, with a keen sense of humour.[24] She was well read, and herself engaged in writing, as a minor novelist under the pseudonym of Elinor Hume. She and Shaw corresponded about their writing and about their shared interest in music and art for several years. Physical love-making was excluded, by mutual agreement, from their relationship. But the correspondence, as far as one can tell from one side of it, provided Shaw with a valuable testing ground for ideas and a fruitful exchange of knowledge.

It was not until he was twenty-nine that Shaw had his first experience of sexual intercourse, with a passionate and possessive woman many years his senior, Mrs Jenny Patterson. Mrs Patterson was a widow who had moved to London from Dublin after the death of her husband, and took singing lessons from Mrs Shaw. Shaw recorded in a diary he was keeping at the time the steps which led to Mrs Patterson's conquest of him on his 29th birthday. On July 4 1885 he records his visit to Mrs Patterson's house after meeting some friends: 'stayed until 1. Vein of conversation distinctly gallant.' A week later, having come home in the evening to find Mrs Patterson at his mother's house he 'walked to her house by way of the park. Supper, music and curious conversation, and a declaration of passion. Left at 3. virgo intacta still.' Finally, he records elsewhere in the diary, 'on the 26th July, my 29th birthday, begins an intimacy with a lady of our acquaintance. I was an absolute novice. I did not take the initiative in the matter.'[25] As her letters and Shaw's comments reveal, Jenny Patterson loved Shaw with obsessive intensity.[26] Shaw, for his part, seems to have responded with mixed feelings, rather like those of Don Giovanni in a short story he wrote two years after meeting Jenny Patterson: 'I found the romantic side of our intercourse, which seemed never to pall on her, tedious, unreasonable, and even forced and insincere except at rare moments, when the power of love made her beautiful, body and soul.'[27]

Shaw's affair with Mrs Patterson came to an end in 1893. By

that time he had met and fallen deeply in love with the actress
Florence Farr Emery, who played the leading female role,
Blanche Sartorius, in his first play, *Widowers' Houses*, and Louka in
Arms and the Man at the Avenue Theatre in 1894. Jenny Patterson
reacted with extreme jealousy to his new love affair, and Shaw
was more than once subjected to violent scenes of reproach. His
relations with the two women had a direct influence on the
writing of his first two plays. It was a rather cruel irony that the
aggressive young woman played by Florence Farr in *Widowers'
Houses* was partly modelled on the character of Jenny Patterson.
Act I of his next play, *The Philanderer*, was 'founded on a very
horrible scene' which occurred on 4 February 1893 when Jenny
Patterson burst in on Shaw and Florence at the latter's home in
the evening and became violent and abusive.[28] Shaw concluded
one of his letters to Florence Farr with an invitation to a concert,
and a reference to Psalm XLII: 'The hart pants for cooling
streams.'[29] He had just been denouncing the behaviour of Jenny
Patterson.

Relations with women to whom he was strongly attracted
physically seem always to have produced in Shaw an intense
inner conflict, an experience of feelings 'tyrannical but irresistible'. He sought relief from that tyranny in other companion-
ships in which sex had a lesser part or no part at all. He tended to
cast his women friends into roles, as either his good angels or his
femmes fatales, a tendency which is reflected in his treatment of
female characters in the plays. A pattern of contrasts begins with
his 'trifler', Alice, and his 'serious friend', Elinor Huddart, and is
seen again in the character of his relations with Jenny Patterson
and Florence Farr, Stella Campbell and Ellen Terry, and in the
contrast between Charlotte and various women with whom
Shaw had flirtations after his marriage. Shaw's marriage with
Charlotte, physically unconsummated, though from all appearances deeply satisfying in other respects, seems to have been a
philanderer's haven, a retreat from, though not a solution to,
conflicts which continually recurred in Shaw's relations with
women.

One difficulty for Shaw was that the romantic visions of his
childhood were not matched by real men and women.
Cultivation of the Uranian Venus in childhood, he thought, is
both delightful and necessary:

All young people should be votaries of the Uranian Venus to keep them chaste: that is why Art is vitally important. I was steeped in romantic opera from my childhood. I knew all the pictures and antique Greek statues in the National Gallery of Ireland. I read Byron and everything of romantic fiction I could lay my hands on. . . . From our cottage on Dalkey Hill I surveyed an enchanting panorama of sea, sky, and mountain. I was overfed on honey dew. The Uranian Venus was bountiful.[30]

But the Uranian Venus and the honey dew of Dalkey Hill may create expectations which are disappointed in ordinary life. 'The difficulty about the Uranian Venus' is that 'she can . . . sterilize us by giving us imaginary amours on the plains of heaven so magical that they spoil us for real women and real men.' Whatever contrast he found between dream and reality, Shaw was certainly not indifferent to the 'celestial flood of emotion and exaltation' which sexual experience produced for him; nor did he regard sex in an irreverent way. But he found relations which were never consummated left 'the longest and kindliest memories'.[31]

In reviewing Shaw's treatment of sexual themes in the plays it is more appropriate to see him as an advanced Victorian rather than as a failed D. H. Lawrence. The theme of filial revolt is certainly important in Shaw's work; but it is not true to say, as Eric Bentley does, that hostility between parents and children replaces sexual feeling as an emotional centre in the plays.[32] Rather, the two themes tend to be intricately intertwined. In *Widowers' Houses*, *Mrs Warren's Profession* and *Man and Superman* the relations between parents and children have a direct bearing on the love relation; and the two sets of relations are explored together in ways which illuminate the determinative economic, social and political forces which surround the love relation. In *Arms and the Man*, *Misalliance* and *Fanny's First Play* the evolving patterns of sexual relations are closely associated with filial repudiation, or outgrowing, of parental influences and ideals. Raina Petkoff's transference of her affections from Sergius to Bluntschli in *Arms and the Man* is anticipated in her speech to her mother: 'I know Sergius is your pet. I sometimes wish you could marry him instead of me.' In *You Never Can Tell* Gloria Clandon's discovery of unsuspected depths of passion in her nature is accompanied by rueful complaint about the inadequacy of her 'education' by her mother.

William Archer may have been judging by not very Rabelaisian standards when he declared that Shaw's plays 'reek with sex', but there is nevertheless a strong presence of erotic feeling in Shavian drama, which is often overlooked by critics wishing to emphasize intellectual paradox (the tag sticks to Shaw's critical treatment of stereotypes despite its inadequacy) and wit. In scenes such as those between Blanche Sartorius and Harry Trench at the end of *Widowers' Houses*, Gloria and Valentine in *You Never Can Tell*, Ann and Tanner in *Man and Superman*, Shaw deals more directly with sexual attraction than any of his predecessors and early contemporaries in the Victorian and Edwardian theatre. It is true that in Shaw's drama sex is frequently in conflict with other impulses and motives – this becomes a major theme in *Three Plays for Puritans* – but generally in his plays sexual attraction is treated with un-Victorian candour, and sexual motivation has full play in the characterization. The leading female characters especially, whether volatile and tempestuous like Julia Craven, or comically unprepared like Gloria Clandon, or humorously purposeful like Ann Whitefield or frankly appetitive like Hypatia and Sweetie, tend often to behave in ways of which Shaw's mother would not approve. R. L. Stevenson's exclamation about the women in Shaw's novel, *Cashel Byron's Profession*, 'I say, Archer, my God, what women!' could be applied with equal justice to the women in the plays.

Shaw did succeed to a certain extent in upsetting Victorian conventions about women and their role in society. His second play, *The Philanderer*, lampoons Victorian images of the womanly woman and the manly man and interestingly explores the predicament of the New Woman in the character of Grace Tranfield and, through glimpses of the relation between Sylvia and Charteris, the possibilities of a kind of male – female comradeship which the conventions of the duel of sex preclude. Female characters such as Vivie Warren, Major Barbara, Lina Szczepanowska, Saint Joan and Epifania Ognisanti compete with men on a more than equal footing in the world of action. But, as Elsie Adams has pointed out, there do remain strong traces of familiar literary stereotypes in Shaw's portrayal of women. Oversimplifying the case a little, Adams holds that what we find in the plays are 'permutations of basic literary types: temptress, mother, goddess'.[33] There are qualifications to be made about individual cases, but such a pattern is certainly present in Shaw's female portraiture. Ann Whitefield, Lady Cicely, and Barbara, or Saint Joan, spring to mind as ready examples of the three basic types, and one can see how Shaw's own experiences as son and lover would have reinforced, or perhaps have been the primary imaginative source, of such conceptions.

The many conflicting impulses in his attitude to women are summed up in a letter to Stella Campbell: 'I want my Virgin Mother enthroned in heaven. I want my Italian peasant woman. I want my rapscallionly fellow vagabond. I want my dark lady. I want my angel – I want my tempter.'[34] Only in comparatively few instances do we have any sense of a synthesis of spiritual or moral authority and sexual power in Shaw's female universe. Very rarely are his Venus Aphrodite and his Venus Urania one and the same person. Jennifer Dubedat, the *arrestingly good-looking* heroine of *The Doctor's Dilemma*, Mrs George in *Getting Married*, who speaks in her trance of the mystical union of sex ('I gave you eternity in a single moment') and Lina Szczepanowska are amongst the rare examples in which a full synthesis of female powers is realized.

By the time he reached London in 1876 Shaw's self-education in literature and the arts was extensive. He mentions as very early reading ('when I was two months old or so') two books far apart in spirit but both significant as influences, *The Pilgrim's Progress* and *The Arabian Nights*. Shaw's comments on Bunyan were sometimes far from complimentary, and he saw his narrowness and limitations quite clearly. But Bunyan's work and the social and religious vision it contains remained active forces in Shaw's mental landscape throughout his life. Mr Valiant for Truth's Speech as he prepares to cross the River – a speech about which Shaw remarked 'the heart vibrates like a bell to such an utterance as this'[35] – had a potency in Shaw's imagination akin to one of Wordsworth's 'spots of time'. *The Arabian Nights* no doubt helped foster Shaw's delight in exotic Eastern settings, such as those in which he locates some of the later plays, and would have provided a model for the prose rhythms of a scene such as the alternative Prologue of *Caesar and Cleopatra*. Shaw's two child-hood loves are amusingly combined in the scene in *Too True to be Good* (1932) when the Sergeant is discovered reading Bunyan in a pink grotto called The Abode of Love. Shakespeare and Dickens were also childhood favourites of Shaw, and he had a profound and intimate knowledge of both writers. Among the novelists, he also read Scott, Dumas père, George Eliot, Thackeray (but 'tittle-tattle, however well done, remains tittle-tattle') and Trollope ('always surprised to find him so readable'). He read Byron 'very early and all through', Coleridge's *The Ancient Mariner* and Cowper's 'John Gilpin'. He read G. H. Lewes's *Life of Goethe* and 'every translation of Faust [he] could get hold of'. He described his early 'intellectual attitude and affectation' as Mephistophelean, and painted heads of Mephistopheles 'on whitewashed walls in water color as the patron saint of sceptics and deriders'.

Among non-fictional works, he read Tyndall's lectures 'relig-iously', Emerson and Carlyle, John Stuart Mill's *Autobiography* and some of his shorter essays, Robertson's histories, Hume and, a special favourite, the maxims of La Rochefoucauld. Shelley, Blake, Ruskin, Morris, Ibsen, Wagner, Schopenhauer, Comte, Henry George and Marx were soon to become, in his early London days, further influences of major significance.[36]

Of all the writers he read in the Dublin days, Charles Dickens may be singled out as having the most direct and pervasive influence on Shaw's early development as a playwright. His first play, *Widowers' Houses*, is full of Dickensian echoes. The rackrent-ing landlord, Sartorius, and his scruffy rent-collector, Lickcheese, are clearly modelled on the smooth 'Patriarch', Casby, and his rent squeezer in Bleeding Heart Yard, Mr Pancks, in *Little Dorrit*. The scene in which Sartorius reviles Lickcheese for his soft treatment of the tenants directly recalls that in Dickens's novel when Mr Casby berates Pancks for 'a very bad day's work'. Cokane, the obsequious upholder of the proprieties and chaperon of Harry Trench in Shaw's play, fills a role very similar to that of Mrs General in *Little Dorrit*, and both characters underline the importance of surface appearances and ceremony in the social system which they help to uphold. Harry Trench's realization of his own involvement in the corrupt social and economic system portrayed in *Widowers' Houses* is a further Dickensian echo in that it recalls a similar development in the career of Arthur Clennam. *Little Dorrit* continued to be a fruitful influence in later plays, providing, in Mrs Clennam, a model for Mrs Dudgeon in *The Devil's Disciple*, and in the pathetically commonplace business entrepreneur Mr Merdle, whose vast financial empire is discovered to be built on nothing, a model for Boss Mangan in *Heartbreak House*. Another early play, *You Never Can Tell*, draws substantially in its characterization on *Bleak House* and *Great Expectations*. Shaw was not an uncritical reader of Dickens, but the Dickens presence in his own work can be seen both in details and in the larger contours of his social vision and comic manner. With his capacity for appealing both to highbrow and popular taste, his social range, his skill in the creation of sharply individualized personae who yet have significance as social types, his passionately felt concern at the injustices and inequities of his society, and in the searching quality of his social satire, Shaw is the direct heir of Dickens in the tradition of English critical comedy.

Shaw's thinking about society and its injustices was given further shape and direction in London when he was 'swept into the great Socialist revival'[37] of the early 1880s. He was decisively converted to Socialism in 1882 when listening to a lecture by the American radical thinker and author of *Progress and Poverty*, Henry George. In 1884 Shaw was elected a member of the newly-formed Fabian Society, and soon became one of its leading thinkers and its most effective public spokesman. The Fabian Society was a rival organization to that formed by Karl Marx's disciple H. M. Hyndman, the Social Democratic Federation. The fundamental outlook and aims of the Fabians were radical enough. The Fabian Manifesto published in 1884 included the following declarations of opinion:

That the Nationalization of the land in some form is a public duty.

That the pretensions of Capitalism to encourage Invention, and to distribute its benefits in the fairest way attainable, have been discredited by the experience of the nineteenth century.

That under the existing system of leaving the National Industry to organize itself, Competition has the effect of rendering adulteration, dishonest dealing, and inhumanity compulsory.

That since Competition among producers admittedly secures to the public the most satisfactory products, the State should compete with all its might in every department of production.

That Men no longer need special privileges to protect them against Women; and that the sexes should henceforth enjoy equal political rights.

That we had rather face a Civil War than such another century of suffering as the present one has been.[38]

But the distinctive feature of Fabian strategy was to work for gradual reform rather than for violent revolution. The Fabians were an intelligent, well-informed pressure group, whose policy was to permeate existing political parties, especially the Liberal Party, with ideas for reform.

Despite the strongly romantic bias of much of his early reading, the young Shaw arrived in London with, on the surface at least, a markedly rationalistic and analytical cast of mind. He was a vivisector of the emotions, a radical questioner of conventions. In this mood he set about writing the first of five novels, the manuscripts of which were returned by publishers with what for less resilient spirits would have been heartbreaking regularity. 'Even the rats', Shaw later remarked of the first novel, *Immaturity*, 'could not finish it.'[39] But the novels, most notably *Cashel Byron's Profession* and *An Unsocial Socialist*, are far from unreadable in fact, and one can share up to a point Shaw's later respect, mingled with his laughter at their pedantry, for their 'priggish conscientiousness'.[40] One quality which often comes through impressively is a certain wry dissonance in what we see of the psychology of the heroes (and some of the heroines) and in their relations with society. Unhappy and often unstable them- selves, they present an angular but tough-minded front of hostility to the sentimentalities of romance and to the social order as they find it. The dry, off-beat conclusion to *Immaturity* has a quality of understatement that Shaw achieved effectively again at the end of some of his early plays: 'As Smith recrossed the bridge, he stopped and stood in one of the recesses to meditate on his immaturity, and look upon the beauty of the still expanses of white moonlight and black shadow which lay before him. At last he shook his head negatively and went home.'

The second novel, *The Irrational Knot*, is important as marking what Shaw considered to be a major turning point in his development as a thinker. This novel is dominated by the presence of a highly intelligent, uncompromisingly honest electrical engineer and inventor, Ned Connolly. Connolly, in whose portrayal there is clearly a good deal of self-parody by Shaw, is good-humoured, musically gifted, thrifty yet generous, and always right. He is, in some ways, a monster of rationality, and the defects of his virtues begin to emerge in his marriage (the irrational knot of which is tied in a very rational spirit) to Marian, an attractive young woman with an upper class social background. Whilst being a 'monotonously amiable' husband, Connolly crushes Marian's spirit with his intellectual superiority and tacit contempt for her abilities. The two become distant from one another and Marian is driven into a disastrous affair with a handsome gentleman of leisure and minor poet, Sholto Douglas. At the end of the affair, Connolly arrives to pick up the pieces, but the marriage cannot be resumed.

Shaw later declared that this early novel had carried him 'as far as [he] could go in Rationalism and Materialism', and that thereafter he took 'the unreasonable instinctive man' as his theme: 'I finished with rationalism (except as a butt) in my second book'.[41] An important passage in the novel itself anticipates this change of course. Marian Connolly and her friend Elinor are discussing love and marriage when Marian (expressing ideas which would not look out of place in an essay by D. H. Lawrence) says:

> I took up the Bible last night for the first time since my marriage; and I thought what fools we two used to be when we made up our minds to avoid all the mistakes and follies and feelings of other people, and to be quite superior and rational. 'He that observeth the wind shall not sow; and he that regardeth the clouds shall not reap.' It is all so true, in spite of

what Ned says. We were very clever at observing the wind and regarding the clouds; and what are we the better for it? How much irreparable mischief, I wonder, did we do ourselves by letting all our little wisdoms stifle all our big instincts.[42]

Shaw exaggerates in saying that he 'finished with rationalism' in this novel: but *The Irrational Knot* establishes tensions which are of fundamental importance in his art, and points forward to the repeated conflicts in the plays between the 'little wisdoms' of reason and philosophy and the inexorable energies of the 'big instincts'. In the writing of *The Irrational Knot* Shaw discovered the limitations of reason as a means of coming to terms with the forces which govern the workings of the human heart and the realities of human relations. In doing so he was beginning to define a major theme of his later work as a dramatist. The theme is finely summed up in the comic image of Professor Higgins, man of reason and codifier of language and manners, having his slippers thrown at him by the disorderly and justly furious human being, Eliza Doolittle.

W. B. Yeats once described Shaw as 'a notorious hater of romance'.[43] One can see why Yeats, with his very different artistic goals, and perhaps having in mind the memory of a double bill at Florence Farr's Avenue Theatre in 1894 when *Arms and the Man* was playing with *The Land of Heart's Desire*, should have thought this about Shaw; and Shaw tended to encourage the idea himself. But the description is a misleading one. Shaw was certainly critical of the conventions of operatic and, later, Hollywood romance, and the public persona he presented was often that of the thoroughly prosaic, commonsensical drains-and hygiene-in-the-St Pancras-vestry man, the street-corner Socialist. But one does not have to look very far below the surface to find a quite different personality, that of a man sensitive to natural beauty, deeply responsive to and extraordinarily well versed in music and opera, literature and art, with a passion for perfection of detail in acts both of creation and performance. He scoffed at the idolatrous worship of Shakespeare of his time, but would condemn as 'earless' an actor who missed the scansion of a syllable of Shakespeare's verse.[44] For polemical purposes he sometimes posed as a philistine; but he had a profound respect for art, and a strong bias towards the romantic in his literary and musical tastes. Beneath the Mephistophelean sceptic and derider was a Faustian idealist and dreamer. The clash between his Mephistophelean and Faustian selves is the source of a continuing psychomachy in Shavian drama which reaches creative high points in such scenes as the Dream in *Man and Superman* and the final encounter between Broadbent and Keegan in *John Bull's Other Island.*

Shaw's fundamental intellectual loyalties are not with nineteenth-century rational materialism; and his drama can be approached more fruitfully if he is seen not as a hater of romance but as one who created new forms of romance in the context of critical attacks on romantic stereotypes. Like his prosaic and anti-heroic, but courageous and attractive, Captain Bluntschli in *Arms and the Man,* he had 'an incurably romantic disposition'.

Whatever the precise nature of his adolescent dreams on Dalkey Hill, they would clearly not in themselves be the stuff of great comic drama. Indeed, had Shaw developed only that side of his nature he might have become, at best, a minor late-Victorian poet. The distinctive marks of Shaw's mature character are a robust critical intelligence, a gaiety of mind which had at its command an inexhaustibly fertile comic imagination, together with extraordinary generosity and courage. It was his possession of qualities such as these which enabled him to become such a formidable opponent of the enemies of the human spirit and the common weal in his time. But for comedy not to be merely brittle and superficial, it needs to carry as an undercurrent a sense of both the painful and joyful aspects of human experience. Shaw's childhood and youth provided him with enough experience of both to last him a lifetime. Very late in his life Shaw wrote as follows on the family decision to go to live at Dalkey:

> I had one moment of ecstatic happiness in my childhood when my mother told me that we were going to live in Dalkey. I had only to open my eyes to see such pictures as no painter could make for me. I could not believe that such skies existed anywhere else in the world until I read Shakespear's 'this majestical roof fretted with golden fire', and wondered where he could have seen it if not from Torca Cottage. The joy of it has remained with me all my life.[45]

NOTES

1. *Shaw: An Autobiography, 1856–1898*, selected from his writings by Stanley Weintraub (London: Max Reinhardt, 1970) p. 63.
2. Ibid., p. 31.
3. *Everybody's Political What's What*, 2nd edn (London: Constable, 1945) p. 180.
4. *Sixteen Self Sketches* (London: Constable, 1949) p. 7.
5. Preface to *Immaturity* (London: Constable, 1930) p. xxiv.
6. Ibid., p. xxii.
7. This is recorded by Thomas Demetrius O'Bolger in Chapter 1 of his unpublished biography of Shaw, now held in the Houghton Library, Harvard University, Cambridge, Mass. (bMS Eng. 1046.9 [25]).
8. *Sixteen Self Sketches*, p. 13. Elsewhere Shaw wrote of his mother: 'Her almost complete neglect of me had the advantage that I could idolize her to the utmost pitch of my imagination. . . . It was a privilege to be taken for a walk or a visit with her, or on an excursion' – Preface to *London Music in 1888–89* (London: Constable, 1937) p. 13.
9. Preface to *London Music in 1888–89*, p. 10.
10. *Sixteen Self Sketches*, p. 14.
11. Letter to O'Bolger, Feb. 1916 (Houghton Library, Harvard University, bMS Eng. 1046.9 [5]) p. 27.
12. Ibid., p. 3.
13. *Shaw: An Autobiography, 1856–1898*, p. 305, n. 1.
14. *Sixteen Self Sketches*, p. 114.
15. *Bernard Shaw and Mrs Patrick Campbell: Their Correspondence*, ed. Alan Dent (London: Victor Gollancz, 1952) p. 96.
16. A valuable study of the relationships resulting from this has been made by Peter Ure in his essay 'Master and Pupil in Bernard Shaw', *Essays in Criticism*, vol. XIX, no. 2 (1969) pp. 118–39.
17. *Bernard Shaw: Collected Letters 1874–1897*, ed. Dan H. Laurence (London: Max Reinhardt, 1965) pp. 6, 17.
18. Preface to *The Irrational Knot* (London: Constable, 1931) p. xv.
19. *Collected Letters 1874–1897*, p. 19.
20. The set of Act III of *Pygmalion*, with its Cecil Lawson landscape painting and Pre-Raphaelite décor is clearly a recollection of the Lawson house (cf. Preface to *Immaturity*, pp. xli–xliii).
21. Ibid., p. xl.
22. *Collected Letters 1874–1897*, p. 7.
23. Ibid., p. 75.
24. A large collection of Elinor Huddart's letters to Shaw is preserved in the British Library (MS Add. 50535–7).
25. St John Ervine, *Bernard Shaw: His Life, Work and Friends* (London: Constable, 1956) pp. 152–3.
26. Jenny Patterson's letters to Shaw are preserved in the British Library (MS Add. 50544–5).
27. 'Don Giovanni Explains', in *The Black Girl in Search of God and Some Lesser Tales* (London: Constable, 1934) p. 177.

28. See Hesketh Pearson, *Bernard Shaw: His Life and Personality* (London: Methuen, 1961) p. 117 and St John Ervine, *Bernard Shaw: His Life, Work and Friends*, pp. 166–7.

29. *Collected Letters 1874–1897*, p. 297.

30. *Sixteen Self Sketches*, p. 114.

31. Ibid., p. 115.

32. In a letter to Frank Harris Shaw wrote: 'Archer's early complaint that my plays reeked with sex was far more sensible than the virgin–eunuch theory which the halfpenny journalists delight in' (16 October 1916, T.l.s in Houghton Library, Harvard University, fMS Eng. 1046.11, p. 5). For Bentley's discussion see his *Bernard Shaw*, 2nd British edn (London: Methuen, 1967) p. 179.

33. Elsie Adams, 'Feminism and Female Stereotypes in Shaw', in *Fabian Feminist: Bernard Shaw and Woman*, ed. Rodelle Weintraub (Pennsylvania and London: Pennsylvania State University Press, 1977) p. 157.

34. *Bernard Shaw and Mrs Patrick Campbell*, p. 90.

35. *Our Theatres in the Nineties*, 3 vols (London: Constable, 1948) vol. III, p. 2.

36. The above account of his Dublin reading is principally based on Shaw's replies to questions put to him in correspondence by Thomas Demetrius O'Bolger (Houghton Library, Harvard University, bMS Eng. 1046.9). Unless otherwise indicated, all quotations in the above account are from that source. See also Stanley Weintraub (ed.), *Shaw: An Autobiography*, *passim*.

37. Letter to Hamlin Garland, cited in Archibald Henderson, *George Bernard Shaw: Man of the Century* (New York: Appleton-Century-Crofts, 1956) p. 216.

38. The full manifesto is reproduced in Henderson, ibid., pp. 220–1.

39. Archibald Henderson, *George Bernard Shaw: His Life and Works* (London: Hurst & Blackett, 1911) pp. 46–7.

40. Preface to *Immaturity*, p. xxxix.

41. *Shaw: An Autobiography, 1856–1898*, p. 96, and reply to O'Bolger (Houghton Library, Harvard University, bMS Eng. 1046.9, p. 20).

42. *The Irrational Knot*, pp. 252–3.

43. W B Yeats, *Autobiographies* (London: Macmillan, 1955) p. 134. Yeats added to this description the words 'whose generosity and courage I could not fathom'.

44. Referring to a performance of the role of Richard III by Richard Mansfield in 1889, Shaw wrote:

> when in that deliberate staccato—
>
> I am determinéd to be a villain,
>
> he actually missed half a bar by saying in modern prose fashion, 'I am determin'd to be a villain', I gave him up as earless. (*London Music in 1888–89*, p. 83).

45. *Sixteen Self Sketches*, p. 72.

2 Critical Perspectives

An artist to the tips of his fingers.
(Beatrice Webb, of Shaw)

I

As in his lifetime, so in the years following his death in 1950 critical opinion about Shaw has been sharply divided. The same dramatist whom one critic describes as 'a great creative genius',[1] and another regards as a writer of plays which 'can scarcely prove other than lastingly delightful',[2] is seen by others as a spent force[3] and 'as a creative artist only a minor figure'.[4] His plays continue to be performed more frequently in the English theatre than those of any other playwright except Shakespeare.[5] But his reception in academic circles is often unenthusiastic or hostile. His powers as a dramatic artist are often acclaimed,[6] but a strong critical tradition persists in which he is seen as a playwright who sacrificed artistic integrity to the designs of purveying ideas and orchestrating debate about social problems. Judged by some to be the greatest English dramatist since Shakespeare and Jonson, Shaw is yet seen in some critical accounts as a writer of thesis plays.

This book is written in the conviction that Shaw was indeed a great creative genius, and one who deserves recognition as a major contributor to the English and European dramatic traditions. The defence of this view must, of course, rest finally on close appraisal of individual plays. The purpose of this chapter is to explore Shaw's dramatic art in more general terms, and to provide critical perspectives which may help to define and illuminate the nature of that art. It is argued here that examination of Shaw's dramatic language, his use of non-verbal devices and his treatment of form reveals an extraordinarily resourceful and versatile creativity. In some plays, it may be conceded, he strayed into areas of creativity over which he had imperfect command. The astringency and edge which are essential qualities in his successful works occasionally desert him. At its best, however, Shaw's work is remarkable not only for its vigour and wit but also for qualities of imaginative subtlety and depth which are less commonly acknowledged.

Shaw's own perceptions about the nature of his art, and the information he provides about his creative processes, though we cannot regard them as conclusive, deserve close attention. In a letter written in 1919 to the inquisitive and sometimes obtuse Professor O'Bolger, Shaw wrote:

> There is an economic link between Cashel Byron, Sartorius, Mrs Warren and Undershaft: all of them prospering in questionable activities. But would anyone but a buffleheaded idiot of a university professor, half crazy with correcting examination papers, infer that all my plays were written as economic essays, and not as plays of life, character, and human destiny like those of Shakespear or Euripides?[7]

In his accounts of his creative processes Shaw tells us that the original impulses of his plays lay not in ideas or theses about social problems but in scenes, moments, chance remarks and recollections of people, in actual or imagined occasions by which his imagination was stirred. Writing to Henry Arthur Jones in 1894, Shaw described the imaginative genesis of his plays as follows: 'things occur to me as scenes, with action and dialogue – as moments developing themselves out of their own vitality. I believe you will see as I go on that the conception of me as a doctrinaire, or as a sort of theatrical Joyce (of *Scientific Dialogues* fame), is a wrong one.'[8]

In answer to Archibald Henderson's question, 'do you usually develop your play from a central idea?', Shaw replied ('*oracularly*'): 'The play develops itself. I only hold the pen.' He went on to explain that sometimes the first thing in his head was a situation like the arrest in *The Devil's Disciple*, or a remark made in his presence which was 'pregnant with a whole play'.[9] Shaw shows his affinities with Romantic traditions of thought in his view of works of art as organic forms: 'real plays . . . are no more

constructed than a carrot is constructed. They grow naturally.'[10]
He spoke, in the same discussion with Archibald Henderson, of
his experience that in the process of creation the central
motivation of what was happening always remained hidden from
view until after the work was completed, like the core of meaning
in a dream: 'I must warn you that the real process is very obscure;
for the result always shows that there has been *something behind* all
the time, of which I was not conscious, though it turns out to be
the real motive of the whole creation.'[11]

The evidence of the plays, it can be shown, is consistent with
Shaw's remarks about the ways in which they formed themselves
in his mind. Devices of imagery, motif and plot in Shavian drama
have a function which is somewhat analogous to that of the
conceit in metaphysical poetry. In Shaw's plays sensuous
particulars are the defining instruments of ideas; and critical
understanding of his work depends upon an openness of response
to the ways in which his theatrical artistry and intellectual
preoccupations worked together. Obviously, in any one play the
possible 'real' motives of the initial creative impulse are numerous. But often there can be discerned in the plays images and
motifs which function as nodal points in the imaginative and
thematic life of the work as a whole. Examples of these are the
clothing imagery in *Widowers' Houses*; the incest theme in *Mrs
Warren's Profession*; Mr Whitefield's will in *Man and Superman*; the
dream motif in *John Bull's Other Island*; the images of the ship and
of light and darkness in *Heartbreak House*. In the plays, economic,
political and religious themes are explored. But that statement
needs to be distinguished from the naive conception that the
plays are simply dramatizations of preconceived ideas about
social problems, or dramatic versions of what is said in the
prefaces. In Shavian drama the destinies of individuals are seen
to be inextricably linked with the fate of society at large. But
Shaw's engagement with social issues does not undermine the
vitality and integrity of his plays as works of art.

Typically, the end of a play by Shaw leaves us not so much
with the sense of a proven thesis as with an awareness of open-
ended possibilities and irreducible complexity. It is true that in
his first play, *Widowers' Houses*, possible socialist solutions to the
problems revealed in the play are clearly implied. His third play,
Mrs Warren's Profession, is obviously critical of the system of

predatory capitalism which has directed the destinies of the individual characters. But already in this latter play the complexity of Shaw's treatment of social themes is evident. At the end of the well-portrayed quarrel with which *Mrs Warren's Profession* closes, the rightness of Vivie's decision to sever relations with her mother and Frank may be acknowledged, but only with an accompanying sense of her diminished humanity and bleak self-isolation, and with the realization that her future career in actuarial calculations is hardly likely to contribute to a change in the structure of society. Later plays display a similarly open-ended quality. In *Man and Superman*, for example, the final speech of the still rebellious Tanner, who embodies most of the play's more positive affirmations, is greeted with '*universal laughter*'. *Heartbreak House* ends on deeply ambiguous notes of tragi-comedy. *Saint Joan* concludes with an unanswerable question. At the end of a late play, *The Simpleton of the Unexpected Isles*, Pra and Prola, the Priest and Priestess of Life, dedicate themselves to the 'surprise and wonder' of the future, having rejected all plans as mere 'jigsaw puzzles'.

But to say that the plays are open-ended is not to say that they lack discernible patterns of meaning, or that they fail to function as instruments of social criticism. The plays convey clear criticisms and affirmations, in spite of their rapid shifts of focus and sympathy, and the complexity – especially in the early and middle period of Shaw's career as a dramatist, up to and including *Heartbreak House* – of their portrayal of character. The value of Shaw's drama as a thorn in the flesh of society is that it remains critical whilst not being easy to discard as presenting a partisan or limited view.

II

In Shaw's dramatic art imaginative use is made of all the resources of the theatre. The plays demonstrate a mastery of both verbal and non-verbal forms of communication. Shaw's lucid, supple and robust dramatic prose creates an impressive range of dramatic effects. He is sometimes charged with an incapacity for rendering passionate emotion in his dialogue. This view is belied by such passages as Blanche Sartorius's scene with Trench at the end of *Widowers' Houses*, Mrs Warren's denunciation of Vivie as 'a bad daughter and a stuck-up prude', Jack Tanner's cry 'Oh, that clutch holds and hurts', near the end of *Man and Superman*, Eliza Doolittle's final quarrel with Higgins, and Ellie Dunn's exclamation, 'O, I hope so', at the end of *Heartbreak House*. Such passages can be cited as a few of the many instances where strong emotional resonances are present. But Shaw's modes of seriousness are not always, or even often, modes of solemnity. As an inventor of comic dialogue his resources range from the pungent wit of such moments as the opening exchange between Tanner and Mendoza in *Man and Superman*:

> MENDOZA:. . . [*posing loftily*] I am a brigand: I live by robbing the rich.
> TANNER: [*promptly*] I am a gentleman: I live by robbing the poor. Shake hands.

to the finely drawn humour of character and situation in a speech such as this by the profoundly philistine Broadbent in *John Bull's Other Island*: 'Dont sneer, Larry: I used to read a lot of Shelley years ago. Let us be faithful to the dreams of our youth [*he wafts a wreath of cigar smoke at large across the hill*]', to the engaging burlesque of such passages as the conversation between the housebreaker and Tarleton in *Misalliance*, when the former produces his accusing photographs:

> THE MAN: Look here, upon this picture and on this [*He holds out the two photographs like a hand at cards, and points to them with his pistol*].
> TARLETON: Good. Read Shakespear: he has a word for every occasion.

The rhetorical virtuosity of Shaw's dramatic prose is exemplified in his creation of satirical tirades, such as those of Napoleon in *The Man of Destiny*, the Devil and Don Juan in *Man and Superman*, Undershaft in *Major Barbara*. In the Shavian tirade brilliantly organized rhythmical and syntactical harmonies provide a unifying and directing force, as torrents of words develop cumulative energy before breaking into summary denunciatory statements:

you will never find an Englishman in the wrong. He does everything on principle. He fights you on patriotic principles; he robs you on business principles; he enslaves you on imperial principles; he bullies you on manly principles; he supports his king on loyal principles and cuts off his king's head on republican principles. His watchword is always Duty; and he never forgets that the nation which lets its duty get on the opposite side to its interest is lost.[12]

Shaw's verbal humour sometimes has an epigrammatic quality, as, for example, in one of Undershaft's numerous suggestions concerning his son Stephen's future, in *Major Barbara*: 'He knows nothing; and he thinks he knows everything. That points clearly to a political career.' But, unlike the wit of the dandies in Oscar Wilde, which tends to be more detachable from its dramatic context, humour in Shaw is usually closely associated with the portrayal of character and action. In the following exchange between Undershaft and Stephen the comedy of the more general satire is greatly enriched by knowledge of Stephen's character, and a consequent sense of the perfection of Undershaft's final choice of career for him:

UNDERSHAFT:	And what does govern England, pray?
STEPHEN:	Character, father, character.
UNDERSHAFT:	Whose character? Yours or mine?
STEPHEN:	Neither yours nor mine, father, but the best elements in the English national character.
UNDERSHAFT:	Stephen: Ive found your profession for you. Youre a born journalist. I'll start you with a high-toned weekly review. There!

The visual aspects of the plays testify further to the validity of Shaw's claim to high regard as a dramatic artist. The plays convey a strong sense of place; and the visual dimensions supplied by setting, costume and the physical appearance of the actors play an important part in the creation of meaning. The picture-postcard quality of the set for Raina's bedroom in *Arms and the Man*, with its view of the starlit snowy peak of the Balkans through the window, its painted wooden shrine with an ivory figure of Christ, its large photograph of the conventionally handsome Sergius, establishes by visual means an atmosphere of romantic sentiment which is soon to be rudely intruded upon by the arrival of Bluntschli. In Act I of *You Never Can Tell* the dentist's chair provides a comic image of pain, which is both literally and metaphorically related to the opening movement of the play's action, whilst the glimpse of the sea through the window is linked with later images in the play, and is significantly echoed early in Act I in a detail of costume. Act I of *Caesar and Cleopatra* opens with the striking image of a Sphinx cradling the girl Cleopatra in its paws. This image forms the imaginative and thematic centre of the dialogue which follows. Recalling a similar moment in Ibsen's *Peer Gynt*, Caesar hails the Sphinx as a symbol of the constant, contemplative and immortal part of his own self, whilst Cleopatra is associated with its connotations of primitive, destructive and revengeful power.

In *John Bull's Other Island*, *Major Barbara* and other plays, scenic transitions contribute significantly to the development of meaning. Act I of *John Bull's Other Island* is set in the London office of the civil engineering firm of Doyle and Broadbent, where the paraphernalia of plans, tracing paper and mathematical instruments reflects the pragmatic materialism of Broadbent's outlook. The Celtic world of poetry and dreams and religious devotion which Broadbent comes to conquer is conjured up visually at the beginning of Act II, for which the setting is Rosscullen at sunset, a '*hillside of granite rock and heather*', a round tower and a lonely white road winding past the tower to lose itself in the distant mountains. In *Major Barbara* the location of the action changes from the comfortable library of Lady Britomart's house in Wilton Crescent to the scenes of the Salvation Army shelter and the munitions factory, which literally force into view social realities which are largely ignored by Lady Britomart herself and Stephen.

Shaw makes skilful use of various other forms of the visual language of the theatre. The actress, Lillah McCarthy, who played several leading roles in Shaw's plays, makes illuminating comment on the non-verbal aspects of Shaw's art in her autobiography, *Myself and My Friends*:

The old tricks of production never count with him. He snatches his characters, his way of dressing them, his conception of their movements, from the streets, from anywhere, from people he actually knows. Here is an instance. We were preparing for the death scene in 'The Doctor's Dilemma'. When Dubedat, the artist, dies, Jennifer, his wife, goes from the room whilst the doctors bend over him. She returns, not in black and sombre clothes, but in a lovely flaming gown and a jewelled head-dress. London is shocked. . . .

[Dubedat's] was not a creed that could be served by a widow draped in mourning. I must return to the body of my husband in gorgeous raiment.[13]

Shaw had employed a similar visual device in *Man and Superman*. For her first appearance in Act I of that play, the stage direction tells us, Ann Whitefield has *'devised a mourning costume of black and violet silk'*, so that meanings in addition to the fact that she is in mourning for the death of her father are immediately conveyed in her appearance. Eliza Doolittle appears on the stage after her bath in Act I of *Pygmalion* as *'a dainty and exquisitely clean young Japanese lady in a simple blue cotton kimono printed cunningly with small white jasmine blossoms'*. The disguise deceives even her father, and his deferential 'Beg pardon, miss' makes a succinct point about the relations between class and appearance. In *Heartbreak House* Hector's character as dandified playboy, with shades of a quixotic T. E. Lawrence, and the idle game-playing of the inhabitants of the house, are emphasized by his appearance late in the play in a *'handsome Arab costume'*.

Shaw's strongly active visual imagination is also revealed in his descriptions of the physical appearance and deportment of the characters. If they cannot always be followed to the letter, the descriptions nevertheless provide lively guides for the actor and producer, supplementing what is created in the dialogue, as to the distinctive essence of a role. Before the term was invented Shaw was well aware of the forms of expression described by behavioural psychologists as 'body language'. Referring to a controversy about his description of one of H. G. Wells's visits to Russia, Shaw wrote: 'I cannot withdraw the word 'trotted' as descriptive of Wells' entry into the Kremlin. A man's mood is always reflected in his locomotion'.[14] Vivie Warren's repudiation of conventional forms of female behaviour is visually conveyed at the beginning of *Mrs Warren's Profession* in her manner of shaking hands, closing the garden gate and moving a chair. Mrs Whitefield in *Man and Superman* ('*a little woman, whose faded flaxen hair looks like straw on an egg*') is described as having '*an odd air of continually elbowing away some larger person who is crushing her into a corner*'. One of her attempts in Act I at asserting her tenuous authority over Ann is marked by her '*rising and shaking her widow's weeds straight*'.

The stage direction descriptions do not replace character cues in the dialogue. Linguistic definition of individual character and personality is clearly provided in the diction and rhythms of Shavian dialogue. Rather, the descriptions provide for the actor, producer and reader another dimension of character definition. They are evidence of the fully rounded quality of Shaw's art as a dramatist, of the creative energy and delight which went into the making of all aspects of his plays.

III

Critical indecision about Shaw's achievement and stature is matched by considerable uncertainty as to what kind of play-wright he is. Because it underwent so many metamorphoses during his long career, the generic character of his drama eludes easy description. His distinctive dramatic prose and recurrent thematic concerns give some stamp of unity to his work as a whole. But in the long journey from *Widowers' Houses* (1892) to *Far-Fetched Fables* (1948)[15] Shaw experimented with a very wide range of dramatic forms. In this respect he was both an extensive creative borrower and a bold innovator. It is now well recognized that his work has substantial links with popular dramatic forms of the nineteenth-century English theatre.[16] From the beginning, however, the relation between his work and the popular tradition was critical and parodic in character. He adapted familiar structures and conventions of forms such as the well-made play, the farce and melodrama, the romantic opera, the military adventure story, historical and religious dramas and even (in *Androcles and the Lion*) the pantomime, in ways which, combined with other influences, such as those of Ibsen and Wilde, helped to establish new standards of sophistication in the theatre and to revitalize the drama's engagement with 'life, character, and human destiny'. But in the course of his development Shaw moved progressively further away from Victorian formal models, and from naturalistic conventions.

Shaw's work can be seen to fall into three main periods of development: an early period in the 1890s, a middle period from *Man and Superman* (first performed 1903) to *Heartbreak House* (first performed 1920), and a late period beginning with *Back to Methuselah* (first performed 1921). Beginning in the 1890s with plays which rely upon relatively tight plot structures, he went on in the first two decades of the twentieth century to develop forms which, in contrast, are remarkable for their fluidity and freedom from close plotting constraints. The development of action in some plays of this middle period (such as *John Bull's Other Island, Getting Married, Misalliance* and *Heartbreak House*) involves skilfully controlled discontinuities in narrative, and kaleidoscopic shifts of view in the presentation of character relations, which are somewhat reminiscent of the techniques of Chekhov.[17] In many of the plays of the late period, Shaw makes a complete break with naturalism. In plays such as *Back to Methuselah, Too True to be Good* and *The Simpleton of the Unexpected Isles* setting and characterization become openly symbolic or allegorical, and fantastic incidents abound. In such works Shaw's art comes close to that of writers of science fiction and of utopian and dystopian fable. In the treatment of political subjects in this period, caricature and burlesque are constant ingredients of plays in which satirical sketches of national and European leaders strut before us like figures in an animated cartoon.

The main line of Shaw's development might be loosely summed up as a movement from naturalism to distinctive forms of comic and tragi-comic fantasy. But the label 'naturalistic' never sits quite comfortably on Shavian drama. The settings of many of the works of the early and middle period – in hotels, drawing rooms, studies and offices and the like – lend some semblance of a solid basis in familiar reality. Character portrayal in the plays before *Back to Methuselah* is usually fairly detailed in its attention to individually distinguishing features of personality, and verisimilitude is added by the fact that Shaw so often cuts through patterns of feeling suggested by fictional conventions to a substratum of more plausible motives and impulses. But even in this period Shaw's playful comic imagination continually takes us beyond the confines of naturalistic convention. Writing to Shaw in 1893 about *Widowers' Houses*, Oscar Wilde spoke admiringly of his fellow-dramatist's 'superb confidence in the dramatic value of the mere facts of life', and praised the 'horrible flesh and blood of [his] creatures'.[18] This is an understandable response to *Widowers' Houses*. But already in 1893 Shaw was writing his second play, *The Philanderer*, in which the 'mere facts of life' are treated with a colouring of extravagant satirical comedy. In the comedy of *The Philanderer*, especially that surrounding the manly sentiments of the theatre critic, Cuthbertson, and the failure of Dr Paramore's medical theory, Shaw laid the foundations of a style which was to be characteristic of the plays of his early and middle periods, and for which the phrase 'fantastic fidelity' seems most appropriate.[19] More complete departures from naturalism in the late period are anticipated in such scenes as Caesar's address to the Sphinx in *Caesar and Cleopatra*, the Dream sequence in *Man and Superman* and in most of the action in *Androcles and the Lion*, a work which carries the sub-title 'A Fable Play'.

In his essay 'J. M. Synge and the Ireland of his Time' (1910), W. B. Yeats writes of 'that Irish fantasy which overflowing through all Irish literature that has come out of Ireland itself . . . is the unbroken character of Irish genius'.

Our minds, [Yeats writes in the same essay] being sufficient to themselves, do not wish for victory but are content to elaborate our extravagance, if fortune aid, into wit or lyric beauty. . . . This habit of the mind has made Oscar Wilde and Mr Bernard Shaw the most celebrated makers of comedy to our time.[20]

Certainly there is a great deal of free-ranging extravagance of the kind to which Yeats refers here in Shavian comedy: one thinks of the distance from 'Zolaesque exactitude'[21] of such episodes as Androcles' rapturous waltz with the lion at the end of the Prologue to his play, or of the Angel descending amidst a hail of bullets in *The Simpleton of the Unexpected Isles*. Up to a point, it is possible to assent to Yeats's drawing together of the plays of Shaw, Wilde and Synge in the suggestive comment that 'fantasy gives the form and not the thought'.[22] But, in Shaw's case at least, some qualification needs to be made, since Shaw's thought and concern about social issues, his 'trick of zeal',[23] as Yeats calls it in a memorable understatement, cannot be disregarded as shaping influences on the plays. It is to this subject, of the relations between Shaw's intellectual outlook and the formal characteristics of his work, that we must now turn.

IV

Shaw was not alone in the English theatre of the 1890s as a writer of plays which engage with controversial social and moral questions. In 1882 William Archer, in the introduction to his *English Dramatists of To-day*, had roundly condemned the shallowness and philistinism of both the drama and the audience of the time. 'A drama which opens the slightest intellectual, moral, or political question', he wrote, 'is certain to fail.' The British public, he complained, 'will laugh always, cry sometimes, shudder now and then, but think – never'.[24] But in the nineties, as Archer himself was able to relate,[25] a new drama was developing alongside the old. The two most prominent English dramatists of the nineties, Arthur Wing Pinero and Henry Arthur Jones, were finding audiences receptive to plays in which such subjects as the Victorian double standard in sexual morality, the plight of the fallen woman, marital infidelity and female liberation were canvassed. At their best, Pinero and Jones treat such subjects with some sympathy and insight, but the plays of both dramatists suffer from the same fundamental flaw, evasiveness. However challenging the beginnings and middles of their plays may be, the ends are always written with an eye to the strict boundaries of Victorian moral sympathies. Both dramatists are vulnerable to the criticism which Shaw made of Pinero in a review of *The Notorious Mrs Ebbsmith* (1895), that 'he has no idea beyond that of doing something daring and bringing down the house by running away from the consequences'.[26] The plays of Pinero and Jones provide textbook examples of the relations which can exist between artistic form and ideological context. Whatever threats may be posed in the plays to the norms of Victorian morality, the movement of the action is invariably towards a facile and unconvincing return to the proprieties.[27]

One older contemporary, on the other hand, who could not be accused of 'running away from the consequences' was Ibsen. It was Ibsen, above all nineteenth-century creative writers, with the possible exception of Wagner, who provided for Shaw a standard of imaginative daring and seriousness in the theatre against which the performances of playwrights such as Jones and Pinero could be measured. Shaw's first encounter with Ibsen was not with the so-called social drama, but with *Peer Gynt*, in viva voce translations by William Archer.[28] Shaw responded keenly to the poetry and symbolism and tragi-comic artistry of Ibsen. In some ways the character of his reaction to Ibsen's dramatic art is more clearly revealed in the reviews Shaw wrote of early performances of the plays in London than in the major critical essay written in 1891, *The Quintessence of Ibsenism*. Writing of a performance of *The Wild Duck*, for example, he said:

> Where shall I find an epithet magnificent enough for The Wild Duck! To sit there getting deeper and deeper into that Ekdal home, and getting deeper and deeper into your own life all the time, until you forget that you are in a theatre; to look on with horror and pity at a profound tragedy, shaking with laughter all the time at an irresistible comedy.[29]

Admiring as he did the profound exploration of individual character and individual relationships in Ibsenian drama, Shaw was also deeply impressed by the challenge which plays such as *A Doll's House* and *Ghosts* threw out to nineteenth-century social ideals. Shaw's own plays are not often reminiscent of Ibsen's in their tonal qualities and structural design, but undoubtedly Ibsen's example was strongly influential in helping to shape the stance of opposition to contemporary society from which Shaw's early plays were written. Like Ibsen, and unlike Pinero and Jones, Shaw was able to create characters whose revolt does not melt at last into conformity, or death by suicide or fever, in order to please sentimental audiences.

Shaw's opposition to the Victorian social order – to its economic and political foundations, its sustaining ideals in relation to such topics as marriage and the family, duty and patriotism, its codes of conduct and conceptions of good form and good taste, its evasive sentimentality – had significant implications for the formal characteristics of the plays he wrote in the late nineteenth and early twentieth centuries. The structures of these plays either run counter to, or subtly re-direct, conventional patterns of comedy in several ways. In *Widowers' Houses* Shaw preserves the outline of a well-made play about young lovers overcoming obstacles in the way of their becoming married. But the comic pattern of the play is sharply distorted by the fact that the prospective marriage is seen not as a happy resolution of problems, but as an unpleasant act of consent to a social system which is clearly seen to be based on callous exploitation and uncontrolled acquisitiveness. In each of the other two plays in the *Plays Unpleasant* volume possible resolutions of the action in the form of romantic attachments fail to be realized. The endings of the two plays arise naturally from what has gone before, and they reflect a refusal on Shaw's part to undermine the insights he provides in these works into problems arising from new conceptions of male and female roles and the corrupting of filial and sexual relations by external social and economic forces.

In *Arms and the Man* and *Man and Superman* comic structure is affected by Shaw's critical treatment of nineteenth-century romàntic stereotypes. In these two plays male characters who, in different ways, reflect nineteeth-century romantic ideals take second place in the affections of the leading female characters to the distinctively Shavian heroes, Bluntschli and Tanner; and the plots of the plays develop in accordance with a shifting of sympathies from one kind of romantic ideal to another.

Most of the plays which Shaw wrote before the First World War, however radical their criticism, carry an underlying assumption that the ills of society are possibly remediable. The first major sign of tension within, if not complete breakdown of, this assumption appears in the Dream scene in *Man and Superman*. The device of the dream in *Man and Superman* provided Shaw with the freedom he needed for a wide-ranging survey of human nature and for a critical exploration of man's destructive and creative impulses. One leading idea in *Man and Superman* (to be developed further in *Back to Methuselah*) is the notion that through co-operation, by means of the will and the intelligence, with the evolutionary energies of the universe, the Life Force, Man might eventually evolve into a more altruistic and less self-destructive form of creation. But this theme is surrounded in the play by irony and scepticism. The Life Force ideas, which Shaw developed out of certain lines of nineteenth-century evolutionary thought have, with some justification, been regarded as a sign that his world view was fundamentally optimistic. But they can equally be seen as symptomatic of profound disillusionment with humanity in its present state. Viewed in one way, the Life Force theories can be seen as instruments of radical satire, in that they involve the notion that it is only by developing into a different kind of creature altogether that man can hope to survive. Like the Houyhnhnms in *Gulliver's Travels*, Shaw's fictional images of the Superman and of the He-Ancients and She-Ancients are serio-comic fantasies which throw into sharp relief the author's vision of man in his present state of development as a creature of savage and destructive folly.

The sombre vision of mankind which is presented by the Devil in the Dream scene of *Man and Superman* is framed by a relatively buoyant, and relatively conventional, comic structure. The stately and witty conduct of the debate in Hell itself suggests perspectives of civility and order, which are not completely cancelled by our recognition that the Devil *is*, after all, a gentleman. But the Devil's arguments about man were not put to rest by the end of *Man and Superman*. The pessimistic themes of that play recur as a strong undercurrent in *John Bull's Other Island* and *Major Barbara*, and they emerge again with scarcely contained violence in *Heartbreak House*. *Heartbreak House* is a portrait of a disintegrating society, and the thematic concerns of the play are mirrored in its fragmented, episodic and dream-like form. Instead of ending the play with a tying-up of plot strands, Shaw brings his characters to the edge of Armageddon in a final scene which is charged with a mixture of ecstatic exhilaration and fierce satire.

In the plays of the final period of his development one can sense an increasing measure of agreement on Shaw's part with the verdict of his Dutch Judge in *Geneva* (1938) who, presiding over an international court attended by caricatures of Mussolini, Hitler and Franco, together with other representatives of the conflicting ideologies of the twentieth century, declares that 'Man is a failure as a political animal'. There is an impression, too, in the late plays of a growing scepticism about the possibility of bridging the dangerous gulf between enlightened intelligence and the centres of power. In the poorly furnished office of the International Committee for Intellectual Co-operation,[30] which is the setting of Act I of *Geneva*, the following exchange takes place between the Secretary and a visitor:

HE: . . . How are the intellectual giants who form your committee bringing the enormous dynamic force of their brains, their prestige, their authority, to bear on the destinies of the nations? What are they doing to correct the mistakes of our ignorant politicians?

SHE: Well, we have their names on our note-paper, you know. What more can they do? You cant expect them to sit in this little hole talking to people. I have never seen one of them.

The bright despair of this is typical of the mood of the late plays.

A good deal is said about the plays of the late period in a letter Shaw wrote to Mrs St John Ervine on his way back from a tour of New Zealand in 1934:

My bolt is shot as far as any definite target is concerned and now, as my playwright faculty still goes on with the impetus of 30 years of vital activity, I shoot into the air more and more extravagantly without any premeditation whatever – *advienne que pourra*.[31]

Yet in spite of the come-what-may spirit in which they were evidently written, the formal characteristics of the late plays – the reduction of dramatis personae to caricature and character-type, the picaresque journeys, the projections of future societies, the uses of fable and fantasy – reflect a continuing, if sceptical, quest for a way of coming to terms with the disastrous history of the twentieth century. The precarious balance of Shaw's intellectual stance in the late plays is epitomized in the final scene of *On the Rocks* (1934) in which a rioting mob of unemployed can be heard singing Edward Carpenter's 'England Arise' to a background music of breaking glass, police whistles and '*a percussion accompaniment of baton thwacks*'.

V

The later plays command respect for their lively inventiveness and perceptive grappling with the key problems of twentieth-century Western societies. But it is the works of the early and middle periods of Shaw's career as a dramatist which seem likely to remain the most enduring monuments of his art and mind. Amongst the works of those periods, *Man and Superman*, *John Bull's Other Island*, *Major Barbara* and *Heartbreak House*, with *Caesar and Cleopatra* as their less artistically assured, but impressive, forerunner, stand out as works of major scope and significance. But there are many, less ambitious, works of the early and middle periods, such as *Mrs Warren's Profession*, *Arms and the Man*, *You Never Can Tell*, *The Doctor's Dilemma*, *Misalliance*, *Fanny's First Play*, *Androcles and the Lion* and *Pygmalion*, which by themselves would have secured for Shaw a very substantial reputation.

For some readers and playgoers, *Candida* and *Saint Joan* are the outstanding works in the Shavian canon. Both of these plays clearly have strong audience appeal, but they are also open to the charge that the appeal is made in somewhat suspect ways. *Saint Joan* is admirable for its grandeur of design and its boldly imaginative and intelligent interpretation of the Saint Joan legend. But the play is marred by the obtrusive factitiousness of the language which Shaw created for the central character and, more seriously, by his failure to create a prose poetry which is adequate for the moments of high emotion in the trial scene. The passages of poetical prose in *Candida* are similarly unsuccessful. At crucial points in both *Candida* and *Saint Joan* one senses that emotional effects are being created by too facile, even senti-mental, means.[32]

Shaw's occasional ventures into the realms of poetical prose are less than happy. Yet there are very many aspects of his work which prompt description of him as a great poet of the theatre. The proper spheres of his genius are comedy and tragi-comedy. In those spheres he displays a remarkable fertility of imagination and comedic invention. His comedy is informed with a strong sense of moral commitment and with an enduring concern for the well-being of human society. 'He Was Mankind's Friend' is the apt title of an essay on Shaw by Thomas Mann.[33] It would be wrong to dissociate his work altogether from the category in which it is so often placed, of 'the drama of ideas'. But the plays need to be rescued in critical discussion from that dusty, off-putting mental compartment, with its suggestions of dry abstraction and mechanical design, and recognized for the lively works of theatrical art that they are. Like his character Ann Whitefield in *Man and Superman*, Shaw was 'one of the vital geniuses'.

NOTES

1. Peter Ure, 'Master and Pupil in Bernard Shaw', *Essays in Criticism*, vol. xix, no. 2 (1969) p. 139.
2. J. I. M. Stewart, *Eight Modern Writers* (Oxford University Press, 1963) p. 183.
3. 'Shaw's dynamic as a dramatist has now largely weakened' – Raymond Williams, *Drama from Ibsen to Brecht* (Harmondsworth: Penguin Books, 1973) p. 290.
4. T. R. Barnes, 'Shaw and the London Theatre', in *The Modern Age: The Pelican Guide to English Literature*, ed. Boris Ford, vol. 7 (Harmondsworth: Penguin Books, 1961) p. 213.
5. An analysis of reviews in *The Stage* of London and provincial professional productions from June 1978 to May 1980 indicates that, next to Shakespeare, Shaw was by far the most frequently performed playwright in that period. A count of productions of works by a selected group of playwrights shows the following results: Shakespeare, 96; Shaw, 24; Coward, 12; Ibsen, 10; Chekhov, 8; Wilde, 8; Pinter, 6; Beckett, 3.
6. Amongst recent studies in which the dramatic artistry of the plays receives favourable attention are: Margery M. Morgan, *The Shavian Playground: An Exploration of the Art of George Bernard Shaw* (London: Methuen, 1972); Charles A. Berst, *Bernard Shaw and the Art of Drama* (Urbana: University of Illinois Press, 1973); Bernard F. Dukore, *Bernard Shaw: Director* (London: Allen & Unwin, 1971) and *Bernard Shaw, Playwright. Aspects of Shavian Drama* (Columbia: University of Missouri Press, 1973). Louis L. Crompton's valuable study, *Shaw the Dramatist* (Lincoln: University of Nebraska Press, 1969) is concerned more with the intellectual background and historical setting of the plays than with their dramatic artistry. This was pointed out by Crompton in the preface to the British edition of his work, which has a revised title, *Shaw the Dramatist: A Study of the Intellectual Background of the Major Plays* (London: Allen & Unwin, 1971). An account of earlier criticism of Shaw is provided in the final chapter of my *Writers and Critics* study, *Shaw* (Edinburgh: Oliver & Boyd, 1969).
7. *Sixteen Self Sketches* (London: Constable, 1949) p. 89.
8. *Bernard Shaw: Collected Letters 1874–1897*, ed. Dan H. Laurence (London: Max Reinhardt, 1965) p. 462.
9. Archibald Henderson, *The Table-Talk of G. B. S.* (London and New York: Harper, 1925) pp. 62–3.

10. Ibid., p. 63.
11. Ibid.
12. The speaker is Napoleon in *The Man of Destiny*.
13. Lillah McCarthy, *Myself and My Friends* (London: Thornton Butterworth, 1933) pp. 84–5. Shaw's idea for the head-dress was inspired by Judith Lytton, the beautiful wife of the artist Neville Lytton, who was accustomed to wearing her hair 'strung . . . with bands of sapphires, rubies and pearls' (ibid., p. 85).
14. This is recorded in Kingsley Martin's *Editor: A Second Volume of Autobiography, 1931–45* (London: Hutchinson, 1968) p. 87.
15. The latter was his last dramatic work, not including the puppet play *Shakes Versus Shav* (1949) and a comic sketch, *Why She Would Not* (1950).
16. The fullest and most authoritative study of this subject is still Martin Meisel's *Shaw and the Nineteenth-Century Theater* (Princeton University Press, 1963; Oxford University Press, 1963).
17. Shaw acknowledges Chekhov's influence in the Preface to *Heartbreak House*.
18. *Selected Letters of Oscar Wilde*, ed. Rupert Hart-Davis (Oxford University Press, 1979) p. 112.
19. Michael K. Goldberg, in his article 'Shaw's Dickensian Quintessence', *The Shaw Review*, vol. XIV, no. 1 (Jan. 1971) pp. 14–28, attributes the phrase 'fantastic fidelity' to Dickens himself. However this attribution seems dubious.
20. W. B. Yeats, *Essays and Introductions* (London: Macmillan, 1961) pp. 337–9. Cf. Max Beerbohm's comment: 'Shaw's great gift . . . lay in his wild and irresponsible Irish humour' – cited in S. N. Behrman, *Conversations with Max* (London: Hamish Hamilton, 1960) p. 138.
21. A phrase employed by an early reviewer of *Widowers' Houses*.
22. Yeats, *Essays and Introductions*, p. 339.
23. Ibid., p. 339. Yeats includes Oscar Wilde in this comment.
24. William Archer, *English Dramatists of To-day* (London: Sampson Low, Marston, Searle & Rivington, 1882) p. 9. Archer concludes these strictures with some remarks which may have given Shaw the idea for the title of the first volume of his plays:

> Especially it [the British public] will have nothing to do with a piece to whose theme the word 'unpleasant' can be applied. This epithet is of undefined and elastic signification, but once attach it to a play and all chance for it is past. Nothing can be more deplorable. Theatrical audiences are seldom entirely composed of young ladies' boarding-schools, and in a world constituted as ours is, the serious facts of life cannot be seriously treated without touching on subjects which may be classed as 'unpleasant'.

25. In the last four chapters of *The Old Drama and the New: An Essay in Revaluation* (Boston, Mass.: Small, Maynard, 1923).
26. *Our Theatres in the Nineties*, 3 vols (London: Constable, 1948) vol. I, p. 63.
27. The plays which best illustrate this are Jones's *The Case of Rebellious Susan* (1894), *Michael and his Lost Angel* (1896) and *The Hypocrites* (1906); and

Pinero's *The Profligate* (1889), *The Second Mrs Tanqueray* (1893) and *The Notorious Mrs Ebbsmith* (1895).

28. 'Ibsen first fascinated me when in the scraps that Archer translated to me viva voce I recognized my own youth in Peer Gynt, with painting and music and poetry added' (MS reply to O'Bolger, Houghton Library, Harvard University, bMS Eng. 1046. 9, p. 9).

29. *Our Theatres in the Nineties*, vol. III, p. 138.

30. A Committee with the title 'Organization of Intellectual Co-operation' was established by the League of Nations. Its membership included: Henri Bergson, Mme Curie, Albert Einstein and Gilbert Murray (see Gilbert Murray, *Liberality and Civilisation* (London: Allen & Unwin, 1938) p. 45).

31. St John Ervine, *Bernard Shaw: His Life, Work and Friends* (London: Constable, 1956) p. 555.

32. The critical problems raised by *Candida* are examined in detail in Chapter 6 below. *Saint Joan* is omitted from this study, not in a spirit of dismissal, but from a belief that the play has had more than its due of critical attention in recent years. A collection of critical essays on the play has been edited by Stanley Weintraub – see his *Saint Joan, Fifty Years After* (Baton Rouge: Louisiana State University Press, 1973). See also the works by Crompton and Morgan in the references cited above (note 6).

33. In the *Listener*, 18 Jan. 1951.

3 The Economics of Love

Married! The Captain is a bold man and will risk anything for money.

> (Gay, *The Beggar's Opera*)

She was in love with him, which was natural . . . but romance was not the game which he was playing.

> (Trollope, *The Way We Live Now*)

HECTOR: . . . Why wont you let me own up?
VIOLET: We cant afford it. You can be as romantic as you please about love, Hector; but you mustnt be romantic about money.

> (*Man and Superman*)

The first and third of the works in Shaw's *Plays Unpleasant* volume, *Widowers' Houses* and *Mrs Warren's Profession*, lend themselves to discussion together because of their common concern with the ways in which private spheres of love, friendship and family relations are affected by the economic organization of society as a whole. Defending her profession, as a manager of a chain of brothels, Mrs Warren describes some of the connections between economics and love in very bald terms:

The only way for a woman to provide for herself decently is for her to be good to some man that can afford to be good to her. If she's in his own station of life, let her make him marry her; but if she's far beneath him she cant expect it: why should she? it wouldnt be for her own happiness.

In *Widowers' Houses* the relations between father and daughter, and daughter and lover, are seen to be dominated and polluted by economic considerations. Harry Trench, the young lover in the play, is drawn by an irresistible combination of forces into a marriage which signifies his acquiescence in a system of economic exploitation which he despises. Unlike Clennam in *Little Dorrit*, Trench is not redeemed from his more or less innocent initial complicity in corruption by marriage to a pure young woman. In *Mrs Warren's Profession* the only way in which Vivie Warren, in contrast to Trench, achieves a degree of integrity is by complete repudiation of her closest personal ties, ties which are also deeply affected by economic factors. The economic and social realities revealed to her in the course of the play are such as to make 'love's young dream' repugnant to her.

Confusions between acquisitive and romantic interests in the love relation are familiar enough as a topic of literary satire. But Shaw treats this subject with an unusually sharp focus in the two early plays under discussion here, and perceptively reveals its broader social bearings. His approach to the topic differs from that of, say, Trollope in *The Way We Live Now*, where again the economic dimensions of the love relation are a major concern. In Trollope's world of upper-class cads and fortune hunters in *The Way We Live Now*, the forms of behaviour which come under critical scrutiny are lapses from codes of honourable conduct within a social dispensation which is not itself under serious attack. As Walter Allen remarks of the novel, 'it is a detailed study of corruption in society in all its aspects, literary, journalistic, financial, though at bottom what we are faced with is always corruption of manners, of the code of behaviour in decent society'.[1] But in *Widowers' Houses* and *Mrs Warren's Profession* it is the entire structure of 'decent society' itself which is the principal target of attack. Decent society in fact becomes, in these plays, a contradiction in terms, because the forms of decency are revealed to be amongst the means by which a corrupt social system is kept intact. The limitations on moral action and choice which the system imposes for the individual are curtly indicated in a speech by Sir George Crofts to Vivie Warren: 'If youre going to pick and choose your acquaintances on moral principles, youd better clear out of this country, unless you want to cut yourself out of all decent society.'

Widowers' Houses is unquestionably a minor work in the Shavian canon. The methods of the play do not to any great extent adumbrate those of mature Shavian comedy; and, of all

his works for the stage, it is perhaps the one which most carries
with it the air of a social thesis. But despite some crudities it is an
impressive first play. The portrayal of the grey, resigned and
ironical character of the rackrenting landlord, Sartorius, is
particularly well done, as is that of his ruthlessly manipulative
daughter, Blanche. And the analysis which is developed in the
play of the motives and defences of those in power in a society
based on private capital and property ownership remains, in its
essentials, pertinent and challenging.

The plot of *Widowers' Houses* is partly based on that of a 'well-
made' play by the French dramatist Émile Augier, entitled
Ceinture Dorée. The French play concerns the predicament of an
honourable young man who finds that the inherited fortune of
the young lady he intends to marry is tainted by the fact that it
was immorally gained by her father. The marriage is threatened:
but the situation is saved when the young lady's family fortune is
lost in a national crisis, a turn of events which enables the two
lovers to marry with a free conscience and live poor but honest.
The meaning of Shaw's play can be partly defined in terms of its
critical relation to this source. In *Widowers' Houses* no artificial
solution is produced to the problem of tainted income, and the
young man himself is ironically discovered to be as much
dependent upon slum landlordism as the young lady. The young
lady, though initially shocked, is not deeply perturbed by the
discovery of the sordid realities of her father's occupation; and in
the end Trench joins with her in assenting to the corrupt society
which the play depicts.

The critical methods of Shaw's play are in some ways
reminiscent of those of Swift in *A Tale of a Tub*. The civilized
forms of society, its sartorial surfaces (the name of the slum
landlord, Sartorius, is symbolic) are seen in the play both as
masks of primitive and animalistic behaviour and also as part of
the machinery of power. The key for the play's fierce juxtapo-
sitions of mask and reality is set in Cokane's description, in the
opening speech of Act I, of the tourist attractions of Southern
Germany: '. . . We'll leave in the morning, and do Mainz and
Frankfurt. There is a very graceful female statue in the private
house of a nobleman in Frankfurt. Also a zoo. Next day,
Nuremberg! finest collection of instruments of torture in the
world.' With its casual transition from images of aristocratic

culture and female elegance to animals and instruments of torture, this list of tourist attractions presents an impressionistic forecast of the portrayal of capitalist society which emerges in the later action. Blanche, the 'graceful female' associated with private property in the play, combines with her lady-like deportment and outlook a habit of sadistically maltreating her maid with brutal speech and physical violence. Her sexual conquest of Trench at the end of the play is carried out *'in a flush of undisguised animal excitement'*. Sartorius is confronted in his *'handsomely appointed'* villa at Surbiton with the shabby instrument of his profession, Lickcheese, who is hideously unkempt, and described in the stage direction as a *'pertinacious human terrier'*. The appearance of Lickcheese here constitutes an eruption of the underworld which has been largely kept from view in Act I. There, in the garden restaurant overlooking the Rhine, society appears in its formal dress. Sartorius enters splendidly attired in a light frock-coat with silk linings and a white hat. In the course of the dialogue which follows, the deeper social significance of his elegant appearance is brought out. As in the society portrayed by Castiglione in *The Courtier* or in Burke's idealisation of English society in *Reflections on the Revolution in France*, the surface is of the essence. Shortly after Sartorius's entry in Act I, Cokane speaks of social customs such as those practised by Lady Roxdale in London as 'apparently idle ceremonial trifles, really the springs and wheels of a great aristocratic system'. Cokane is a Mrs General-like spokesman for etiquette, respectability and good taste. Through him, Shaw sketches the codes of gentlemanly and ladylike behaviour in which the exploitative society finds its rationale and its sustaining power.

In the portrayal of Lickcheese the clothing motif undergoes further development. Both the physical appearance and the speeches of Lickcheese in Act II show us Sartorius's world stripped of its adornment and revealed in ugly reality. But Lickcheese does not present any basic moral contrast to Sartorius. With more justification than Sartorius, but with the same social effects, he is motivated in his predatory behaviour by family loyalty: he has to allow other children to starve in order to prevent his own children from starving. The play does not point to any possibility of the circle of exploitation being broken by spontaneous revolt on the part of the lower classes. When Lickcheese gets his chance after being dismissed by Sartorius for being insufficiently tough as a rent-collector, he simply becomes a more powerful and successful predator, and takes on the appropriate costume. The reappearance of Lickcheese as a 'swell' in Act III has more significance than description of it as a *coup de théâtre* would suggest. His circus-manager style of dress, though comical in immediate effect, is an image of his new social role. His sealskin overcoat, the wonder of the parlormaid, who immediately associates it with gentlemanliness ('Quite the gentleman, sir! Sealskin overcoat, sir'), is '*lined throughout with furs presenting all the hues of the tiger*'. Draped triumphantly on Blanche's chair as it is shortly after his arrival, the coat, with its bizarre mixture of animal skins, points to the predatory nature of his new-found strength.

The entry of Lickcheese encapsulates, in a moment of broad farce, ideas about the connection between Darwinism and Capitalism which found fuller expression later in Shaw's career in the Preface to *Back to Methuselah*, where, in the section headed 'Why Darwin Pleased the Profiteers Also', Shaw points out that 'Darwinism was so closely related to Capitalism that Marx regarded it as an economic product rather than as a biological theory.'[2]

In *Widowers' Houses* Lickcheese demonstrates, in the broadest colours, social Darwinism in action: unchecked by political controls and determined interference, the Capitalist society functions at all levels according to Darwinian laws of survival and conquest. Shaw's later critique of Darwinism is anticipated in another way in *Widowers' Houses*, in the treatment of the attitudes which the characters display towards their social predicament. The 'characteristic blight' of Darwinism, Shaw more than once insisted, is 'an unbreathable atmosphere of fatalism'.[3] All the major characters in his first play could be said to illustrate this, but it is Sartorius who makes articulate the pervasive atmosphere of fatalistic consent in his retort to Trench: 'If, when you say you are just as bad as I am, you mean you are just as powerless to alter the state of society, then you are unfortunately quite right.'

In some respects Sartorius can be seen as an early draft for the characterization of Undershaft in *Major Barbara*. The ironical and polite manner in which Sartorius enlightens Trench as to the true nature of the young man's situation is clearly echoed in

Undershaft's dialogues with his son, Stephen, in the later play. But, in contrast with Undershaft, the melancholy and inwardly uncertain, though aggressive, character which Shaw gives Sartorius has no altruistic or philosophical dimensions. He is perceptive and human enough to see that the callousness of Blanche's attitude towards poverty is a sad sign of the success of her education as a lady; but, for his part, the only gesture made towards improving the plight of the poor is in the form of 'charitable' action in which he himself has a pecuniary interest, namely the provision of more tenement houses. As the final act of the play shows, the forces which he and Lickcheese represent readily assimilate and convert to profitable use the humanitarian and progressive ideas which are directed against them.

The connections between sexual and family relations and their economic context emerge in a variety of ways in the play. Language associated with commerce and property readily transfers in point of reference to other areas of human relations. In Act I Sartorius refers to the engagement between Blanche and Trench as a 'transaction'. In Act III Trench's sulky protest to Lickcheese, 'I wont have the relations between Miss Sartorius and myself made part of a bargain',[4] serves only to underline the true basis of the union which is about to be confirmed. A lovers' quarrel in Act II centres around the question of the cash basis of the future marriage. Trench's awkward position in the trap between his affection for Blanche and his newly-awakening understanding of Sartorius's activities is well conveyed in the following passage:

BLANCHE: [getting behind him, and speaking with forced playfulness as she bends over him, her hands on his shoulders] Of course it's nothing. Now dont be absurd, Harry: be good; and listen to me: I know how to settle it. You are too proud to owe anything to me; and I am too proud to owe anything to you. You have seven hundred a year. Well, I will take just seven hundred a year from papa at first; and then we shall be quits. Now, now, Harry, you know youve not a word to say against that.

TRENCH: It's impossible.

BLANCHE: Impossible!

TRENCH: Yes, impossible. I have resolved not to take any
          money from your father.
BLANCHE: But he'll give the money to me, not to you.
TRENCH: It's the same thing. [*With an effort to be sentimental*]
          I love you too well to see any distinction. [*He puts
          up his hand halfheartedly: she takes it over his shoulder
          with equal indecision. They are both trying hard to
          conciliate one another*].

In the final scene between the two, when Blanche enters to find
Trench studying a photograph of herself she delivers a taunting,
hostile speech, the erotic design of which is fulfilled at the end
when she '[. . . *crushes him in an ecstatic embrace as she adds, with
furious tenderness*] How dare you touch anything belonging to me?'
The remark has doubly ironic force, as we are aware, simultaneously, of her determined act of possession of him and of the
basis of their relations in property ownership. Designed as a
deliberate travesty of the conventional happy ending of romantic
comedy, the scene brings together conflicting feelings with
peculiar force. Blanche's speech harps on the ambiguity and
hypocrisy of Trench's position, but, in the embrace, erotic feeling
is mingled with consent to a morally disintegrating social
conspiracy. There is no reason to suppose that in her future
relations with Trench, Blanche would be any less ruthless than
she is with her maid (whose maltreatment in Act II is the result of
the temporary frustration of Blanche's designs on Trench) or
with her father, to whom she makes clear that her love for him is
based on the fact that he has provided her with material security:
'I should hate you if you had not'.

Contemporary critical comments on *Widowers' Houses*, which
Shaw gleefully assembled in a later preface, were, for the most
part, splendidly predictable:

> . . . Mr Shaw's world has not rags enough to cover its nudity.
> [The clothing metaphor is worth remarking on.] He aims to
> show with Zolaesque exactitude that middle-class life is foul
> and leprous. (*Athenaeum*)

> The mere word 'mortgage' suffices to turn hero into
> rascal. (*Speaker*)

In a sense, such comments serve only to echo the meaning of the play itself. But they might also be said to reveal weaknesses in the play's critical methods. Later Shavian comedy is richer, lighter in touch and more generous in its treatment of conservative opponents, and hence less open to dismissal as the 'revelation of a distorted and myopic outlook on society' (*Sunday Sun*).[5] *Widowers' Houses* nevertheless commands respect, both for its courageous challenge to society and for the deeply critical light it casts on the threadbare conventions of Victorian comedy.

The final play of the *Plays Unpleasant* volume, *Mrs Warren's Profession*, has thematic connections not only with *Widowers' Houses* but also with the second play in the volume, *The Philanderer*. Vivie Warren, Mrs Warren's daughter and a mathematics graduate from Cambridge, has much in common with the New Women of the Ibsen Club in *The Philanderer*. In her are combined aspects of the characters of both Grace Tranfield and Sylvia Craven. Her predicament in the play, as the discoverer of the fact that she is living on income derived from a tainted source, is related to that of Trench in *Widowers' Houses*, and, further back in Shaw's artistic evolution, to Trefusis, the hero of *An Unsocial Socialist*. The character of Cokane in *Widowers' Houses* has a more amiably human and credible counterpart in Mrs Warren's artistically inclined friend Praed, who in the last act of *Mrs Warren's Profession* offers to escort Vivie on a European tour like the one Trench and Cokane are embarked upon in Act I of the earlier play. *Mrs Warren's Profession* presents the same jaundiced view of artistic culture in an economically diseased society as did the earlier play; and Mrs Warren herself, as one of the consenting agents of exploitation (though she is treated far more sympathetically) is obviously linked with Sartorius.

In *Mrs Warren's Profession* Shaw again drew on a French source for primary plot material – in this case on a story entitled *Yvette* by Guy de Maupassant. The heroine of Maupassant's story, Yvette, is a lively and innocent young girl who in the course of the narrative makes the discovery that her mother is a courtesan. Appalled by her discovery, she attempts to commit suicide. She is rescued from her attempt by a man who, all the indications of the story suggest, will lead her into the same sort of life as that of her mother. This understanding having been established, the story closes with the mother and daughter embracing one another.

Shaw's play is also linked with a popular genre in the nineteenth-century English and French theatres of plays about repentant 'magdalens'. (Martin Meisel points out that in 1893, when Shaw was writing the play, there were two plays on the London stage about women with a past, *La Dame aux Camélias* and *The Second Mrs Tanqueray*.)[6] The 'magdalens' in these plays were, characteristically, beautiful, careless and improvident women, deeply ashamed of their former life and desperately trying to get back to innocence and respectability. Mrs Warren is a counter-portrait of this conventional type. She is Shaw's Wife of Bath: a vital, generous, vulgar woman, whose hard-headed shrewdness in business is balanced by sentimentality and warm sensuality. She is not ashamed of her past, society having offered her no reasonable alternative courses of action to the one she took; and she doesn't need to 'get back' because she *is* respectable. The money she earns from the chain of brothels which she runs with her crony, Sir George Crofts, enables her to send her daughter to boarding schools and then Cambridge and to live comfortably herself in the pleasant and respectable village of Haslemere in Surrey, where, with apt irony, most of the action of the play is set.

Vivie – the name is perhaps a play on Yvette, and suggests her character as a potentially regenerative force in the society which the play depicts – is intellectually and physically vigorous, unconventional and high-principled. Though candid and vivacious in conversation, she is priggish and, understandably enough, lacking in humour. The narrowness of her mathematical education at Cambridge, her analytical conversational manner and her professional interest in actuarial calculations combine to make her seem, at first, a rather mechanical figure. Her suitor, Frank, supplies Vivie's want of humour, and has moments of wisdom and perception, but is generally a lightweight and feckless character. Vivie's relations with her mother and Frank develop along parallel and related lines. At the beginning of the play she is almost completely estranged from her mother, the two having mostly lived apart during Vivie's school and university days. Mrs Warren treats her with affected maternal gestures, and fails to recognize her adulthood, introducing her to Crofts in Act I as 'my little Vivie'. At the beginning of Act II Mrs Warren has a mildly flirtatious scene with Frank, but then becomes querulously solicitous about Vivie's sexual relations with him. She wishes to dissociate from Vivie the sexual feelings which she has herself towards Frank: 'I wont have any young scamp tampering with my little girl.'

At the end of Act II we reach a substratum of character in the two women in a well-handled scene in which Vivie finds out about her mother's past. At the end of this narrative, with the scene lit by moonlight, Vivie has a moment (which she later recognizes to be illusory) of complete acceptance of her mother, and the curtain falls as they embrace. The moonlit illusion in Act II is echoed in Act III by an odd, escapist love scene between Vivie and Frank, in which Vivie herself plays a maternalistic role. In their embrace the two seek to enshroud themselves in a new illusion of childhood innocence and romance:

FRANK: The babes in the wood: Vivie and little Frank. [*He nestles against her like a weary child*]. Lets go and get covered up with leaves.

VIVIE: [*rhythmically, rocking him like a nurse*] Fast asleep, hand in hand, under the trees.

FRANK: The wise little girl with her silly little boy.

VIVIE: The dear little boy with his dowdy little girl.

FRANK: Ever so peaceful, and relieved from the imbecility of the little boy's father and the questionableness of the little girl's –

VIVIE: [*smothering the word against her breast*] Sh-sh-sh-sh! little girl wants to forget all about her mother.

But this scene is only the prelude to a new awakening. The scene shows that the only way in which Vivie can release sexual feeling and achieve tenderness is by closing off her mind from the realities of her situation as a whole.

In a letter to William Archer written after he had completed the first act of *Mrs Warren's Profession*, Shaw gaily declared that in the play he had 'skilfully blended the plot of *The Second Mrs Tanqueray* with that of *The Cenci*'.[7] Seven years before, Shaw had been closely associated with a production of *The Cenci* sponsored by the Shelley Society.[8] Shaw commented unfavourably on Shelley's play at the time, but clearly his treatment of the theme of incest in *Mrs Warren's Profession* was partly influenced by

Shelley's example in *The Cenci*. It appears from a manuscript draft of the play that at one point Shaw intended to leave no doubt in the audience's mind as to the truth of Crofts's assertion that Frank's father, the Reverend Samuel Gardner, was also the father of Vivie.[9] In the published version of the play he deliberately leaves open the question as to whether the father of Vivie was Gardner or Crofts. This enables him to expand the incest theme in the play, by hinting at the possibility that Crofts's advances to Vivie may be incestuous in character, as well as to suggest the possibility of incest in the relationship between Frank and Vivie.

The atmosphere and tone of *Mrs Warren's Profession* are obviously remote from the Gothic horrors and pseudo-Shakespearean rhetoric of *The Cenci*. Nevertheless, there are clear and significant parallels between the two works. The chief male character in Shelley's play, the Count, is a gross and perverse sensualist whose incestuous assault on his daughter, Beatrice, is the last resort of a jaded appetite:

> Invention palls . . .
> And but that there yet remains a deed to act
> Whose horror might make sharp an appetite
> Duller than mine – I'd do – I know not what.[10]

His vast wealth and powerful political and ecclesiastical connections enable him to make a mockery of justice with 'gold, opinion, law and power'. Eventually in the play the Count's crimes are revenged by Beatrice and others, who conspire to have him murdered. His counterpart in Shaw's play is Sir George Crofts, one of the most thoroughly disagreeable of Shaw's characters, whom the stage direction requires to appear dressed fashionably, but in a style too young for his age, as a '*gentlemanly combination of the most brutal types of city man, sporting man, and man about town*'. The manuscript shows more explicitly than the published play the links between Crofts and Count Cenci, in the treatment there of a brief scene between Crofts and Mrs Warren in Act II. The manuscript has the following passage of dialogue relating to Crofts's feelings about Vivie:

MRS W: Yes: it's the sort of thing that would grow in your

> mind. [*lowering her voice*] How do you know that
> the girl maynt be your own daughter, eh?
>
> CROFTS: [*lowering his*] How do *you* know that that maynt be
> one of the fascinations of the thing? What harm if
> she is?[11]

In the published version, no doubt with the censor in mind, this plot motif was considerably muted. But we are still made aware, through his own words to Praed in Act I, that Crofts may have been Vivie's father; and Shaw clearly wanted to convey by innuendo the substance of the speeches spoken in lowered voices above in a piece of stage business. In the published version, the first sentence of Mrs Warren's speech as it appears above is retained, but the rest is replaced by the following stage direction:

> *He halts in his prowling; and the two look at one another, she steadfastly, with a sort of awe behind her contemptuous disgust: he stealthily, with a carnal gleam in his eye and a loose grin.*

Following Shelley's example, Shaw directs the animus of revulsion about incest against the whole social system which the paternal figures represent. In both plays paternal authority appears in warped and perverse (or in the case of the Rev. Samuel Gardner, ineffectual) forms and its structure is held together by money and social influence. In their scene in Act III Crofts explains to Vivie that the scholarship she held at Newnham was 'founded by [his] brother the M.P. He gets his 22 per cent out of a factory with 600 girls in it, and not one of them getting wages enough to live on.' Society, he tells her, maintains a discreet silence about activities such as those engaged in by himself and Mrs Warren: 'In the class of people I can introduce you to, no lady or gentleman would so far forget themselves as to discuss my business affairs or your mother's.'

Vivie's progress in the play is towards complete dissociation of herself from the society which the play encompasses. The feelings which lead to this are a compound of moral revolt and sexual frigidity, the latter being caused by the knowledge she gains of her mother's profession, and precipitated by Crofts's revolting proposal of marriage. Again the manuscript draft is more explicit in its account of motivation. Shaw completely altered the end of

Act III which had originally contained, amongst other things, two self-analytical speeches by Vivie in which her feelings towards her mother, Crofts and Frank are described as follows:

> VIVIE: . . . From moment to moment it has been growing on me that I must get away from it all – away from the sentiment of the tie I formed under the spell of that ghastly moonlight, away from the very air breathed by my mother and that man, away from the world they are part of. I thought of killing myself.
>
> FRANK: My dear Viv – what about little Frank?
>
> VIVIE: Frank was the most unbearable thought of all; for I knew that he would press on me the sort of relation that my mother's life had tainted for ever for me. I felt that I would rather die than let him touch me with that in his mind.[12]

Although some loss of clarity is involved, the final version of the scene is considerably more forceful dramatically. The thought of suicide (which echoes Beatrice's 'I thought to die' in *The Cenci*)[13] is translated into potential action in the final version when Vivie turns the rifle with which Frank has threatened Crofts against her own breast. Her revulsion from sex is tersely expressed in her cry to Frank, 'Ah, not that, not that. You make all my flesh creep.' Further explanation of her feelings is cut short by her precipitous departure for Chancery Lane.

The actuarial calculations at Honoria Fraser's chambers seem a bleak prospect. But the play does compel us, convincingly enough, to see Vivie's choices in Act IV as being at least understandable. We may wish for a moment of self-appraisal, such as that which Shelley gives Beatrice when, in stating her preference for a sisterly relation with her lover Orsino, she says 'sorrow makes me seem / Sterner than else my nature might have been',[14] but Vivie's resolute negations as she weathers out the emotional storms of the meetings with Frank, Praed and her mother in Act IV have an impressive strength. Chesterton thought the play Shaw's 'only complete, or nearly complete, tragedy',[15] and Shaw himself evidently thought of the play in similar terms: it is subtitled in the manuscript 'A tragic variation on the theme of "Cashel Byron's Profession"'. The point is debatable: Vivie is, after all, alive, alert and busy at the end of the play. Nevertheless her position of lonely and bitter isolation does bring us close to the mood of tragedy, and one could apply to her situation Shaw's comment on tragedy in the Preface to 'Three Plays by Brieux': 'the tragedy of modern life is that nothing happens, and the resultant dulness does not kill. Maupassant's Une Vie is infinitely more tragic than the death of Juliet.'[16]

Vivie's actions have a clear moral and emotional logic. But the sympathies in the final scenes of the play are distributed with an even hand. We see the need for Vivie to reject Mrs Warren, who, in the final analysis, must be judged by her friends, by her consent and contribution to the social forces represented by Crofts and his brother the MP, the 'big people, the clever people, the managing people', to whose authority she appeals in the tense final quarrel with Vivie. But critical thoughts of this kind are far from mind at such moments in the quarrel as when the mother, who has been so anxious to provide a genteel education for her daughter, declares her own defiant hostility to ladylike respectability: 'Imagine me in a cathedral town! Why, the very rooks in the trees would find me out even if I could stand the dulness of it', or in the resounding final stroke of argument which Shaw provides her with before her departure: 'Lord help the world if everybody took to doing the right thing!'

The play demands that a distinction be drawn between the positive energies of Mrs Warren's revolt, as an individual, against pious rectitude and hypocrisy, on the one hand, and, on the other, the corruption of the society which forces her into such unpleasant alternative alliances. In the final act of the play Mrs Warren echoes the declaration of Milton's Satan, 'evil be thou my good': 'From this time forth, so help me Heaven in my last hour, I'll do wrong and nothing but wrong. And I'll prosper on it.' Set against the time-serving advice of the 'lying clergyman' and abstracted from the seedy relation with Crofts, her stance presents itself as, within its obvious limitations, a positive and vital force.

In socio-economic terms, Vivie is not Mrs Warren's direct antithesis. She is, as she tells us, her mother's daughter in thriftiness. At most we can see in Vivie the old society reaching a point of self-consciousness from which change may develop.

Later, in *Major Barbara*, Shaw was to present 'the big people, the clever people, the managing people', who are the villains of *Mrs Warren's Profession*, in an entirely different light, and to explore the possibility of a synthesis of diabolonian vitality and enlightened ethical principle. In *Mrs Warren's Profession* we are left with these forces partially displayed and fully opposed, in a discordant close which is one of the characteristic marks of *Plays Unpleasant*.

NOTES

1. Walter Allen, *The English Novel* (Harmondsworth: Penguin Books, 1958) p. 206.
2. See *The Complete Prefaces of Bernard Shaw* (London: Paul Hamlyn, 1965) p. 531. This passage was deleted in the World's Classics edition of *Back to Methuselah*, published in 1945; but the argument connecting Darwinism and Capitalism remains essentially the same.
3. *Prefaces*, p. 531; cf. ibid., p. 520.
4. Cf. Augier, *Ceinture Dorée*, Act I: 'tu as rencontré un homme pour qui le mariage n'était pas une spéculation. Il cherchait une compagne et non une bâilleuse de fonds' (*Théâtre Complet de Émile Augier*, 7 vols (Paris: Ancienne Maison Michel Levy Frères, 1895–7) vol. III, p. 301).
5. *Prefaces*, pp. 705–6.
6. Martin Meisel, *Shaw and the Nineteenth-Century Theater* (Princeton University Press; Oxford University Press, 1963) p. 143.
7. *Bernard Shaw: Collected Letters 1874–1897*, ed. Dan H. Laurence (London: Max Reinhardt, 1965) p. 403.
8. Ibid., pp. 154–5.
9. The manuscript (British Library MS Add. 50598) has the following passage of dialogue between Mrs Warren and Gardner with a cancelling line running through it:

REV. S. : Ah-er-how old is Miss Warren, pray [?]
MRS W. : You'll not tell Crofts? Honour bright?
REV. S. : Certainly not.
MRS W. : She's twenty three last March.
REV. S. : [*appalled*] Twenty three last March!
MRS W. : Twenty three last March. Go home and figure that out, Sam; and then consider whether you hadn't better talk seriously to Master Frank.

10. Shelley, *Poetical Works*, ed. Thomas Hutchinson, new edn, corr. G. M. Matthews (London: Oxford University Press, 1970) p. 281.
11. British Library MS Add. 50598.

12. Ibid.
13. Shelley, *Poetical Works*, p. 300.
14. Ibid., p. 283.
15. G. K. Chesterton, *George Bernard Shaw* (London: John Lane, 1909) p. 131.
16. *Prefaces*, p. 199.

4 Old Adam and New Eve: *The Philanderer*

> It seems to me you can trust feminists – or any other '-ists', for that matter – only when they speak from personal truth in all its complexity. Such truth is never black or white.
>
> (Betty Friedan, 'Feminism's New Frontier', 1979)

I

In a period of history when such a role was far from fashionable, Shaw was a forceful, eloquent and unpatronizing champion of women's rights. In essays and speeches he repeatedly affirmed his belief in the equality of the sexes, and argued the case for this to be recognized not only in the political, economic and legal organization of society, but also in people's perceptions and attitudes. A recurrent theme in Shaw's treatment of feminist issues outside the plays is that male and female processes of thought and feeling are essentially identical. In a speech delivered in 1913, he declared 'I myself have the rather original view about woman that she is very much the same sort of person as I am myself. But unfortunately that view is one which does not seem to be very general in official circles.'[1]

Feminist issues prompted some of Shaw's most trenchant polemical prose. The quality of his engagement with those issues is well illustrated in the 1913 speech referred to above, a contribution to a protest meeting about the forcible feeding of imprisoned suffragettes. In that speech Shaw was concerned not merely to argue the illegality of forcible feeding, but to bring home to the senses the violence of the act itself:

> If you have a case of somebody eternally keeping their teeth shut, the first thing that occurs to uneducated or rough people

is simply to take an instrument like a chisel and attempt to pry them open. That is an impossible thing to do, because you cannot get the chisel through unless you break the teeth. I want to impress this on you – that for anybody to prise a person's mouth open in that way is to perform an act of extraordinary violence.

The spirit in which such torture was carried out in 1913, Shaw argues, has even less justification than torture carried out in the Middle Ages, because 'the Middle Ages really always did things . . . with some sort of reference as to whether it was the sort of thing God would have done'. The powerful peroration of the speech is a striking example of the proximity, at times, of Shaw's moral vision to central parts of the teaching of Christianity. The themes of his closing remarks are based on two Biblical texts: 'Ye are members one of another', and 'Inasmuch as ye do it to the least of My brethren ["I dont think", Shaw adds to this text, "these gentlemen understand that brethren means sisters as well"] you have done it unto Me.' The chain of being in the human family is continuous, and violence done to one member is violence done to all, to life itself:

If you take a woman and torture her, you torture me. If you take Mrs Pankhurst's daughter and torture her, then you are torturing my daughter. If you take Mrs Pankhurst's mother and torture her, then you are torturing my mother. Let us go further, and say that if you torture my mother, you are torturing me.

These denials of fundamental rights are really a violation of the soul and are an attack on that sacred part of life which is common to all of us, the thing of which you speak when you talk of the Life Everlasting. I say this in not a mystical sense, but the most obvious commonsense, that the denial of any fundamental rights to the person of woman is practically the denial of the Life Everlasting.

Equally impressive, as an example of Shaw's imaginative and incisive treatment of feminist themes, is an essay in which he demolishes the arguments of a book by his friend, Sir Almroth Wright, vulnerably entitled *The Unexpurgated Case Against Woman*

Suffrage. With a parade of 'diacritical judgement', pseudo-scientific discussion and old-fashioned chivalry, Wright, a medical man, had attempted to elaborate a case against female suffrage on the grounds that women are normally less capable of objective thought than men. Shaw aptly refers in this essay to the passage from Isabella's speech in *Measure for Measure*, beginning 'but man, proud man, / Drest in a little brief authority'. In a brilliant display of good-humoured, but devastating, ridicule, Shaw brings the house of cards of Wright's arguments to the ground:

> Shakespear, speaking of himself and Sir Almroth and me and the rest of us as glassy essences and angry apes, is bitter, but within his rights, and entitled, alas! to the verdict; but what sort of figure would Shakespear have cut had he added:
>
>> You must understand, gentlemen, that these remarks are confined strictly to Ann Hathaway, and that I, the Masculine Male Manly Man, am obviously purely intellectual and aniconic in appraising statements; am never over-influenced by individual instances; never arrive at conclusions on incomplete evidence; have an absolutely perfect sense of proportion; cannot be tricked into accepting the congenial as true or denying the uncongenial as false; do not believe in things merely because I wish they were true, or ignore things because I wish they did not exist; but live, godlike, in full consciousness of the external world as it really is, unbiased by predilections and aversions; for· such, gentlemen, is the happy effect of the physiological attachments of Man's mind.[2]

II

The clear stand which Shaw took on feminist issues in essays and speeches is not contradicted in his plays.[3] But in the play which is most directly concerned with feminist themes,[4] *The Philanderer*, a full sense of the complexity of the struggle for emancipation from imprisoning sexual roles is conveyed. In this early comedy of Shaw's, new theories and new ideals regarding the relations of the sexes come into conflict with other passions and old patterns of human behaviour in ways which certainly do not lead to the simple triumph of the theories and ideals.

Some measure of the distance at which the play stands from partisan argument is provided by Shaw's description of it in a letter to R. Golding Bright as a work about 'the fashionable cult of Ibsenism and "New Womanism"', which flourished in the early 1890s as Ibsen's impact was beginning to be felt in England.[5] The 'fashionable cult' is treated with a good deal of playful satire in *The Philanderer*. In Act II, set in the Ibsen Club in London, where it is incumbent on the members to be 'if female . . . not womanly, and if male, not manly', there is much comic play with the affectations of the New Women, who stride about in Norfolk tweed jackets and breeches (worn with or without detachable skirt) rolling cigarettes, insisting rigorously on sexually undiscriminating behaviour, and chiding 'womanly' backsliders such as Julia Craven. But the play's exploration of changing attitudes towards the relations of the sexes operates at deeper levels than this. Despite its predominantly comic spirit and frequent moments of farce, the play's action develops in ways which involve the audience in sharp dilemmas and genuine conflicts of sympathy. The ideals of the Ibsen Club are not dismissed, but they are placed in a context of dramatic action in which 'personal truth in all its complexity' is brought fully into play against the advanced views upheld by the Club.

The action of *The Philanderer* revolves around the triangular relation between Leonard Charteris, Grace Tranfield and Julia Craven. Charteris and Grace are in love and intend to be married; but in the first scene it is discovered through Grace's persistent interrogation of Charteris that his affair with Julia Craven has not been broken off. In the course of the play, Charteris manages to extricate himself from his relationship with the jealously possessive Julia by ruthlessly rejecting her advances and encouraging a romance between her and another member of the Ibsen Club, Dr Paramore. In the meantime he fails to regain the respect of Grace, and the play ends with Julia, having not fully conquered her passion for Charteris, engaged to marry Paramore, and the relation between Charteris and Grace still in ruins.

Charteris is a volatile, intelligent and amusing character in a central line of early Shavian heroes, with Trefusis (in *An Unsocial*

Socialist), Valentine and Tanner. His characterisation bears a close relation to that of the conventional figure of the trapped hero in a bedroom farce:

GRACE: [*deeply hurt, but controlling herself*] When did you break it off?
CHARTERIS: [*guiltily*] Break it off?
GRACE: [*firmly*] Yes: break it off.
CHARTERIS: Well let me see. When did I fall in love with you?
GRACE: Did you break it off then?
CHARTERIS: [*making it plainer and plainer that it has not been broken off*] It was clear then, of course, that it must be broken off.

The love chase in the play is presented more than once in terms of a physical pursuit on the stage, with Charteris as the victim, and in Act III, which is set in Dr Paramore's rooms, he is provided with a chair mounted on castors which he uses as a vehicle for setting a greater or less distance between himself and Julia, as the mood of their interview determines. Charteris is equipped with an impressive armoury of defensive wit, which is mainly deployed against Julia:

JULIA: ...And so you think I'm dying to marry you, do you?
CHARTERIS: I am afraid your intentions have been honorable, Julia.

But his function in the play is more than that of farcical victim and adroit wit. It is through him that the play's critical view of possessiveness and emotional blackmail in love is most clearly articulated ('do I belong to Julia; or have I a right to belong to myself?') and Charteris is perceptive, if ruthless, in his exposure of the contradictions in Julia's position as a professed believer in advanced opinions about marriage:

You regarded marriage as a degrading bargain, by which a woman sells herself to a man for the social status of a wife and the right to be supported and pensioned in old age out of his income. Thats the advanced view: our view. Besides, if you had married me, I might have turned out a drunkard, a criminal, an imbecile, a horror to you; and you couldnt have released yourself. Too big a risk, you see. Thats the rational view: our view. Accordingly, you reserved the right to leave me at any time if you found our companionship incompatible with – what was the expression you used? – with your full development as a human being. I think that was how you put the Ibsenist view: our view.

Charteris's wish to extricate himself from the relationship with Julia is obviously justifiable, but he, too, is the subject of critical treatment in the play. If he does not conform to Mr Cuthbertson's stereotype of manliness, he nevertheless has more than his share of male conceit, and can himself echo the Ibsenian male chauvinist, as when he addresses Grace in the first scene as 'my little philosopher', or in his treatment of Julia as a 'plaything'. He gets decidedly the worst of the argument in a scene with Julia in Act III, and when at the end she embraces him and calls him a 'miserable little plaster saint' she sounds a distinct note of hollowness in his buoyant rationalism. In this final act of *The Philanderer* (a section of the play wrongly described as tedious by one of its critics, Maurice Valency)[6] Charteris and Paramore exchange roles in more than one respect. Earlier in the play, Paramore has been presented as a grotesque caricature of the medical scientist, a vivisector whose experimental zeal and professional vanity totally inure him to the feelings of his patient, Craven. But in Act III Julia derives a metaphor from Paramore's profession to make a telling comment on Charteris's analytical and dissecting mind: 'It is you who are the vivisector: a far crueller, more wanton vivisector than he.'[7] The comparison is enriched by the fact that in the previous scene Paramore has been making clumsy but well-intentioned endeavours to treat Julia as a human being, and repudiating the idea that he is merely interested in her because of her sexual attractiveness.

Despite her melodramatic posturing and obsessiveness, Julia displays a seriousness and intensity of passion which presents a significant challenge to the theorists of the Ibsen Club. Her very unreasonableness is an index of her humanity: 'I'm too miserable to argue – to think', she tells Charteris, 'I only know I love you'.

It is her capacity for feeling that makes her the most vulnerable and, in some ways, most sympathetic character in the play. Her attitude towards her own sexual attractiveness is ambiguous. She taunts Charteris with the comparative unattractiveness of her rivals for his affection and calls Grace a 'creature with no figure'; but at the same time sees her own beauty as a barrier in her relations with men. In the quarrel she has with Grace in Act II the latter accuses her of being the type of woman who degrades the image of the sex in men's eyes: 'I see, by you, what wretched childish creatures we are! . . . I will not give myself to any man who has learnt how to treat women from you and your like. I can do without his love, but not without his respect.' But, in the same exchange, the coldly analytical tone of Grace's speeches, where reason is mingled with sexual jealousy, invites little sympathy. In this scene the metaphor of the vivisector seems as much applicable to her as it is to Charteris. Moreover, we see elsewhere in the play, and especially in her self-revelatory speeches to Paramore at the beginning of Act III, that Julia's image as a child and impersonal sex object is partly created by male attitudes towards her. In her explanation of her plight, Julia shows both the need for and the failure of the Ibsen Club ideals:

PARAMORE: I'm afraid I'm a bad entertainer. The fact is, I am too professional. I shine only in consultation. I almost wish you had something serious the matter with you; so that you might call out my knowledge and sympathy. As it is, I can only admire you, and feel how pleasant it is to have you here.

JULIA: [*bitterly*] And pet me, and say pretty things to me. I wonder you dont offer me a saucer of milk at once.

PARAMORE: [*astonished*] Why?

JULIA: Because you seem to regard me very much as if I were a Persian cat.

PARAMORE: [*in strong remonstrance*] Miss Cra-

JULIA: [*cutting him short*] Oh, you neednt protest. I'm used to it: it's the sort of attachment I seem always to inspire. [*Ironically*] You cant think how flattering it is.

PARAMORE: My dear Miss Craven, what a cynical thing to say! You! who are loved at first sight by the people in the street as you pass. Why, in the club I can tell by the faces of the men whether you have been lately in the room or not.

JULIA: [*shrinking fiercely*] Oh, I hate that look in their faces. Do you know that I have never had one human being care for me since I was born?

The visual settings of the play's three acts bear a significant relation to its thematic concerns. The most straightforward example of this is the use of Rembrandt's portrait of the 'School of Anatomy' in the set for Act III, reflecting as it does Paramore's profession, the vivisector metaphor and, more generally, the realism of the play's treatment of sexual relations. The settings of Acts I and II are a reminder that the play is partly concerned with theatrical conditions and with the stereotypes of sexual roles and relations which they tend to promote. The precise significance of most of the theatrical engravings and photographs with which the Cuthbertson drawing room is bedecked in Act I would almost certainly be lost on a present-day audience. Those familiar with Shaw's dramatic criticism will recognize that many of the figures represented are familiar butts of Shaw's attack as the self-appointed scourge of decadent nineteenth-century theatrical traditions. The portraits include Irving in a Shakespearean role, and the playwrights Jones, Pinero and Grundy. Dominating the stage is a statuette of Shakespeare surrounded by flowers, the latter being obviously intended to suggest the bardolatry of the owner. The Green Room atmosphere, augmented by the elegant evening dress of the players, emphasizes the faded conventionality of the scene of philandering and lovers' quarrelling which takes place on stage. The conventional and theatrical qualities of the scene are high-lighted in Charteris's brisk summary of the action of Act I in the penultimate speech: 'I came here tonight to sweetheart Grace. Enter Julia. Alarums and excursions. Exit Grace. Enter you and Craven. Subterfuges and excuses. Exeunt Craven and Julia. And here we are.'

Cuthbertson, the drama critic, is invited by Charteris to consult his 'theatrical experience' to find out what has happened in the scene immediately preceding his arrival. The implication of the remark is that the pattern of sex relations which we have just observed, the philandering, the jealous quarrelling and the 'subterfuges and excuses' belong to and are promoted by the theatrical tradition which Cuthbertson and his drawing room represent. The sentimental ideals of the tradition have already been revealed by Craven when he reports Cuthbertson's conversation on the way home from the theatre about passing his life amid 'scenes of suffering nobly endured and sacrifice willingly rendered by womanly women and manly men'. He is not, as Craven naively supposes, referring to experiences in a hospital, but to the offerings of the nineteenth-century popular theatre. In Act II, living up to his reputation as 'the leading representative of manly sentiment in London', Cuthbertson, pounding his chest a moment later to emphasize the point, declares that a woman of Julia's sort 'likes a strong, manly, deep throated, broad chested man'.

In the setting of Act II the statuette of Shakespeare is replaced by a bust of Ibsen, surrounded by decorative inscriptions of the titles of his plays, as the dominant visual image on the stage. But the first words of Act II, the page-boy's bleating repetition of the obviously punningly intended name of Dr Paramore, contain a hint of the ironical relations which exist here between setting and action. For all the emancipated and advanced ideas about rational relations between the sexes which the club stands for, the central thread of action in Act II, Charteris's encouragement of the romance between Paramore and Julia, is strongly reminiscent of the sexual ethos of Act I. There is a sense in which the meaning of the play at this point seems to be *plus ça change, plus c'est la même chose*. Charteris's remark about Cuthbertson's hopeless state of confusion in which ideas about 'the New Woman and the New This, That and The Other' are 'all mixed up with [his] own old Adam' clearly has more general application to the goings on at the Ibsen Club.

It is only in the persons of Grace Tranfield and the cheerful and independently-minded younger sister of Julia Craven, Sylvia, that we see Ibsen discipleship in less adulterated form. Grace's serious, level-headed and objective explanation to Charteris of her reasons for breaking off with him has easily recognizable affinities with Nora's declaration at the end of *A Doll's House*. The brief scene between Charteris and Sylvia offers a glimpse of a relation between the sexes in which a state of friendly equality and comradeship prevails. But neither Grace nor Sylvia can be said to resolve the play's insistent question as to how the old Adam and the old Eve, the energies of sexual passion and ordinary human demands for commitment and proprietorship in love, can be happily reconciled with the Ibsen Club ideals of rational comradeship and individual freedom.

The relations between men and women which the play depicts oscillate in character between extreme poles of emotional rapacity and callous detachment. We may, of course, infer from the play's range of sympathies and comic spirit an author's viewpoint which avoids both extremes. But this point of view is not located in the presentation of any of the main characters. The play's final injunction, delivered by Grace, is 'never make a hero of a philanderer', and its application to Charteris is clearly justified. But Grace herself, in her rejection of Charteris, seems to have arrived at a mainly negative solution to her predicament, in the suppression of passion: 'I will never marry a man I love too much. It would give him a terrible advantage over me: I should be utterly in his power. Thats what the New Woman is like.' The play shows the New Woman as being trapped in a position of sterile neutrality, unwilling to accept both the attitudes of the philanderer and all the risks of entering into a fully committed, passionate relationship.

The discords of feeling which the play produces continue to be felt until its very last moments. In the final tableau, Charteris is surveying the wretchedly unhappy Julia with laughing unconcern whilst the rest of the company look at her anxiously, *'feeling for the first time the presence of a keen sorrow'*. Charteris has obviously won the final round of the battle with Julia but it is, we are aware, a Pyrrhic victory.

NOTES

1. 'Torture by Forcible Feeding is Illegal', *The London Budget*, 23 March 1913; reprinted in *Fabian Feminist: Bernard Shaw and Woman*, ed. Rodelle Weintraub (Pennsylvania and London: Pennsylvania State University Press, 1977) pp. 228–35.
2. 'Sir Almroth Wright's Polemic', *New Statesman*, 18 Oct. 1913; reprinted in *Fabian Feminist*, ed. Rodelle Weintraub, pp. 243–7.

3. Don Juan/Tanner's definition of male and female roles in the Dream scene in *Man and Superman* may be thought an exception to this statement. However, Don Juan/Tanner's view of sexual roles is substantially undermined in the play proper.

4. I leave out of account here *Press Cuttings*, a topical sketch about the Women's War of 1909.

5. *Bernard Shaw: Collected Letters 1874–1897*, ed. Dan H. Laurence (London: Max Reinhardt, 1965) p. 632.

6. Maurice Valency, *The Cart and the Trumpet: The Plays of George Bernard Shaw* (New York: Oxford University Press, 1973) p. 90.

7. Shaw applied the metaphor to himself in a Charteris-like passage of a letter to Bertha Newcombe written in 1896:

> There have been gusts of ice and sulphur lately, it seems. I had a fit of sardonic laughter at my own follies and was accused of cruelty, sacrilege, blasphemy, insult, iconoclasm, Satanism – as you would compendiously say, of being horrid. 'Twas ever thus, Bertha. Your sex likes me as children like wedding cake, for the sake of the sugar on the top. If they taste by an accident a bit of crumb or citron, it is all over: I am a fiend delighting in vivisectional cruelties, as indicated by the corners of my mouth. (*Collected Letters 1874–1897*, pp. 619–20)

5 Romance and Anti-romance in *Arms and the Man*

THE MAN: Ive no ammunition. What use are cartridges in battle?
          I always carry chocolate instead; and I finished the last
          cake of that hours ago.
RAINA: [*outraged in her most cherished ideals of manhood*]
          Chocolate! Do you stuff your pockets with sweets – like
          a schoolboy – even in the field?

(Arms and the Man)

Much of the laughter in *Arms and the Man* arises from the steady deflation of romantic ideas of love and war. Yet it is a misreading of the play to see it as simply an anti-romantic and anti-heroic work. In production, a fine balance of tones needs to be achieved in order to preserve the integrity and meaning of the play. In some words of advice to producers of the play, Shaw wrote of its essential tonal qualities as follows:

> unless the general effect of the play is thoroughly genial and good-humored, it will be unbearably disagreeable. The slightest touch of malicious denigrement or cynicism is fatal. If the audience thinks it is being asked to laugh at human nature, it will not laugh. If it thinks it is being made to laugh at insincere romantic conventions which are an insult to human nature, it will laugh very heartily. The fate of the play depends wholly on the clearness of this distinction.[1]

For all its Falstaffian perspectives on military valour, the play does not denigrate courage as a human virtue. And within the context of its satirical treatment of 'insincere romantic conventions' a compensating romantic narrative of a less conventional kind is developed.

The two principal, and related, subjects of satire in the play are: the glorification of war, and the so-called Higher Love which is supposed both to stimulate military valour and in turn to be stimulated by it. One dramatic form to which the work is related is the military adventure play, a form which has a long history in England, going back to the Love and Honour drama of the seventeenth century. But nearer at hand as an influence upon the more romantic aspects of the play was a source revealed in the text itself when Raina refers Bluntschli to a scene in *Ernani*, Verdi's opera based on the historical play *Hernani* by Victor Hugo:

> I thought you might have remembered the great scene where Ernani, flying from his foes just as you are tonight, takes refuge in the castle of his bitterest enemy, an old Castilian noble. The noble refuses to give him up. His guest is sacred to him.

In the love plot of *Ernani*, the union of the lovers, Elvira and the aristocratic outlaw Ernani, is threatened in two ways. Ernani has a rival in the form of his enemy, Don Carlo, who is the historical Charles V; but at the same time Elvira is about to be reluctantly united in marriage to a relative (the 'old Castilian noble' referred to in *Arms and the Man*) Don Ruy Gomez de Silva. Ernani, having become involved in a conspiracy against Carlo's life, is captured and pardoned, and the way is temporarily clear for him to marry Elvira. But as the two are about to enter their nuptial chamber they are arrested by the jealous Silva. The opera, as distinct from Victor Hugo's play which ends happily, concludes in a *liebestod* with Ernani committing suicide and Elvira, declaring eternal love, falling dead upon his body.

In the more romantic aspects of its dramatic structure, *Arms and the Man* bears some clear traces of the plot motifs in *Ernani*: the concealment of the fleeing enemy, the point of honour by which the claims of hospitality outweigh enmity, the dramatic discovery of the fugitive's identity and even the alignment of forces which threaten the possibility of marriage between Bluntschli and Raina. (Sergius and Petkoff perform similar functions in this respect to Don Carlo and Don Ruy.)

The characters in Shaw's play translate readily in one's mind into operatic types: Sergius is explicitly described by Bluntschli as being 'like an operatic tenor', and the other personae in the play, from Major Petkoff (basso profundo) to Louka (second soprano), also bear a strong resemblance to stock characters in opera. Raina is an expert on the subject of opera – it is a means of asserting the civilization of the Petkoffs and of Bulgaria – and her imagination is obviously shaped to a considerable extent by operatic conventions. In *Ernani* Shaw would have found presented in sharp outline the stereotypes of exalted love and heroism which are satirised in his play. The opera begins with a chorus of rebels singing the praises of their life of warfare:

> This life, O how joyful!
> With hilt, blade and rifle,
> Our true friends thro' all.[2]

Elvira's thoughts are never far from death when she is speaking of her love for Ernani and the elevated mood of their love relations (typified in such things as the duet 'Ah, morir potessi' in Act II and the dialogue between the two before Don Ruy's entry in Act IV) remains unbroken throughout.

Shaw's satirical treatment of the conventions of romantic opera has some affinities with the methods of early Gilbertian comedy. In Gilbert's *The Palace of Truth* (1870) – a play reminiscent in various ways of *A Midsummer Night's Dream* – the court of King Phanor is transferred to an enchanted palace in which the magic powers compel all the characters to say exactly what is in their minds about one another. Characters are reversed and love partners changed. Poetical compliment turns to plain speaking, and vice versa. A prince tells his adored mistress that she is 'comparatively plain'. A coquette makes advances to several gentlemen whilst demurely explaining her tactics as she proceeds. A normally boorish courtier explains archly that his manners were an affectation designed to

> . . . prove, perchance, a not unwelcome foil
> To Zoram's mockery of cultured taste,
> And Chrysal's chronic insincerity![3]

The comedy in Gilbert's later play *Engaged* (1877), depends on much the same sources of laughter, in candid revelations of prosaic fact and frankly appetitive motives beneath the postures of romance. When writing the scene in Act II of *Arms and the Man* in which Sergius, having rapturously farewelled Raina in accents of the 'higher love', suddenly has his attention caught by the distinctly attractive maid with whom he then proceeds to flirt, Shaw must surely have remembered the scene in *Engaged* where Gilbert puts Cheviot (left similarly alone on the stage) through the same paces:

> CHEVIOT: . . . Dismiss from my thoughts the only woman I ever loved! Have no more to say to the tree upon which the fruit of my heart is growing! No, Belvawney, I cannot cut off my tree as if it were gas or water. I do not treat women like that. Some men do, but I don't. I am not that sort of man. I respect women; I love women. They are good; they are pure; they are beautiful; at least, many of them are.
> [*Enter MAGGIE from cottage: he is much fascinated*] This one, for example, is very beautiful indeed![4]

As Dan H. Laurence in his edition of Shaw's letters points out, William Archer had already communicated his views of *Arms and the Man* to Shaw before writing the review in which he declared that in the second act 'we find ourselves in Mr Gilbert's Palace of Truth', and described the play as 'a fantastic, psychological extravaganza, in which drama, farce, and Gilbertian irony keep flashing past the bewildered eye'.[5] Shaw, in one of his most illuminating commentaries on his own work, pointed out the vital distinctions between his and Gilbert's comedy:

> I must really clear that Gilbert notion out of your head [he wrote to Archer] before you disgrace yourself over Arms and The Man. You have a perfect rag shop of old ideas in your head which prevent your getting a step ahead.
>   Gilbert is simply a paradoxically humorous cynic. He accepts the conventional ideals implicitly, but observes that people do not really live up to them. This he regards as a failure on their part at which he mocks bitterly. This position is

precisely that of Sergius in the play, who, when disilluded [*sic*], declares that life is a farce. It is a perfectly barren position: nothing comes of it but cynicism, pessimism, and irony.

I do not accept the conventional ideals. To them I oppose in the play the practical life and morals of the efficient, realistic man, unaffectedly ready to face what risks must be faced, considerate but not chivalrous, patient and practical, and I . . . represent the woman as instinctively falling in love with all this even whilst all her notions of fine-mannishness are being outraged. . . . It is this positive element in my philosophy that makes Arms and The Man a perfectly genuine play about real people, with a happy ending and hope and life in it, instead of a thing like [Gilbert's] 'Engaged' which is nothing but a sneer at people for not being what Sergius and Raina play at being before they find one another out.[6]

The 'mechanical topsyturvyism' of early Gilbertian comedy leads, in Shaw's view, only to a comically cynical view of human nature and human ideals. In contrast, Shaw's comedy does not simply negate romance. Rather, what he achieves in the play is a rejuvenation of a typical romance structure, by attaching to well-tried dramatic situations an unconventional set of values and affirmations. Instead of the romance of conventional fiction, it offers the romance of reality, of the discovery of true feeling beneath the social accoutrements of spurious and assumed feeling. It is in terms such as these that the relations between Raina and Bluntschli are developed in the play, their romantic intimacy increasing as her romantic attitudes are progressively discarded:

BLUNTSCHLI: . . . When you strike that noble attitude and speak in that thrilling voice, I admire you; but I find it impossible to believe a single word you say . . .

RAINA: [*wonderingly*] Do you know, you are the first man I ever met who did not take me seriously?

BLUNTSCHLI: You mean, dont you, that I am the first man that has ever taken you quite seriously?

RAINA: Yes: I suppose I do mean that. [*Cosily, quite at her ease with him*] How strange it is to be talked to in such a way!

The candid, friendly and amiable person that such moments in the play discover in Raina is consistent with the image of the human being who, to her mother's annoyance, times to perfection her pretty entrances by listening for cues 'off-stage'. But it is a quite different persona from the actress who poses regally for Sergius and who becomes caught up in the rhetoric and fantasies of the Higher Love. In the process of un-masking the postures of the Higher Love, the play shows us not an emptiness beneath, but the possibilities of deeper and more meaningful forms of intimacy.

In some respects, the alternative romance which develops between Raina and Bluntschli follows fairly conventional lines. The amatory possibilities of their relations are already established in Act I, in Raina's moments of maternal solicitousness for her fugitive guest, and, conclusively, in the penultimate line of Act I, spoken as she surveys the un-wakeable and potentially compromising figure on her bed: 'the poor darling is worn out. Let him sleep.' Feelings other than those expressed in the present dialogue on stage are conveyed by the report of Raina's sending a photograph of herself to Bluntschli with the inscription 'Raina, to her Chocolate Cream Soldier: a Souvenir'. It is noteworthy, too, that Bluntschli is allowed the democratic or republican equivalent of aristocratic rank, when he is revealed to be the owner of a large chain of hotels. In writing the play, Shaw judged to a nicety the degree to which conventions could be altered, and the degree to which they had to be allowed to run their course.

Bluntschli does much more in the play than represent the practical life and morals of the efficient, realistic man.[7] This describes a leading aspect of his character; but it does not convey the mobility of wit and sharpness of insight which he is given in the dialogue. And it is not a contradiction but a natural development of the image we have formed of him earlier when he says in Act III that he is a man of 'an incurably romantic disposition':

I ran away from home twice when I was a boy. I went into the army instead of into my father's business. I climbed the balcony of this house when a man of sense would have dived into the nearest cellar. I came sneaking back here to have

another look at the young lady when any other man of my age
would have sent the coat back—

With this revelation, Shaw transfers the aura normally
associated with the brooding Byronic hero in nineteenth-century
literature to a quite different character type. The plain-speaker
becomes the man of mystery. Shaw underlined this with a happy
revision of the last line of the play. In the MS draft, the play
ended on a comparatively weak line, with Sergius saying of the
departed Bluntschli 'What a man! What a man!'[8] The play as
published ends with a line suggesting more sharply the way in
which ordinariness attains extraordinary dimensions in
Bluntschli, as well as providing a satirical comment on his
machine-like efficiency – 'What a man! Is he a man!'

The concept underlying the characterisation of Bluntschli, of
the visionary pragmatist or romantic realist is traceable to
Carlyle, whom Shaw mentions in connection with *Arms and the
Man* in the Preface to *Three Plays for Puritans*. The idea of such a
synthesis of forces exercised a considerable influence on Shaw's
imagination in the early period of his dramatic career, the
portraits of Caesar and Undershaft being further explorations of
it. Shaw's comments on Carlyle's conception of the 'true hero of
history' throw light on the treatment of Bluntschli, Sergius and
the idea of the hero in *Arms and the Man*:

> Carlyle, with his vein of peasant inspiration, apprehended the
> sort of greatness that places the true hero of history so far
> beyond the mere *preux chevalier*, whose fanatical personal
> honor, gallantry, and self-sacrifice, are founded on a passion
> for death born of inability to bear the weight of a life that will
> not grant ideal conditions to the liver. This one ray of
> perception became Carlyle's whole stock-in-trade; and it
> sufficed to make a literary master of him. In due time, when
> Mommsen is an old man, and Carlyle dead, come I, and
> dramatize the by-this-time familiar distinction in Arms and
> the Man, with its comedic conflict between the knightly
> Bulgarian and the Mommsenite Swiss captain. Whereupon a
> great many playgoers who have not yet read Cervantes, much
> less Mommsen and Carlyle, raise a shriek of concern for their
> knightly ideal as if nobody had ever questioned its sufficiency
> since the middle ages.[9]

It is principally through Bluntschli that the play's critical view of romantic notions about military valour and the *preux chevalier* is expressed. Catherine Petkoff's excited reverie early in Act I about the cavalry charge in which Sergius was involved – 'Cant you see it, Raina: our gallant splendid Bulgarians with their swords and eyes flashing, thundering down like an avalanche and scattering the wretched Serbs and their dandified Austrian officers like chaff' – provides the foil for Bluntschli's later, grimly prosaic account of what happens in cavalry charges:

> It's like slinging a handful of peas against a window pane: first one comes; then two or three close behind him; and then all the rest in a lump. . . . You can tell the young ones by their wildness and their slashing. The old ones come bunched up under the number one guard: they know that theyre mere projectiles, and that it's no use trying to fight. The wounds are mostly broken knees, from the horses cannoning together.

In the midst of discussion of the play's complicated relations of love in Act III, a sharply graphic reminder of the horror of the war in the background is provided in Bluntschli's report of the death of his friend: 'Burnt alive. . . . Shot in the hip in a woodyard. Couldnt drag himself out. Your fellows' shells set the timber on fire and burnt him, with half a dozen other poor devils in the same predicament.'

Like Bluntschli, Sergius is not a uni-dimensional character. But the mobility Sergius displays takes the form of vacillation between intransigent or extreme postures. Shaw rings various changes on Cunninghame Graham's celebrated remark in Parliament, 'I never withdraw',[10] as the keynote of Sergius's character. Whichever of the 'half dozen Sergiuses who keep popping in and out of [his] handsome figure' tends to do so in the shape of a rigid pose. Sergius can find no middle ground between views of life as romance and views of it as empty farce: 'Raina: our romance is shattered. Life's a farce.' Apart from its recollections of Cunninghame Graham, Sergius's character is an amalgam of various nineteenth-century literary ideals. In Act I, in an ironic speech which prepares the audience for her later self-discoveries in the play, Raina confesses to her mother that 'it came into my head just as he [Sergius] was holding me in his arms and looking

into my eyes, that perhaps we only had our heroic ideas because
we are so fond of reading Byron and Pushkin, and because we
were so delighted with the opera that season at Bucharest'. In the
stage direction before Sergius's first entry in the play, Shaw
identifies his sensibility with '*what the advent of nineteenth century
thought first produced in England: to wit, Byronism*'. Byronism, in the
account which follows, is seen as a mixture of sensitive, ironic
intelligence, scorn at the failure of people (including the Byronic
individual himself) to live up to ideals, cynicism, and a '*mysterious
moodiness*' such as that of Childe Harold. Shaw has this figure
defeated in both love and, in terms of strategic skill, war, by a
character who has more in common with Sidney Webb than with
Childe Harold.[11]

Yet Shaw is careful not to make Sergius merely an object of
ridicule in the play. Like Raina, Sergius has engaging flashes of
candour, as when he tells Louka that the Higher Love is a 'very
fatiguing thing to keep up for any length of time'. And Shaw gives
him a fine moment of moral victory over Bluntschli in the final
scene of the play when it is revealed that the latter has all along
been thinking of the twenty-three-year old Raina as a girl of
seventeen:

SERGIUS: [*with grim enjoyment of his rival's discomfiture*]
Bluntschli: my one last belief is gone. Your
sagacity is a fraud, like everything else. You have
less sense than even I!

Occasionally Sergius appears as a more knowing person than
Bluntschli; and his spirited, virile character is not always
presented in an unfavourable or ridiculous light.

The comedy of *Arms and the Man* is not completely devoid of
political overtones, even though this is a comparatively minor
aspect of the play. In the final scene of the play, Shaw gently
underlines the fact that Bluntschli is a 'good Republican' and a
'free citizen'. Louka's engagement with Sergius constitutes some
challenge to the rigidities of the class system in Bulgaria, though
we feel that her most likely course after marriage would be to
become herself a bastion of upper-class power. But in her Act III
scene with Sergius, she has turned the play's preoccupation with
courage very clearly in a new direction. She describes as

schoolboyish Sergius's notion of the brave man as one who will 'defy to the death any power on earth or in heaven that sets itself up against his own will and conscience', and substitutes her own definition of 'true courage' as a willingness to become *déclassé* for love: 'if you felt the beginnings of love for me you would not let it grow. You would not dare: you would marry a rich man's daughter because you would be afraid of what other people would say of you.' She is not, of course, a disinterested pleader. But her spirited rejection of servanthood, set off as it is by Nicola's docile but adroit submission to it, is one feature of the play which extends its revolutionary thrust beyond the spheres of love and honour.

The unions which are foreshadowed at the end of the play hardly lend themselves to close analysis in political terms. But an ending in which the hussar marries a maidservant, and the well-bred young lady a hotel keeper, has more than a slight air of calculated indecorousness. Through the distancing perspective of Shaw's toyland Bulgaria, an English Victorian audience could no doubt afford to smile at the discovery of man alive and woman alive beneath the inhibiting conventions of a military caste system, and views of love and war based on romantic opera.

NOTES

1. Shaw, 'Arms and the Man: Instructions to Producer' (undated typescript in the Humanities Research Centre, University of Texas at Austin).
2. *Verdi's Opera Ernani, Containing the Italian Text, with an English Translation, and the Music of all the Principal Airs* (Boston, Mass.: O. Ditson, 1859) p. 5.
3. W. S. Gilbert, *Original Plays*, First Series (London: Chatto & Windus, 1884) p. 191.
4. W. S. Gilbert, *Original Plays*, Second Series (London: Chatto & Windus, 1930) p. 49.
5. *Bernard Shaw: Collected Letters 1874–1897*, ed. Dan H. Laurence (London: Max Reinhardt, 1965) p. 427.
6. Ibid., p. 427.
7. The part of Bluntschli calls for carefully controlled acting, as Shaw points out in his 'Instructions to Producer':

Bluntschli, a Coquelin [French actor who created the title role in Rostand's *Cyrano de Bergerac*] part, must be played by a good actor; but the part is not difficult: 'it plays itself'. Nevertheless it is possible to make dangerous mistakes in it. If the note of melodrama is kept up too long in the first Act, the play will go to pieces. His first laugh must come from his reply to Raina's 'Some soldiers, I know, are afraid of death'; and thereafter, whenever Raina is melodramatic, he is terre à terre. But if he is not careful, he may make the audience conclude that he is a coward. He must therefore seize certain moments to shew that he is a brave man. These moments are, first, when he gives Raina the cloak, and prepares to climb down the window later on in spite of the fusillade outside [*sic*]. On both these occasions Raina saves him from the risk he is prepared to run; and it is these sincere moments which must make the play real and sympathetic to the audience in spite of the apparent bizarrerie of its continual violations of the conventions of theatrical romance.

8. British Library, MS Add. 50601, A-C.
9. *Collected Plays*, vol. II, pp. 45–6.
10. The dashing and colourful character and writings of Cunninghame Graham made a strong impression on Shaw, as he explains in the 'Notes to Captain Brassbound's Conversion: Sources of the Play', which appeared in the first edition of *Three Plays for Puritans*. There Cunninghame Graham is described as 'a fascinating mystery to a sedentary person like myself', and the borrowing of the famous remark is acknowledged: 'I promptly stole the potent phrase for the sake of its perfect style, and used it as a cockade for the Bulgarian hero of Arms and the Man.'
11. Shaw identifies Webb as his model for Bluntschli in a letter to H. C. Duffin of 5 January 1920 (British Library, MS Add. 50517).

6 The Case against *Candida*

Only *one* thing struck me at the time as wrong. Towards quite the end of a play to say 'Now let's sit down and talk the matter over'. Several people took out their watches and some of them left to catch a train, or a drink!

(Ellen Terry to Shaw, 30 August 1897)

Initially, at least, Shaw seems to have invested a great deal of emotional capital in *Candida*. Some indication of the extraordinary quality of his investment is provided in one of his letters to Ellen Terry:

One does not get tired of adoring the Virgin Mother. Bless me! you will say, the man is a Roman Catholic. Not at all: the man is the author of Candida; and Candida, between you and me, is the Virgin Mother and nobody else. And my present difficulty is that I want to reincarnate her – to write another play *for* you.[1]

Shaw's next 'Mother' play was *Captain Brassbound's Conversion* in which the part of Lady Cicely was, we are told, modelled on Ellen Terry. Shaw was not at his best when he was writing for, or under the influence of, Ellen Terry. Despite his initial enthusiasm about *Candida*, Shaw later came to regard it as 'an overrated play',[2] a judgement which remains pertinent. A great deal of critical attention has been paid to the play, particularly to such enigmatic aspects as Shaw's claim that his intention was 'To distil the quintessential drama from pre-Raphaelitism'[3] or the use of Titian's 'Assumption of the Virgin' in the set, or the question as to what is 'the secret in the poet's heart'. *Candida* could almost have been written with critical 'casebooks' in mind. But speculation about the more exotic questions of interpretation which arise in the play seems a little beside the point when more fundamental problems of characterisation, action and tone demand attention.

Candida is often praised for its characterization, a view perhaps encouraged by the stage directions which, even for Shaw, are unusually elaborate in their descriptions of the dramatis personae. Yet it is precisely in the matters of the conception and execution of the character portrayals in the play that the most acute critical problems arise.

It can be readily conceded that Shaw was very successful in his portrayal of the public persona of his Christian Socialist clergyman, Morell. Morell epitomizes the qualities conjured up by the phrase 'muscular Christianity'. His speeches in the play are consistent with the opening stage direction description of him as a '*vigorous, genial, popular man of forty, robust and goodlooking, full of energy, with pleasant, hearty, considerate manners*'. Samples of his rhetoric (such as the Act I speech to Marchbanks, beginning 'Then help to kindle it in them') adequately, and indeed with admirable subtlety, convey his qualities as a morally earnest and successful public speaker. We learn from his silent worshipper, Prossy, that his devoted curate, Lexy, imitates Morell by pronouncing 'knowledge' as 'knoaledge' in church, as well as in other mannerisms: 'Yes, you do: you imitate him. Why do you tuck your umbrella under your left arm instead of carrying it in your hand like anyone else? Why do you walk with your chin stuck out before you, hurrying along with that eager look in your eyes?' In many respects, Shaw's portrayal, in Morell, Prossy and Lexy, of a certain type of Anglican clergyman and his entourage is one that could hardly be improved upon.

The major difficulty with Morell's characterization arises in Shaw's treatment of his relations with Candida. The problem was perceptively pinpointed by a very early critic of the play, Oliver Elton. Reviewing a production of the play in 1898, Elton commented on Morell's joyful reception of Candida's judgement in favour of himself at the end of the play as follows: 'it is some strain on belief that even Morell should welcome his reward with such rapture when receiving it as the corollary of his weakness from his direst critic who has upset his whole theory of himself'.[4] Candida is indeed Morell's 'direst critic', and she does much to 'upset his whole theory of himself'. In Act I Marchbanks taunts Morell with the Biblical text describing the feelings of the wife of

David as she watches him 'leaping and dancing before the Lord': 'and she despised him in her heart'.[5] This stinging allusion to Candida's feelings about Morell's enthusiastic sermons is recalled in Act III. In the final scene of the play Candida puts this taunt aside by saying that she only 'said something like it in jest'. But her real contempt for Morell's life's work has already been made clear. In Act II she says to him, *with the fondest intimacy*': 'Put your trust in my love for you, James; for if that went, I should care very little for your sermons: mere phrases that you cheat yourself and others with every day.' Morell's persistent uxoriousness in the face of such assaults becomes increasingly difficult to accept as credible as the play continues.

The problems surrounding the characterization of Morell are closely related to confusions in Shaw's conception – or rather conceptions – of the character of Candida. Shaw clearly intended Candida to be seen as an extremely powerful character. In line with his remarks to Ellen Terry, a stage direction in the play suggests a *'spiritual resemblance'* between Candida and the Titian portrait of the Virgin in the set. But Shaw obviously had difficulty in finding satisfactory ways of representing this power in dramatic terms. Having decided to show her as being entirely without interest in either Christian Socialism or poetry, he fell back on unctuous maternalism as her most positive form of communication. Her characteristic expression is described as one of *'amused maternal indulgence'*. At the end of the play she makes a long speech which is seemingly meant to show her in an attractive light, and to solve the issues which have been raised in the preceding action about her relations with Morell and Marchbanks. Instead, the speech shows her as arch, condescending and self-congratulatory.

Shaw's association of Candida with the Virgin Mary is in striking contrast with later comments which he made about her character, in a letter to James Huneker:

Candida is as unscrupulous as Siegfried: Morell himself sees that 'no law will bind her'. She seduces Eugene just exactly as far as it is worth her while to seduce him. She is a woman without 'character' in the conventional sense. Without brains and strength of mind she would be a wretched slattern or voluptuary.[6]

The various comments which he made about Candida point to conflicting impulses in Shaw's creation of the part which are continually reflected in the play, and which lead to a disquieting uncertainty as to whether she is to be admired for spiritual authority and beauty of character or seen quite unsympathetically as a power-seeking coquette.

A brief summary of her role in Act III will sufficiently indicate the problems of interpretation and tone which arise in the portrayal of Candida. At the opening of Act III, she is discovered sitting by the fire looking intently at the point of a brass poker which she holds upright in her hand, whilst Marchbanks reads poetry to her. If, as seems the unavoidable conclusion, the poker is not only a sword of Damocles but also a comic phallic symbol, this is in keeping with Candida's behaviour in the scene up until the time of Morell's entry.[7] She is bored by the poetry and proposes a talk instead. Marchbanks is reluctant because he is afraid of placing himself in a dangerous position, but she is persuasive: 'Come and sit down on the hearth-rug, and talk moonshine as you usually do. I want to be amused. Dont you want to?' This brings him to a place by her feet on the rug and leads to the obviously compromising position in which they are discovered by Morell. Candida leaves the room shortly after Morell's entry and returns to find the two men quarrelling. She immediately sides with her husband and turns on Marchbanks, in the manner of an enraged headmistress:

CANDIDA:	You have been annoying him. Now I wont have it, Eugene: do you hear? . . .
MARCHBANKS:	Oh, youre not angry with me, are you?
CANDIDA:	[*severely*] Yes I am: very angry. I have a good mind to pack you out of the house.

If there were anything in the text to suggest that Candida is in effect punishing herself in this onslaught on Marchbanks it would be easier to accept. Instead, it seems to be an example of almost ludicrous duplicity on her part.

The scene between the three principals is interrupted by the revellers from Burgess's dinner party, and with their departure we have the improbable auction scene with which the play ends. Candida makes her choice of the 'weaker of the two', Morell, and then sits them all down to talk things over. The seating is clearly intended to reflect their final relationships:

> CANDIDA: [*smiling a little*] Let us sit and talk comfortably over it like three friends. [*To Morell*] Sit down, dear. [*Morell, quite lost, takes the chair from the fireside: the children's chair*]. Bring me that chair, Eugene. [*She indicates the easy chair. . . . She sits down. He takes the visitors' chair himself, and sits, inscrutable. When they are all settled she begins, throwing a spell of quietness on them by her calm, sane, tender tone*].

Candida then proceeds to explain to the two men that the reason why Morell can be 'strong and clever and happy' is that she has continued to play the same protective and supporting role as was played by his mother and three sisters. But what is made clear in the speech and its setting is that the price which Morell ('my boy') has to pay for Candida's loving care is his own unmanning, his reduction in status in his relationship with her to that of a child. Candida emerges from this speech not so much as the loving partner of Morell as his emotional castrator and dominator. At the end of the speech Morell, '*quite overcome*', kneels beside her chair and embraces her with '*boyish ingenuousness*'. From this embrace Candida smilingly addresses to Marchbanks the question: 'Am I your mother and sisters to you, Eugene?' Marchbanks, apparently seeing the truth about Candida's relations with men at this point, decides that it is time for him to depart. But even that gesture of defiance and independence is undermined by the fact that he does not leave the house before kneeling (as does Captain Brassbound before Lady Cicely) to receive benediction from Candida.

In this last scene of the play, the tensions in Candida's role, the clashes between her loving Madonna and unscrupulous Siegfried personae, become overwhelming. Her speeches in this scene convey the impression not of successful realization of a complex character (or, as Paul Lauter suggests, a deliberate subversion of a stereotype[8]) but of artistic failure. There is an awkwardness in her final speeches, which arises from the radical incongruity of the tonal qualities called for in the stage direction ('*calm, sane, tender*'; '*With deepening gravity*'; '*With sweet irony*') and the implications of the words she speaks.

Uncertainties of tone and conception are also apparent in the characterization of Marchbanks. One critic maintains that 'The greatness of *Candida* as a play depends . . . upon the masterful depiction of a young man of genius.'[9] But whilst it is true that there are strong dramatic moments in Marchbanks's exchanges with Morell, some of the more serious let-downs in the play occur at precisely those points when Shaw was endeavouring to present Marchbanks in his character as a poet. (Jimmy Porter's contemptuous reference to his friend Cliff as 'a proper little Marchbanks' in John Obsorne's play *Look Back in Anger* is a more penetrating comment on Marchbanks's character than those provided by many critics.) John A. Mills argues that the poetical and rhetorical passages in Marchbanks's speeches are intended to be seen in a critical light.[10] But tell-tale stage directions and dramatic contexts tend, alas, to suggest otherwise.

MARCHBANKS: [*softly and musically, but sadly and longingly*] No, not a scrubbing brush, but a boat: a tiny shallop to sail away in, far from the world, where the marble floors are washed by the rain and dried by the sun; where the south wind dusts the beautiful green and purple carpets. Or a chariot! to carry us up into the sky, where the lamps are stars, and dont need to be filled with paraffin oil every day.

MORELL: [*harshly*] And where there is nothing to do but to be idle, selfish and useless.

CANDIDA: [*jarred*] Oh, James! how could you spoil it all?

MARCHBANKS: [*firing up*] Yes, to be idle, selfish, and useless: that is, to be beautiful and free and happy: hasnt every man desired that with all his soul for the woman he loves? Thats my ideal . . .

It can, of course, be argued that there is an implicit criticism of Marchbanks's poetical speech within the play in that at the end of Act III he makes his Nietzschean and Carlylean declaration 'I no longer desire happiness', and thus transcends the escapist ideal suggested in the languorous, Swinburnesque lines here. But then it is too late, and everything about the passage just quoted, the rhythms of Marchbanks's speech, the reactions of Candida and Morell, as well as the stage direction, indicates that the 'shallop' speech can only be played 'straight' by the actor. The dramatic context indicates that this piece of adolescent effusiveness is meant to present an unironical glimpse of the poet in action.

Even less satisfactory are the by now almost unactable lines that Marchbanks has at the end of the play: 'Out, then, into the night with me! . . . I know the hour when it strikes. I am impatient to do what must be done. . . . The night outside grows impatient.' Apart from the bombastic writing here there is also a problem of decorum, in the sense in which the word is used in classical rhetorical theory. In a play such as Ibsen's *The Lady from the Sea* (which closely parallels *Candida* in its basic dramatic situation) the poetic strains are indigenous to the action. In *Candida* they stand out awkwardly against a background of prosaic domesticity. More than once in talking about the play Shaw brings to mind characters who appear in Wagner's operas. If Candida is like Siegfried in her fearless amorality,[11] the night into which Marchbanks walks is the 'holy night' of Tristan. Counselling the members of a Rugby school literary society on the question of 'the secret in the poet's heart', Shaw recommended a course of reading in poetry about the night, in which they were to finish up with 'Wagner's *Tristan and Isolde*, where you will find the final and complete repudiation of the day and acceptance of the night as the true realm of the poet'.[12] But the comparison with Tristan draws attention to Shaw's failure to deal adequately with themes of such heroic scale in terms of the prose conventions operating in *Candida* (*Man and Superman* is more successful in this respect), and to the comparative vagueness of the night image in the play. For all we are told in the play, Marchbanks's flight into the night could be seen as no less escapist than the shallop fantasy, as an image which again defines the poet as one who turns his back on mundane realities rather than as one who finds his subject, as Yeats puts it, in 'the foul rag-and-bone shop of the heart'.

In a footnote to his discussion of Marchbanks in his study *Bernard Shaw and the Art of Destroying Ideals*, Charles A. Carpenter cites a letter of Shaw's to Ellen Terry in which he offered some advice about her daughter Edith. Edith had declared that she would never marry because 'she would not stay where she was not entirely happy':

> Tell Edy that the two things that worthless people sacrifice everything for are happiness and freedom, and that their punishment is that they get both, only to find that they have no capacity for the happiness and no use for the freedom. . . . Tell her to go and seek activity, struggle, bonds, responsibilities, terrors – in a word, life; but don't mention me as the prompter of this highly edifying lecture.[13]

The letter is illuminating for what it tells us about Shaw's thinking on the subject of happiness as a goal of human endeavour. But its value as a gloss on Marchbanks's situation at the end of *Candida* is less certain. Marchbanks does indeed renounce the quest for happiness. But the play does not, as the letter to Ellen Terry so admirably does, find expression for the Shavian alternative, of embracing 'activity, struggle, bonds, responsibilities, terrors – in a word, life'. On its own, without the accretions of explanation and comparison, Marchbanks's plunge into the night is less than satisfactory as an image of his arrival at maturity.

The actor Richard Mansfield's principal complaint about *Candida* was that it is all 'talk-talk-talk'.[14] Shaw might have objected that substantial developments occur in the three main characters' relations. But the play certainly has a very slight thread of plot, and it is questionable whether what action the play does contain is adequately unified. The minor characters, Prossy, Lexy and Burgess, have no vital bearing on the main action, and the intrusion of the tipsy revellers in Act III conveys the impression of a not fully realized dramatic symbol. It is possible that the off-stage party held by Burgess is a distant echo of the carousal in *Hedda Gabler* in which Lövborg rediscovers his Dionysian self. (In discussing *Candida* in his letters, Shaw more than once suggested that Mansfield should follow up the playing of Marchbanks with a performance as Lövborg, with Janet Achurch, who was cast as Candida in the proposed New York production, as Hedda.)[15] The revellers are at odds with the principles of order and restraint which ordinarily prevail in the Morell household ('You know our rules: total abstinence'), and their behaviour might conceivably be regarded as an oblique signal of the challenge to domestic ideals which Marchbanks's departure will complete. But Marchbanks is not one of the revellers, and if the tipsy scene is meant to appear as a symbol of subversion and to be thus related to Marchbanks's final speeches, the point is not clearly made.

The end of the play, with the depressing vistas it opens up of Candida mothering the 'big baby' Morell through even more years of 'stale perorations', and with Marchbanks, who suddenly acquires a manly voice, striking a pose of martyred resolution before passing out into the night and his dubious future as a poet, is material for comedy rather than high drama; and for once Shaw's usually reliable instinct in these matters failed him. Professor H. F. Brooks is on record as having remarked that 'people who have trouble with their mother-images have trouble with Candida'.[16] But the difficulties, both in the role and the play, are surely not confined to the minds of a particular class of beholders. They are all too apparent in the text.

NOTES

1. *Bernard Shaw: Collected Letters 1874–1897*, ed. Dan H. Laurence (London: Max Reinhardt, 1965) p. 623.
2. Ibid., p. 668
3. *Collected Plays*, vol. I, p. 373. For discussion of Shaw's treatment of Pre-Raphaelite themes in *Candida* see Elsie B. Adams, 'Bernard Shaw's Pre-Raphaelite Drama', *PMLA*, vol. LXXXI, p. 2 (Oct. 1966) pp. 428–38.
4. 'Miss Janet Achurch and Mr Charles Charrington in "Candida"', *Manchester Guardian*, 15 Mar. 1898; excerpt reprinted in *A Casebook on 'Candida'*, ed. Stephen S. Stanton (New York: Crowell, 1962) pp. 175–7.
5. 2 Samuel 6:16.
6. James Huneker, 'The Truth about *Candida*', *Metropolitan Magazine*, vol. xx (Aug. 1904) p. 635.
7. The poker business creates difficulties of tone in the theatre. Elton remarked in his review that 'Once, when a red-hot poker in some way served as a symbol of chaste separation, a wild humour was half apparent' (*A Casebook on 'Candida'*, pp. 175–7).
8. '*Candida* and *Pygmalion*: Shaw's Subversion of Stereotypes', *The Shaw Review*, vol. III, no. 3 (Sep. 1960) pp. 14–19.
9. Maurice Valency, *The Cart and the Trumpet: The Plays of George Bernard Shaw* (New York: Oxford University Press, 1973) p. 123.
10. John A. Mills, *Language and Laughter: Comic Diction in the Plays of Bernard Shaw* (Tucson: University of Arizona Press, 1969) p. 78.

11. Shaw saw Wagner's Siegfried as 'a type of the healthy man raised to perfect confidence in his own impulses by an intense and joyous vitality which is above fear, sickliness of conscience, malice and the makeshifts and moral crutches of law and order which accompany them' (*The Perfect Wagnerite*, 4th edn (London: Constable, 1923) p. 64).

12. *A Casebook on 'Candida'*, p. 168.

13. *Collected Letters 1874–1897*, p. 693; cited by Charles A. Carpenter, *Bernard Shaw and the Art of Destroying Ideals* (Madison: University of Wisconsin Press, 1969) p. 234.

14. *Collected Letters 1874–1897*, p. 523.

15. Ibid., pp. 499, 501.

16. See Margery M. Morgan, *The Shavian Playground: An Exploration of the Art of George Bernard Shaw* (London: Methuen, 1972) p. 72, n.1.

7 You Never Can Tell

There is no country of the Expected. The Unexpected Isles are the whole world.

(The Simpleton of the Unexpected Isles)

'Is there a law in your world, not to sleep in a fixed Land?'
'Yes', said the Lady. 'He does not wish us to dwell there.'
(C. S. Lewis, *Perelandra*)

'The dullest trash I ever revised'; 'a frightful example of the result of trying to write for the theatre de nos jours'.[1] Such were among the several dyspeptic judgements which in some moods (near the time of its completion) Shaw made of *You Never Can Tell*. In the preface to *Plays Pleasant*, he gives the play only brief mention as a work written in ways which would temper the brilliancy of *Arms and the Man* and accord more with the requirements of managers in search of 'fashionable comedies for West End theatres':

> I had no difficulty in complying, as I have always cast my plays in the ordinary practical comedy form in use at all the theatres; and far from taking an unsympathetic view of the popular preference for fun, fashionable dresses, a little music, and even an exhibition of eating and drinking by people with an expensive air, attended by an if-possible-comic waiter, I was more than willing to shew that the drama can humanize these things as easily as they, in the wrong hands, can dehumanize the drama.[2]

But Shaw's early comments on the play do much less than justice to *You Never Can Tell*. It is a deftly written, high-spirited, but serious, comedy which ranks itself as one of the outstanding achievements of the early period of his career as a dramatist.

Later, Shaw seems to have revised his early judgements of the play. The comments he made to William Archer, in a letter written in 1906, are very much closer to the true spirit and achievement of *You Never Can Tell*: 'The thing is a poem and a document, a sermon and a festival, all in one.'[3]

You Never Can Tell is Shaw's festive comedy; a celebration with feasting, music and dance as accompaniments, of life's contradictions of expectation, system and reason and of the possibilities it always holds out of fruitful change and development. More clearly than any other of the early plays, *You Never Can Tell* gives the lie to views of Shaw as an arch-rationalist and trumpeter of the intellect as a means of solving the problems of human relations. Throughout the play, settled prejudices and ideas are undermined by the contrariness of experience and by unpredictable shifts in perspective and feeling. The spirit of the play's title reigns over its action. Hardened attitudes are modified. Seemingly inviolable principles and decisions become irrelevant. The poised intellectuality of the young lovers is seen to conceal vast gaps in their emotional experience, and to create unnatural barriers in the way of fulfilment of their real needs and desires. The class structure turns out to be less rigid than it appears. Outrageous coincidences are part of the essence of both plot and themes. The realities of pain, bitterness and discord are not underestimated in the play. But the stress falls on hopeful possibilities: life and chance appear in their benign aspects. The inclusion of the twins in the cast is but one reminder of the possibilities of playful and exuberant benignity in the workings of the life force, which the play generally invites us to rejoice in. The action moves from an opening scene of pain, overshadowed by a figure of crabbed age, to a closing scene of revelry – the occasion is a ball held 'for the benefit of the Life-boat' – in which youth, vitality and hope are the prevailing forces.

Although it bears many of the marks of a play written to suit the conventions of 'fashionable comedies for West End theatres', close study of *You Never Can Tell* reveals it to be a work of surprising depths. If the fashionable surface of the play belongs to the late nineteenth century, its roots go down to what are thought to be the primitive origins of comedy, in rituals and games designed to exorcize the painful aspects of human experience and to celebrate the temporary triumph of life, growth and harmony over their opposites. Key metaphors in the play's design are introduced in deceptively simple ways. The drawing of a troublesome tooth, the drinking of wine, the ball in aid of the Life-boat, the seaside setting of the play, are so unremarkable at the literal level of response that their significance as metaphor can easily be overlooked.

The main characteristics of the play's metaphorical texture can be readily illustrated from the events of its opening and closing scenes. The first act is set in a dentist's operating room at a seaside resort. Valentine, the young dentist, has just completed the operation of extracting a tooth from one of the twins, Dolly, whose face as the play opens shows a '*rapidly clearing cloud of Spartan endurance*' as she utters the first words of the dialogue, 'Thank you'. This opening scene announces the pattern and function of the subsequent comic action. In the play painful and deep-rooted problems of human relations will be grappled with, and a final release from pain (if not a complete solution to the problems) will be achieved.

The second extraction performed in Act I is a more complicated affair. Valentine's second patient is the elderly estranged husband and father, Crampton. The metaphorical dimensions of this operation are brilliantly foreshadowed in Dolly's joking reference to *Macbeth*. In a speech which fuses the ideas of physical and psychological pain, she advises Crampton on the subject of a black 'twinge of memory': 'Have it out. "Pluck from the memory a rooted sorrow''. With gas, five shillings extra.' In the course of the operation, revelations of the 'rooted sorrow' of Crampton's broken marriage and his bitterly resentful feelings about his wife and children are interlaced with discussion of the surgical task in hand. At the end of Act I Crampton suffers a mock death as he succumbs to the gas which, on principle, he has forbidden Valentine to use:

> CRAMPTON: [*clutching at the arms of the chair as he falls back*] p! take care, man! I'm quite helpless in this po—
> VALENTINE: [*deftly stopping him with the gag, and snatching up the mouthpiece of the gas machine*] Youll be more helpless presently.
> *He presses the mouthpiece over Crampton's mouth and nose, leaning over his chest so as to hold his head and*

shoulders well down on the chair. Crampton makes an inarticulate sound in the mouthpiece and tries to lay hands on Valentine, whom he supposes to be in front of him. After a moment his arms wave aimlessly, then subside and drop. He is quite insensible. Valentine throws aside the mouthpiece quickly; picks the forceps adroitly from the glass; and –

After this 'death' a slow and faltering progress (Susanne Langer is surely wrong in saying that the characters in comedy do not develop)⁴ towards some modification of Crampton's cantankerous severity begins. The 'death' is also a means of survival for Valentine, since the bargain was that a completely painless extraction would mean the waiving by Crampton of six weeks' rent which the young man owes for his premises and is unable to pay.

The device of the fancy dress ball in Act IV enabled Shaw to heighten the stylistic register of the play, and to introduce several non-verbal expressions of its final affirmations. A festive atmosphere is established in the setting of Act IV, with its lighted lamps on stage, Chinese lanterns and starlit night in the background, and the sound of the band playing dance-music. Near the beginning of the act, the appearance at the window of the '*grotesquely majestic stranger*', Bohun, in his domino, false nose and goggles, is a further early signal of the movement towards a resolution of the play's action in revelry. After Bohun's entry and introduction, coffee is ordered; but the order is changed to one for spirits and claret cup, with only Gloria modifying this Dionysian decision by asking for cucumber as well. The gradual invasion which takes place during the act of the on-stage action by the fancy dress ball reaches a climax with the brilliant, dancing entry of the twins in harlequin and columbine costumes. The columbine's costume is a salute to summer and fertility: '[*her*] *petticoats are the epitome of a harvest field, golden orange and poppy crimson, with a tiny velvet jacket for the poppy stamens*'. After this entry, all the characters, with the exception of the abject Valentine, are drawn into the dance. The selection of partners for the dance brings together youth and age in several surprising combinations.

Under the spell of the artifice and make-believe of the fancy dress ball the more sombre characters in the play present their

most agreeably human selves. Crampton loses his severity, and
Mrs Clandon allows herself to be whirled away in dance by the
harlequin. Bohun's self-assertive authority is seen in its most
genial light as he claims a dance with Gloria in his 'grandest
diapason'. Once again it is Dolly who provides in a jest an insight
into the function of comedy, as she remarks on the humanizing
effect of Bohun's resumption of his fancy dress:

> [He claps on the false nose and is again grotesquely transfigured].
> DOLLY: . . . Oh, now you look quite like a human being.
> Maynt I have just one dance with you? Can you
> dance?
> Phil, resuming his part of harlequin, waves his bat as if
> casting a spell on them.

The fantastic artifice of the fancy dress ball, this passage suggests,
is a form of magic which has the effect of bringing out the more
amiable humanity of those involved in its dances, of encouraging
their more friendly and sociable ranges of feeling. The ball may
thus be seen as an epitome of the larger artifact of the play which
contains it.

In the thematic pattern of the play, feeling and intellect are
largely opposed forces. The opposition seems too simple when it is
stated in such abstract terms. But it is not so in its dramatic
context. You Never Can Tell does not often sound like a 'sermon'.
But in so far as Shaw's casual description of it as such can be said
to have relevance, the main text of its teaching is perhaps
contained in the following passage of dialogue between
Crampton and Gloria:

> GLORIA: [firmly] You see! Everything comes right if we
> only think it resolutely out.
> CRAMPTON: [in sudden dread] No: dont think. I want you to
> feel: thats the only thing that can help us.

For both participants in this exchange, the play's action provides
a gradual education in feeling. Gloria, we see, has both to
discover and to come to terms with her feelings. Crampton needs
to modify and soften his. They both need to find some humility.
Gloria's attempt to discuss matters with her father 'coolly and
rationally' in Act II ends in failure. Their final reconciliation

comes about in a simple moment of mutual surrender:

	[*She stops beside him and looks quaintly down at him*]. Well, father?
CRAMPTON:	[*submissively*] Well, daughter?
	They look at one another with a melancholy sense of humor, though humor is not their strong point.
GLORIA:	Shake hands [*They shake hands*].
CRAMPTON:	[*holding her hand*] My dear: I'm afraid I spoke very improperly of your mother this afternoon.
GLORIA:	Oh, dont apologize. I was very high and mighty myself; but Ive come down since: oh, yes: Ive been brought down. [*She sits down on the floor beside his chair*].

The conflicts which take place within Gloria's character mirror those which have occurred in the past between her parents. In her person are combined characteristics of both her parents; and the conflicting impulses and sympathies which this creates are expressed when she says to Crampton: 'My feelings – my miserable cowardly womanly feelings – may be on your side; but my conscience is on hers.' Gloria's coming to terms with her father is intimately connected with the development of her relationship with Valentine, and with the discovery of aspects of her own personality which, under the influence of her mother's educational principles and outlook, have been suppressed. Both relationships reveal to her the passionate nature she has inherited from her father which she has previously endeavoured to deny as an unwanted tyranny, just as in the past her mother has denied Crampton himself. The cause of the breakdown of her parent's marriage is revealed so succinctly and obliquely as to be almost hidden from view:

MRS CLANDON:	I never discovered his feelings. I discovered his temper, and his – [*she shivers*] the rest of his common humanity.
M'COMAS:	[*wistfully*]. Women can be very hard, Mrs Clandon.

Mrs Clandon's admission that she never discovered her

husband's feelings is consistent with other aspects of her characterization in the play. In some respects, Mrs Clandon's character
is reminiscent of that of Mrs Alving in Ibsen's *Ghosts*, a woman
whose incapacity for affection is seen to be one of the prime causes
of the tragic action which is unfolded in the play. Mrs Clandon
has another literary forebear in Mrs Jellyby in Dickens's *Bleak
House*. Mrs Jellyby is portrayed by Dickens as a woman who is so
preoccupied with humanitarian causes that she overlooks the
immediate human needs of her own family. She is a philanthrop-
ist whose charity does not begin at home: 'O don't talk of duty as
a child, Miss Summerson; where's Ma's duty as a parent? All
made over to the public and Africa, I suppose!'⁵ Mrs Clandon is
high-principled and altruistic, a reader, like the young Shaw, of
Mill, Huxley, Tyndall and George Eliot, champion of women's
rights and author of purportedly advanced, but actually old-
fashioned, treatises on family relations, and other sociological
topics, the titles of which are reeled off with sardonic flippancy by
Dolly and Philip in Act I. But Mrs Clandon's intellectual and
humanitarian pursuits are accompanied by failures and lack of
perception in the primary relations of her own life, with her
husband and her children. The heartfelt reproach which Gloria
directs to her mother at the end of Act II after her unexpectedly
passionate encounter with Valentine – 'Why didnt you educate
me properly?' – is particularly wounding because it strikes
simultaneously at Mrs Clandon's central pretensions and central
failings. Mrs Clandon is certainly presented in a critical light in
the play. Yet Shaw's portrayal is considerably softened by the
occasional suggestions he provides in her characterization of a
more tender, decorously flirtatious self which has never come into
full flower.

Shaw achieves a similar richness and complexity in the
characterization of Crampton. In his first appearances in the
play he is shown as a man full of prejudices, bitterness and anger.
But his need for affection, his clumsy gestures towards expressing
affection, and his fear of exposing himself to further wounds are
skilfully shown in his scene with Gloria in Act II. Crampton's
marriage and character represent the reverse of the fortunate
accidents which the play celebrates. This is brought out in the
eloquent speech in which M'Comas puts the case for Crampton
to Mrs Clandon in Act III:

Think of the people who do kind things in an unkind way! people whose touch hurts, whose voices jar, whose tempers play them false, who wound and worry the people they love in the very act of trying to conciliate them, and who yet need affection as much as the rest of us.

The qualities of humility, tact and grace which Crampton lacks and needs to acquire are precisely those which are unfailingly displayed by Walter Bohun, the hotel waiter whose likeness to Shakespeare's bust at Stratford prompts the twins to rename him William. Comparison between the two paternal figures is encouraged by the fact that Philip claims to be reminded of his own father by 'William', and by his declaration when the true father appears: 'William: at the very outset of your career as my father, a rival has appeared on the scene.' When Crampton acquires some of the benevolence and tolerance (as in the matter of judging the children's manner of dress) of his 'rival', the waiter, he becomes more fit for the paternal role. Significantly, it is Crampton who helps Dolly down from the precarious pose which her Act IV entry as columbine leaves her in. By this act of service he demonstrates the new character of his relations with his children in the closing movements of the play's action. In the early part of the play Crampton is seen as being puritanically opposed to self-indulgence, and yet at the same time prone to give way to violent passions. Valentine's Act I comment on Crampton's custom of cleaning his teeth with 'plain yellow soap' points the way towards the process of mollification which Crampton later undergoes: 'Well, your teeth are good, I admit. But Ive seen just as good in very self-indulgent mouths.' When Crampton departs to watch the dancing in Act IV he has learned the uses of both indulgence and control: 'What harm will it do, just for once, M'Comas? Dont let us be spoil-sports. . . . We must indulge them a little.'

You Never Can Tell abounds in character pairing. In addition to the twins and rival 'fathers' there are also two contrasting lawyers: the friendly and humane family solicitor, M'Comas, and the imposing and aggressive QC, Bohun, whose eyebrows resemble early Victorian horsehair upholstery, and whom Valentine describes as 'the very incarnation of intellect'. In the little allegory which is embedded in the events of Act IV, it is true that the family reunion is presided over by Intellect. It is Intellect, in the shape of Bohun's marshalling of facts and extracting of objective statements of positions ('Youre going to tell me about your feelings, Mr Crampton. Dont. . . . Tell us exactly what you want') which brings the family situation into focus. But what is revealed about the situation is that it is only by adjustments in feeling that the oppositions can be resolved. 'You can do nothing but make a friendly arrangement', Bohun finally declares. But that is what M'Comas has been implying all along.

Under the inspection of Bohun's sceptical intelligence life is seen in a completely negative light. Comically sounding the barren depths of what reason can tell us about life, he says 'It's unwise to be born; it's unwise to be married; it's unwise to live; and it's wise to die.' This Act IV speech of Bohun's momentarily puts us in touch again with the underlying themes of pain in the play. But its sour denials are immediately countered by the waiter's retort: 'Then, if I may respectfully put a word in, sir, so much the worse for wisdom!'

The seaside setting of *You Never Can Tell* has significant connections with its thematic concerns. The action of the play takes place on *terra firma*. But the image of the sea, as a place of hazard, unpredictability and turbulent depths, is a strong background presence. There are various ways in which the sea is alluded to in the play. In the course of writing, Shaw altered the name of the hotel in which the major part of the action takes place from The Granville to The Marine.[6] Valentine's operating room in Act I has a broad window with a sea view which Dolly comments upon and Gloria, on her first entry, gazes at. The description of Gloria's costume shows that Shaw wanted part of it to be a visual echo of the sea background:

> *Her tailormade skirt-and-jacket dress, of saffron brown cloth, seems conventional when her back is turned; but it displays in front a blouse of sea-green silk which scatters its conventionality with one stroke.*

The hotel terrace in Act II overlooks the sea, and at the break-up of the luncheon party most of the diners retire to the beach. At the beginning of Act III we learn that Valentine, who is 'unaccustomed to navigation', has been out boating on the bay with the twins. In Act IV (which begins with the sound of dance-music '*drowning the sound of the sea*') Philip as harlequin briefly undergoes a further transformation into an Ariel-like figure when he is sent to summon Bohun: 'From the vasty deep. I go. [*He makes his bat quiver in the air and darts away through the window*].'

In the manuscript draft of the play, the Act II speech of Valentine's which precipitates Gloria's sudden capitulation to passion employs the sea as an image of subconscious feelings, and thus explicitly brings it into relation with the play's thematic concerns:

VALENTINE: . . . Now that I think down into it seriously, I dont know whether I like you or not.
GLORIA: I am sorry.
VALENTINE: But I know what I feel. Do you see the sea there? Do you know how strongly it affects us? You can imagine the waves are its breathing, and it is troubled and stirred to its great depths by some emotion that cannot be described. Well, in my heart –
GLORIA: [suddenly] Oh, stop telling me what you feel: I can't bear it.[7]

In the published text Valentine's speech appears in substantially revised form, and the rather stilted exposition is replaced by a direct appeal, with an accompanying gain in dramatic effect. But the sea image remains in vestigial form: 'Oh, dont pity me. Your voice is tearing my heart to pieces. Let me alone, Gloria. You go down into the very depths of me, troubling and stirring me.' Later in the scene between the two in Act IV, the image is recalled in more than one speech:

GLORIA: . . . You dragged me down to your level for a moment this afternoon . . .
VALENTINE: . . . Because I was being tempted to awaken your heart: to stir the depths in you. . . . When the great moment came, who was awakened? who was stirred? in whom did the depths break up?

What both Valentine and Gloria learn in the play is that

whatever rational constructions we set upon experience, or attempt to order experience by, the forces of the subconscious, 'the depths', remain inexorable, and are likely to influence behaviour in unexpected and subversive ways. The development of the relationship between Gloria and Valentine is thus a major variation on the theme of the play's title.

The book which Gloria takes to read by the sea is (ironically enough in view of the final development of her role) John Stuart Mill's *The Subjection of Women*. With such emancipating texts, as well as with the sociological and scientific education provided by her mother, she seems equipped, cap-à-pie, to cope with any emotional emergencies. But, partly through Valentine's rather chauvinistic conversation with Mrs Clandon in Act III ('I learnt how to circumvent the Women's Rights woman before I was twenty-three'), and partly through what takes place in the love scenes themselves, we are made sharply aware of the distance between the dictates of reason and the commands of passion in Shaw's presentation of the love relation in the play. It is Valentine who gives expression to the idea which the play conveys, of Nature as an omnipotent force which dwarfs the pretensions of both human reason and individual identity. The Nature of *You Never Can Tell* is reminiscent of the benign, all-powerful Dame of Alanus and Chaucer. Describing his feeling of helplessness in the grip of Gloria's attractiveness, Valentine says it is

> As if Nature, after letting us belong to ourselves and do what we judged right and reasonable for all these years, were suddenly lifting her great hand to take us – her two little children – by the scruffs of our little necks, and use us, in spite of ourselves, for her own purposes, in her own way.

In some respects *You Never Can Tell* is a surprisingly conservative play. It is most appropriate that its action should be presided over by a gentle waiter who bears a strong resemblance to Shakespeare. On the other hand, the final development of the relationship between Gloria and Valentine does not follow a conventional pattern, and there is considerable irony in Shaw's handling of the denouement of the love plot, especially in the treatment of Valentine. As one who dangerously describes

intellect as 'a masculine speciality', Valentine's cleverness is
similar to that of Charteris in *The Philanderer*. In most of his
appearances in the play he is presented as being highly self-
confident and intellectually adroit. This being so, the more
ignominious is his defeat and collapse in the last moments of the
duel of sex in Act IV. When the point of commitment is reached,
Valentine becomes virtually inarticulate, and the remark about
his being 'unaccustomed to navigation' acquires additional
richness. The imperious Nature he spoke of earlier has become
personified as Gloria, and his capitulation to her is like a
drowning. Gloria's overwhelming of Valentine turns the tables
on the nimble overwhelmer of Crampton at the end of Act I:

VALENTINE: [*half delighted, half frightened*] I never could:
youd be unhappy. My dearest love: I should be
the merest fortune-hunting adventurer if –
[*Her grip of his arms tightens; and she kisses him*].
Oh Lord! [*Breathless*] Oh, I – [*he gasps*] I dont
know anything about women: twelve years
experience is not enough. [*In a gust of jealousy she
throws him away from her; and he reels back into a
chair like a leaf before the wind*].

It was Shaw's original intention to make Gloria's seaside
reading Schopenhauer's misogynistic essay 'On Women'.[8] Mill is
more appropriate, but the Schopenhauer essay left its mark on
the play, and indeed on Shaw's thinking about the relations
between the sexes for some time to come. Schopenhauer sees
women as the vehicles of primary natural energies which
overwhelm any other manifestation of humanity which threatens
to oppose them. In the 1891 translation, by Shaw's fellow music
critic on *The Star*, Belfort Bax, Schopenhauer says:

Young, strong, and fine men are called by nature for the
propagation of the human race, in order that the race may not
deteriorate. This is the fixed WILL of nature, and the passions of
women are its expression. This law takes the precedence in age
and force of every other. Woe therefore unto him who so places
his rights and interests that they stand in the way of it; no
matter what he says and does, they will be mercilessly crushed
on the first important occasion.[9]

The domineering Gloria Clandon who, at the conclusion of the love scene in Act IV, orders Valentine to get up and to have 'no false delicacy' about announcing that they have agreed to marry one another certainly seems to be modelled on Schopenhauerian lines. But, if so, the mood of the end of the play does not allow us to dwell upon the fact in the grim and crabbed mood of Schopenhauer's essay. At least in the benign perspective offered by the waiter, the terrors of Schopenhauerian women and monstrous and aggressive lawyers can be seen to be possibly tolerable; and at all events it is his philosophical commendation of marriage, steering a sagacious course between optimism and pessimism, which concludes the play:

> WAITER: [*contemplating the defeated Duellist of Sex with ineffable benignity*] Cheer up, sir, cheer up. Every man is frightened of marriage when it comes to the point; but it often turns out very comfortable, very enjoyable and happy indeed, sir – from time to time. *I* never was master in my own house, sir: my wife was like your young lady: she was of a commanding and masterful disposition, which my son has inherited. But if I had my life to live twice over, I'd do it again: I'd do it again, I assure you.

The glow, exuberance and edge of the comedy in this play make it one of the most engaging of Shaw's early works. The orchestration of voices in ensemble scenes such as the luncheon party in Act II is handled with impressive virtuosity, and the dialogue throughout shows a fine control of cadence and tempo. The play's affinities with 'fashionable comedies for the West End' are certainly apparent, but the subtlety and richness of the treatment of character and themes have a transforming effect on its conventional materials. If the play can be said to be related to a nineteenth-century tradition of farcical comedy, the relation is by no means a matter of simple derivation. In *You Never Can Tell* the materials of farce become the basis of high comedy.

NOTES

1. *Bernard Shaw: Collected Letters 1874–1897*, ed. Dan H. Laurence (London: Max Reinhardt, 1965) pp. 799, 801.

2. *Collected Plays*, vol. i, p. 376.
3. Letter to William Archer, 10 July 1906, in Charles Archer, *William Archer, Life, Work and Friendships* (London: Allen & Unwin, 1931) p. 295.
4. 'Because the comic rhythm is that of vital continuity, the protagonists do not change in the course of the play, as they normally do in tragedy' (Susanne K. Langer, *Feeling and Form* (London: Routledge & Kegan Paul, 1953) p. 335).
5. Charles Dickens, *Bleak House*, ed. Norman Page (Harmondsworth. Penguin Books, 1971) p. 96.
6. The original name appears in the manuscript draft of the play held in the British Library (Ms Add. 50605).
7. British Library, MS Add. 50605.
8. British Library, MS Add. 50605.
9. *Selected Essays of Arthur Schopenhauer, Translated with Biographical Introduction and Sketch of his Philosophy* by E. Belfort Bax (London: H. G. Bohn, 1891) p. 342.

8 Puritanism and Revolt in *Three Plays for Puritans*

> I am more nearly a Quaker than anything else that has a denomination.
>
> (Shaw)

I

The collective title which Shaw gave to *Three Plays for Puritans* perhaps suggests a greater degree of homogeneity in the plays than they actually exhibit. Nevertheless, there are common thematic patterns in the three plays, and the title has more than one kind of relevance. The 'Puritans' of the title seem intended to be both pleased and displeased by the dedication. On the one hand, the plays can be said to be 'for Puritans' in that they attack puritanical rigidity and narrowness of thought and outlook, and the conceptual stereotypes underlying middle-class morality. ('It annoys me to see people comfortable when they ought to be uncomfortable', Shaw declares in the Preface, 'and I insist on making them think in order to bring them to conviction of sin.')[1] On the other hand, the plays can also be seen to be 'for Puritans' in more favourable senses of the term. They are each marked by a deliberate avoidance of sentimental and conventionally romantic resolutions of action. They show the inadequacy of established religious and ethical codes. And they each present central characters who are, in different ways, outside and superior to the religious and moral systems which prevail in the societies in which they move. The ethical codes which are implied in their behaviour, though not denominational in character, are very close to the central teachings of the New Testament.

In the Preface which he wrote for the three plays in 1900, Shaw lays stress on the fact that they were written in a mood of profound dissatisfaction with the sentimentalities of nineteenth-century dramatic and non-dramatic fiction, with the syndrome in which 'love-interest', carefully stripped of its real erotic content and made fit for genteel audiences, is regarded as the *sine qua non* of success in play and novel alike, and the motivating force in each and every situation.[2] Shaw's perception about the handling of sexual themes on the stage in the nineteenth century was that it not only tended to be prudish and prurient, but also that it involved a drastic impoverishment of the drama in terms of the range of human experience which could be treated. Shaw puts this point of view memorably as follows:

> It may seem strange, even monstrous, that a man should feel a constant attachment to the hideous witches in Macbeth, and yet yawn at the prospect of spending another evening in the contemplation of a beauteous young leading lady with voluptuous contours and longlashed eyes, painted and dressed to perfection in the latest fashions. But that is just what happened to me in the theatre.[3]

The stories of *The Arabian Nights* are called to witness against the nineteenth-century drama both for their greater frankness and freedom in the treatment of sex and for their larger range of fictional resources:

> In The Arabian Nights we have a series of stories, some of them very good ones, in which no sort of decorum is observed. The result is that they are infinitely more instructive and enjoyable than our romances, because love is treated in them as naturally as any other passion. There is no cast iron convention as to its effects; no false association of general depravity of character with its corporealities or of general elevation with its sentimentalities; no pretence that a man or woman cannot be courageous and kind and friendly unless infatuatedly in love with somebody (is no poet manly enough to sing The Old Maids of England?): rather, indeed, an insistence on the blinding and narrowing power of lovesickness to make princely heroes unhappy and unfortunate.[4]

The Preface to *Three Plays for Puritans* certainly throws light on

Shaw's rather contrary handling of sexual relations in the three plays; and the plays themselves present an amusing challenge to conventions in this respect. But there may also be found in the Preface some explanation of the factitiousness which enters into the resolution of the potential love situations which are presented in the plays. At least two of the plays, moreover, *The Devil's Disciple* and *Caesar and Cleopatra*, are vulnerable to the charge that the treatment of sex, so far from presenting a robust alternative to Victorian prissiness, tends to be itself skittish and evasive. In both plays erotic interest is clearly present in the relations between the male and female leads, but is in the end firmly cancelled in ways which suggest the demonstration of a thesis rather than the inevitable conclusion of the action. Shaw once remarked in a letter to William Archer that in writing *Captain Brassbound's Conversion* he had followed the, for him, unusual procedure of writing to a rough plan of exposition, which made the first act 'smell a little of the workshop'.[5] There are points, it must be admitted even in a sympathetic examination, at which all three of the *Plays for Puritans* convey that impression.

II

In form, *The Devil's Disciple* is a return to the combination of melodrama and military adventure story which Shaw had made use of in *Arms and the Man*. As he did in the earlier play, Shaw exploits the dramatic devices and conventions of popular dramatic forms, but at the same time places their characteristic assumptions in a critical light. He points out in the Preface that 'Every old patron of the Adelphi pit' would have recognized such familiar theatrical standbys as 'the reading of the will, the oppressed orphan finding a protector, the arrest, the heroic sacrifice, the court martial, the scaffold, the reprieve at the last moment'.[6] The play is frankly sub-titled 'A Melodrama', and its extremes of characterization and situation answer to the expectations which this creates.

Richard Dudgeon appears in Act I as almost a caricature of the sardonic, romantic rebel. At the meeting between son and mother, Shaw tells us that Dudgeon's '*lip rolls up horribly from his dog tooth as he meets her look of undisguised hatred*'. Mrs Dudgeon, acknowledged by Shaw to be practically 'a replica of Mrs

Clennam' in *Little Dorrit*,[7] is described as a woman of '*hard, driving, wrathful*' ways; and such dialogue as she has provides little opportunity for her to be shown in any other moods but those of vindictive bitterness and hatred. In the Council Chamber scenes in Act III, however, we see the melodramatic situation through a critically distancing perspective provided by the stock responses of horror and indignation expressed by Judith Anderson, on the one hand, and the suave, polite and jocular spirit of the exchanges between Dudgeon and Burgoyne on the other. In the brief scene which precedes Dudgeon's trial Burgoyne provides a comically blatant reminder of the play's genre with the tart question he addresses to his subordinate, 'May I ask are you writing a melodrama, Major Swindon?'

With such self-conscious techniques, the play throws a critical light on two of the most familiar conventions of the melodramatic form. The first is the convention embodied in the sharp differentiation between hero and villain in melodrama, that good and evil are instantly identifiable according to immutable moral laws and universally accepted outward signs, and that characters belong wholly either to one or the other category. The second is that all self-sacrificing, heroic action is inevitably motivated by the love of a man for a woman, or vice versa. In rebelling against the latter convention, Shaw was no doubt expressing an entirely justifiable reaction to a tedious fictional cliché. The themes of this play are in tune with a remark Shaw made to Frank Harris in a letter of 16 October 1916: 'The infatuated Amorism of the nineteenth century, like its Bardolatry, made it necessary for me to say with emphasis that Life and not Love is the supreme good.'[8] But the difficulty he experienced in making this point dramatically convincing can be sensed in the awkward rhetoric and expository tone of Dudgeon's crucial speech in the scene with Judith in Act III:

> If I said – to please you – that I did what I did ever so little for your sake, I lied as men always lie to women. You know how much I have lived with worthless men – aye, and worthless women too. Well, they could all rise to some sort of goodness and kindness when they were in love [*the word love comes from him with true Puritan scorn*]. That has taught me to set very little store by the goodness that only comes out red hot. What I did

last night, I did in cold blood, caring not half so much for your husband, or [*ruthlessly*] for you [*she droops, stricken*] as I do for myself. I had no motive and no interest: all I can tell you is that when it came to the point whether I would take my neck out of the noose and put another man's into it, I could not do it. I dont know why not: I see myself as a fool for my pains; but I could not and I cannot. I have been brought up standing by the law of my own nature; and I may not go against it, gallows or no gallows.

The style of *The Devil's Disciple* precludes close entanglement, on the part of either author or audience, with the underlying psychological motives of the three main characters, and with the nature of their relations with one another. It is true that Shaw does provide some hints as to the inner realities of the relations of Dudgeon, Judith and Anderson. But it is a justifiable criticism of the play that it leaves too many questions about the relations of the principal characters unanswered. There is clearly an atmosphere of *dangeur* (in the sense in which that term is applied to erotic tension and possibility in medieval romance) in the scene between Dudgeon and Judith when they are left together by Anderson early in Act II. Dudgeon reminds us of Marchbanks when he speaks of the 'almost holy' atmosphere of the Anderson house; and he helps us to understand his feelings towards Judith when he says, again reminding us of Marchbanks, that it would be against his nature to become domesticated. In the same scene, the relations between Judith and Anderson are very lightly touched upon when Judith, with something like a slip of the tongue, reveals her sensitivity to the fact that Anderson is a good deal older than she. But the treatment of these relations, at least in their psychological dimensions, remains sketchy.

An early draft of the play indicates that Shaw had originally intended to make much more of the relation between Judith and Anderson, and indeed to make the final development of their relation a pivotal point in the play's dénouement. It was originally intended to be explicitly revealed that Judith's feelings for her husband had always been less than passionate. At the end of the play she was to reveal that her romantic association with Dudgeon had had the effect of awakening passionate feelings within her towards her husband:

JUDITH:	I never really loved him before: I only pretended to, like most wives. He never could have taught me himself what love is. But you taught me. And now I love *him*. Isn't that funny?
RICHARD:	Quite right. He is a better man than I am.
JUDITH:	But I wish I could have taught you to love, too. Is that wicked, do you think?
RICHARD:	If it is, then I shall always remain the Devil's Disciple.[9]

But Shaw evidently realized that such psychological insights would not fit happily into the general style of the end of the play. He clearly wanted, and achieves, bold theatrical effects: the strong character contrast between the blustering Major Swindon and the suave Burgoyne; the solemn entry into the market place of Dudgeon and his judges with the military band playing the Dead March from *Saul*; the breathless arrival of Anderson as the first stroke of noon is heard from the town clock; the ceremonious playing of the British Grenadiers giving way to the jaunty Yankee Doodle music in the last moments of the play, and the crowd surging forward to carry Dudgeon off in triumph.

The play makes most sense as a theatrical fantasy on the subjects of revolt and the throwing off of outmoded or perverse authority. The historical setting allows Shaw to bring the gravest rebellion in English history (child America impudently throwing off parental England) into association with other forms of rebellion, son versus mother, healthy disrespect versus pious conventionality, the comic spirit versus that of sentimental romance. But these themes are suggested rather than fully realized in the play. It is arguable that it was not until he came to the writing of *Major Barbara* that Shaw was able to make fully articulate his interest (noticeable in his dramatic work from Mrs Warren's declaration about prospering in wrong at the end of her play) in the life-enhancing possibilities of setting aside the categories of good and evil, or of exploring the potentially beneficent powers of apparently sinister persons and philosophies.

Underlying *The Devil's Disciple* as possible shaping influences are Blake's *Marriage of Heaven and Hell* and, perhaps more directly a curious poem which the author, Robert Buchanan, sent to Shaw in 1895, entitled *The Devil's Case*, which praises in semi-humorous quatrains the Promethean virtues of the Devil, and condemns the abject condition of 'slaves of Heaven'.[10] But in Shaw's play, just as the form prevents deep psychological analysis, so does it tend to bar any substantial exploration of what it is that makes Dudgeon the Devil's Disciple. We see that his revolt is directed against the joyless religiosity represented by his mother. He is a purer Puritan. But the alternatives are so starkly presented and the characters so sketchily portrayed that it is difficult to become involved with them at any profound level. In the final analysis it has to be said that the play becomes trapped in the limitations of the genre which it sets out to exploit and show up. The trap for the critic, on the other hand, is to treat the work too seriously. At least its expansive, central jokes – the hero's protestation that he is *not* in love with the lady he is preparing to lay down his life for, the clergyman's discovery that he is really much more fitted to be a military commander than a man of God – have about them a liberating gaiety.

III

Each of the *Three Plays for Puritans* deals in one way or another with the subject of revenge. In *The Devil's Disciple*, Mrs Dudgeon (the name is obviously descriptive in her case) is portrayed as a woman living her life out in a state of impotent vindictiveness and bitter recrimination over injustices, imagined or otherwise, committed against her in the past, and in the course of the play's action. In *Caesar and Cleopatra*, Caesar's forbearance from revenge is seen as one of the cardinal defining features of his superior civility and greatness, and is pointedly contrasted with the vengeful behaviour of Cleopatra in ordering Pothinus to be slain by Ftatateeta. His clemency has strategic advantages as well; but this pragmatic insight does not undermine the point that Caesar approaches the godlike in character, is able to address the Sphinx as belonging to the same order of being, precisely because of his capacity to rise above the ordinary human instinct to exact revenge for injuries suffered. Shaw provides in the play an intelligent interpretation of Caesar's well-known virtue of *clemen-*

tia. In *Captain Brassbound's Conversion* the entire action depends upon the Captain's desire to carry out revenge against his uncle for a wrongdoing committed against his mother. The actual means by which his revenge plot is frustrated is the timely arrival of the American cruiser; but the more profound change which takes place, the one to which the title refers, is that Brassbound is converted by Lady Cicely from a spiritually impotent state, in which the only direction in his life is provided by melodramatic, revengeful feelings, to one in which he achieves a new self-command. Each of the three protagonists in the plays is distinguished by the quality of magnanimity. Dudgeon's heroic altruism, Caesar's clemency, Lady Cicely's inspired diplomacy, all affirm the possibility of transcending the petty motivations and limitations of ordinary human nature. Shaw's treatment of the three main personae in the *Plays for Puritans* adumbrates the more direct handling of ideas about the superhuman in the play which follows this group, *Man and Superman*.

Dudgeon, Caesar and Lady Cicely each emerge in their plays as New Testament figures in societies dominated by Old Testament codes. In each play it is specifically the non-institution-bound individual who approximates most closely in action and outlook to Christian ideals. This supplies what is perhaps the deepest sense in which the plays are 'for Puritans'. They reflect a deeply engrained Protestantism in Shaw, the bias of which takes it far outside the traditional Protestant moulds. Of the two formal representatives of Christianity in the plays, Anderson and Rankin, the former is a Presbyterian, the second a son of the Free Church of Scotland. But the two plays in which they appear celebrate forms of religious obligation and action which do not depend upon affiliation to a church. In this context it may be recalled that when Shaw responded to a request for funds for a church dedicated to Saint Joan in 1927, the note which he wrote to accompany his donation read: 'As I am more nearly a Quaker than anything else that has a denomination, and Joan was the spiritual mother of George Fox, I can hardly refuse an infinitesimal percentage of the money I have made out of her.'[11]

In the *Three Plays for Puritans* it is the inspired outsider (or, in the case of Lady Cicely, highly unconventional person) rather than the denominational man of religion who most vividly recalls the example of Christ. It is Dudgeon, rather than Anderson, who prepares to lay down his life for his friend. It is Lady Cicely, the mere Sunday school teacher, who effects the significant conversions, rather than Rankin the professional missionary. It is Caesar, who regards the Egyptian religious practices as 'hocuspocus' and superstition, who opens up the prospect of more enlightened ethical principles than those belonging to the worship of Ra, and who, obliquely in his own words, is placed in the company of Christ:

> If one man in all the world can be found, now or forever, to know that you did wrong, that man will have either to conquer the world as I have, or be crucified by it.[12]

In the third play of the group, however, *Captain Brassbound's Conversion*, we see an important development, in that here some aspects of the 'outsider' consciousness are themselves placed in a critical light.

IV

Although Shaw completed the play in 1898, *Caesar and Cleopatra* was not professionally performed in England until 1907, when it opened first at Leeds and then in November at the Savoy Theatre. Amongst the witnesses of the production was W. B. Yeats, who recorded his impressions in a letter to Florence Farr:

> I saw *Caesar and Cleopatra* with Forbes Robertson in it twice this week·and have been really delighted and what I never thought [to] be with work of his, moved. There is vulgarity, plenty of it, but such gay heroic delight in the serviceable man.[13]

Shaw could hardly have wished for a better response to the play than this, and might have defended its 'vulgarity' as being germane to the play's themes. Caesar's attitude to art is, like Shaw's, deeply ambiguous. His feelings towards the patrician amateur artist, Apollodorus (whose motto, pleasantly borrowed from a later age, is 'Art for Art's sake'), is far from contemptuous. It is a discussion of Apollodorus that prompts Caesar's reflection on the Romans' 'brutal life of action' and the dullness of the Roman character: 'That is the worst of us Romans: we are mere doers and drudgers: a swarm of bees turned into men. Give me a good talker – one with wit and imagination enough to live without continually doing something!'

Caesar and Cleopatra might, in fact, be regarded in some senses as another play, after *Candida*, about Pre-Raphaelitism. Apollodorus is sumptuously dressed with '*deliberate aestheticism*', and his sword is '*designed as carefully as a medieval cross*'. In Act IV Apollodorus calls himself Cleopatra's knight, and evokes the code of medieval chivalry when he reproaches Cleopatra for not allowing him to defend her honour in 'fair duel'. Caesar is the only Roman who shows any real appreciation of Apollodorus, and this fits with the side of his character which is enraptured with the idea of tracking the Nile 'to its cradle in the heart of the regions of mystery' and with the man who, as Cleopatra unhistorically tells us, 'loves music'. On the other hand, Caesar is also, paradoxically enough, a super-philistine. His response to the burning of the library at Alexandria is exciting, and its extra-historical context of the artistic and literary culture of *fin de siècle* England gives it added point:

THEODOTUS: What is burning there is the memory of mankind.
CAESAR: A shameful memory. Let it burn.
THEODOTUS: [*wildly*] Will you destroy the past?
CAESAR: Ay, and build the future with its ruins.

Caesar is like the Cromwell of Marvell's 'Horatian Ode'.

The scene of the burning of the library is followed almost immediately by the arrival of the delicate and attractive Sicilian, Apollodorus, the 'worshipper of beauty', who tells the Roman sentinel that his motto of Art for Art's sake is 'a universal password'. At this point, the play see-saws between denunciation and approbation of the artistic sensibility. It is not far-fetched to think of Cleopatra herself, as she enters in Act V, '*cold and tragic*', in her cleverly chosen black dress, as being intended to be viewed as an exotic work of art. Caesar's cheerful and relatively unconcerned farewell to Cleopatra is the play's final, puritan, judgement on Pre-Raphaelite aestheticism. Caesar has already, before Cleopatra's entry, given Apollodorus an answer to the charge that the civilization of Rome is artistically barren:

> What! Rome produce no art! Is peace not an art? is war not an art? is government not an art? is civilization not an art? All these we give you in exchange for a few ornaments. You will have the best of the bargain.

Through the portrayal of Caesar's relations with Apollodorus, the play stretches conventional definitions of art and creativity, and places in a critical light the idea that civilization can be measured only in terms of what a society produces in the way of works of fine art.

With its 'gay, heroic delight in the serviceable man', *Caesar and Cleopatra* can be looked upon as an attempt, on a grander scale than in *Arms and the Man*, to present the pragmatic realist as romantic hero. As such, it makes a robust comment on the escapist, self-isolating tendencies of much of the literature written in England in the last decades of the nineteenth century. Yet in some ways the portrait of Caesar itself seems very much a product of its age. In particular, there are unmistakable traces of Carlyle's description of the heroic character in his lectures *On Heroes, Hero Worship and the Heroic in History*. The characteristic Carlylean hero is the highest point of consciousness of his race, a man with a 'clear deep-seeing eye' and an 'instinctive ineradicable feeling for reality'.[14] Shaw's Caesar is a realist in more than one sense. In his opening address to the Sphinx he appears as a man capable of apprehending Reality in senses not unlike those expressed in Plato's idea of the forms. The Sphinx's steady gaze is directed out of the world to the 'home' from which it and Caesar have strayed. It is part of Caesar's consciousness of the eternal, symbolising a 'Reality' besides which history is a mere dream:

> have I not been conscious of you and of this place since I was born? Rome is a madman's dream: this is my Reality . . . an image of the constant and immortal part of my life, silent, full of thoughts, alone in the silver desert.

But he is also, of course, a realist in the more ordinary senses. In his capacity as military leader, he is presented in the play as an inspired opportunist. He is quick to grasp the essential facts of a situation, and, like a good chess player, knows the value of strategic sacrifices.

Shaw's Caesar is a formidable creation. But, arresting and challenging as the play is in many ways, it is difficult to avoid the conclusion that the subject presented stylistic and structural problems for which Shaw was not able to find altogether adequate solutions. The language and humour are often insensitive and heavy-going. The blend of archaism and modern idiom is tolerable enough in the *Hassan*-like exchanges between the guards in the original prologue to the play. But eventually the rotund biblical style has a slowing effect on the play (which is in any case too long), and Shaw's normally buoyant and energetic prose frequently acquires tones of hollow portentousness. In Caesar's speeches, the 'high' style ('Resent! O thou foolish Egyptian, what have I to do with resentment?') mixes uneasily with a bluff, schoolboyish jocularity. More than one joke depends on rather elaborately prepared-for wordplay:

FTATATEETA:	Who pronounces the name of Ftatateeta, the Queen's chief nurse?
CAESAR:	Nobody can pronounce it, Tota, except yourself.
APOLLODORUS:	. . . Rufio threw a pearl into the sea: Caesar fished up a diamond.
CAESAR:	Caesar fished up a touch of rheumatism, my friend.

For much of the play Caesar appears as a rather ponderous comedian, surrounded by dense stooges such as Britannus and, less dense, but still not very bright, Rufio. There is a lack of tension between the superman and his surrounding society, because his intellectual and moral victories are too easily gained. Cleopatra, a possible opponent, is a kittenish acolyte (her education by Caesar turns her, superficially at least, into a New Woman) who is made to raise too many laughs about Caesar's age. Once the challenge to Caesar presented in Act II by Lucius Septimius's reminder of 'the brave Vercingetorix basely strangled' has been met and overcome, nothing else appears to induce in him any moment of self-doubt or serious internal conflict.

Thereafter, such tension as the episodic form of the play allows is provided by comparatively uninteresting external issues, such as the question as to whether or not the Romans will be trapped and overcome by the Egyptian supporters of the young Ptolemy.

It would certainly be an exaggeration to call the play a failure. The measuring of Caesar's strength and vision against Egyptian and Roman primitivism has its moments of convincing grandeur. And the humour is not always weak: one thinks, for instance, of Britannus's explanation of the early Britons' custom of staining their bodies with woad, as a means of preserving, even in death, their respectability. But the shortcomings are there, and they are instructive in what they tell us about the nature of Shaw's strength and weaknesses as a playwright. In writing *Caesar and Cleopatra* it was easy enough for him to equate, in ideological terms, unenlightened Romans and Egyptians with contemporary Englishmen. What he could not do was to transport into ancient Egypt the English social ethos to which he was so sensitively attuned as a writer and which forms the basis of the greater part of his work. To a large extent (though there are many anachronisms and stock characters and situations) he had to invent a society and a language, and the play shows the strain of this. The staple social milieu of Shaw's drama is that of England, and especially the society of London and the Southern counties. And although it is inaccurate to classify his plays as comedies of manners, it is true that his surest touch as a comic dramatist is displayed when his plays are primarily located within that social sphere, whether in precise geographical terms or not. Comparatively minor comic works such as *Arms and the Man* and *Androcles and the Lion* successfully caricature the manners of other societies. But it is significant that in large-scale, 'epically' conceived works of Shaw such as *Caesar and Cleopatra*, *Saint Joan* and *Back to Methuselah*, which in varying degrees betray similar uncertainties in tone and in the quality of their wit, the settings are all outside his normal social milieu both in place and time. It is equally significant that, after Caesar, Shaw's next two successful portraits of men of exceptional vision, Tanner and Undershaft, are placed in the critical context of a contemporary society which is by no means prepared to regard them as colossi under whom it peeps about to find itself a dishonourable grave. The next two supermen are properly domesticated.

V

The social basis of the last of the *Three Plays for Puritans*, *Captain Brassbound's Conversion* presented Shaw with no difficulties. What he did here was to transport dramatic portraits of Ellen Terry (her maid testified to the accuracy of Shaw's portrayal of her mistress in the play, in the character of Lady Cicely) and an English judge to Morocco, where they are met by a cockney layabout and a Scottish missionary, there to reveal the essential similarity between English justice and primitive revenge codes, and to convert a young brigand to a more accurate knowledge of himself. Shaw's intentions in this play are made clearer if we see it in relation to the first two plays in this group. On the surface, the saturnine, rebellious Captain Brassbound is deceptively akin to Richard Dudgeon. Like Dudgeon he is a dark, brooding, Byronic figure, also the child, as we learn in the course of the play, of a harsh, unloving mother. To a certain extent, too, Shaw employs Brassbound in the same role of outsider/critic. It is he who makes most articulate the criticism of criminal punishment as 'the vengeance of society, disguised as justice by its passions', and Lady Cicely describes him as 'one of the Idealists – the Impossibilists'. But in this play the more obvious outsider figure is outwitted by a more subtle one, and the posture of revolt itself is subjected to critical inspection. The critic – hero is himself criticized and the Caesar-like instrument of this criticism, the realist who penetrates prejudices and illusions is here a woman, Lady Cicely, a character reminiscent both of Voltaire's Candide and of Shaw's Candida. She is in some respects a more successful creation than Candida, however, in that we are shown more convincing sources of power, in her astuteness, humour and courage. It is noteworthy that in the previous play, Shaw had associated the spiritual power of Caesar with the female aspect of the Sphinx: 'I am he of whose genius you are the symbol: part brute, part woman, and part god – nothing of man in me at all. Have I read your riddle, Sphinx?'

Captain Brassbound's Conversion, with its presentation of an all-conquering female in a world of males, can be looked upon as, in a sense, a re-writing of *Caesar and Cleopatra*, exploring the power and mystery of the female spirit in more explicit and obvious terms. As such, it provides a conspicuous example of Shaw's persistent tendency to make the female the centre of gravity in his moral universe. One can only guess at what precisely Shaw perceived to be female characteristics in Caesar: his sympathy with the artistic character of Apollodorus, his quick intuitions (as in detecting falsities in Cleopatra's speeches) and the general contrast he presents to insensitive males in the play, are perhaps the qualities hinted at in the enigmatic remarks to the Sphinx. Lady Cicely, on the other hand, with her combination of firmness of character, motherly considerateness, tact and capacity for making psychologically penetrating observations, is easily recognizable as the quintessence of a certain type of upper middle-class Englishwoman. Her victories are won by a special kind of 'cleverness' which includes warmth of feeling and good humour, as Brassbound recognizes in a self-critical speech in the last scene of the play:

> Since you saw me for the first time in that garden, youve heard me say nothing clever. And Ive heard you say nothing that didnt make me laugh, or make me feel friendly, as well as telling me what to think and what to do. Thats what I mean by real cleverness.

The conversion of Captain Brassbound is a delicate process, occupying almost the entire length of the play. The Moroccan setting, many of the details of which Shaw borrowed from a work on Morocco by Cunninghame Graham, provides both an ironic context of unsuccessful Christian missionary activity – Rankin's conversions are all illusory – and the adventure story, a clash with natives, which brings Brassbound's attitudes of hostility and revolt to a head in a plot of revenge. The conversion begins as an unplanned struggle for power and leadership between Lady Cicely and Brassbound. Where the latter threatens and kicks, the former manages efficiently and humanely. People, including apparently ruthless natives, are human beings, to be treated with proper dignity and love. In the first full-scale encounter between them, in Act II, Lady Cicely begins by undermining the satanic pose. Calling him Mr Hallam, the name which associates him with his uncle, instead of using his 'outsider' nickname, Black Paquito, she attacks the melodramatic assumptions which underlie Brassbound's false self-image: 'Men are always thinking that they are going to do something grandly wicked to their enemies; but when it comes to the point, really bad men are just as rare as really good ones.' She then exposes the false premise in his whole desire for revenge. The mother whom he is avenging he, in fact, detested and suffered hell from as a child. We see that the posture of revolt is adopted by Brassbound not because of a wrong that he feels genuinely concerned about, but rather to give some kind of shape to his own life. This is the situation when we reach the highly-charged final phase of the last scene. After a speech in which he declares his complete moral bankruptcy, Brassbound surprisingly proposes marriage. At this – the metaphors of 'commander' and 'subordinate' underlining the point – there is a sudden levelling up in the balance of power between the two, and momentarily Lady Cicely offers herself to him. But in the last moments of the scene, a further twist occurs as the two are broken from their trance of locked wills by the sound of gunfire from the Thanksgiving, and Brassbound accepts not her hand in marriage but her gift (by her offering of herself to him) of independent identity and self-mastery. He has 'blundered somehow on the secret of command at last' and thanks her 'for a man's power and purpose restored and righted'.

The discussion here impinges on the thesis of Richard Ohmann's study of Shaw's style in his *Shaw: The Style and the Man*. In a central chapter of Ohmann's study, entitled 'The Posture of Opposition', he provides extensive evidence for his contention that Shaw's prose is saturated with stylistic devices which indicate that his most characteristic attitudes were those of opposition and denial. 'Throughout his life Shaw wrote as an *opponent*', and 'Enemy of the people (for their own good) is . . . a role that meshes naturally with Shaw's ideas. It is also intensely congenial to him just as a stance.'[15] There is certainly a great deal of truth in this description; but there is also considerable risk of distortion if it is applied without qualification to the plays.

The victor in *Captain Brassbound's Conversion* is not the obvious opponent of society, but a lady who is highly skilled in the courteous forms of social exchange and who can only be called an outsider from, or opponent of, society in strictly qualified senses. The 'posture of opposition', we see in the final scene, is precisely what has prevented Brassbound from attaining any maturity. A piece of comic business at the conclusion of the trial underlines the point by placing the 'posture of opposition' in an absurd light. Celebrating their escape from conviction, Brassbound's men go into a wild dance which reaches its climax when Drinkwater is '*rapt . . . into an ecstasy*', and '*becomes as it were a whirling dervish*'. Seemingly carried away by this spectacle, Brassbound strides forward at the end to invite the crew to join him in stamping on 'the captain's tall hat', the symbol of his own authority. Instead of reacting enthusiastically as expected, his followers are shocked by his '*iconoclasm*', and Brassbound himself is abashed into picking up the hat and calling himself a fool.

Clearly the *Three Plays for Puritans* can be said, in certain senses, to reflect a posture of opposition. But, at least by the time he came to write the third of the plays, Shaw's attitude towards the diabolonian opponent of society has undergone a significant shift.[16] The play indicates a growing awareness that a stance of simple opposition to society and its behavioural norms can be not only counter-productive in its effects but also symptomatic of insecurity and imperfect self-knowledge. In *Man and Superman* Shaw returned to this subject of the relations between revolt and convention in different terms and on a larger scale.

NOTES

1. *Collected Plays*, vol. II, p. 495.
2. Ibid., vol. II, pp. 23–5.
3. Ibid., vol. II, pp. 17–18.
4. Ibid., vol. II, p. 24.
5. British Library, MS Add. 45296.
6. *Collected Plays*, vol. II, p. 31.
7. Ibid., vol. II, p. 33.
8. Houghton Library, Harvard University, fMS Eng. 1046.11, p. 6.
9. British Library, MS Add. 50606B.
10. See British Library, MS Add. 50529. Robert Buchanan, *The Devil's Case* (London, n.d. [1894]). The title-page of Buchanan's poem carries as part of an epigraph the blasphemous words 'Diabolus Hominum Salvator'.
11. MS in the Houghton Library, Harvard University (Autograph file).
12. The notion that Shaw viewed Caesar as an historical anticipation of Christ is discussed by H. Ludeke in 'Some Remarks on Shaw's History Plays', *English Studies*, vol. XXXVI, pp. 239–46; cited by Margery M. Morgan, *The Shavian Playground: An Exploration of the Art of George Bernard Shaw* (London: Methuen, 1972) p. 243.
13. *The Letters of W. B. Yeats*, ed. Allan Wade (London: Macmillan, 1954) p. 500.

14. Thomas Carlyle, *On Heroes, Hero Worship and the Heroic in History* (1840) lecture IV.
15. Richard M. Ohmann, *Shaw: The Style and the Man* (Middleton, Conn.: Wesleyan University Press, 1962) pp. 74, 76.
16. The force of Ohmann's argument about Shaw's style is weakened, I think, by the fact that it is mainly based on Shaw's non-dramatic writing.

9 Comedy and Philosophy in *Man and Superman*

In the name of human vitality WHERE is the charm in that useless, dispiriting, discouraging fatalism which broke out so horribly in the eighteen-sixties at the word of Darwin, and persuaded people in spite of their own teeth and claws that Man is the will-less slave and victim of his environment? What is the use of writing plays? – what is the use of anything? – if there is not a Will that finally moulds chaos itself into a race of gods with heaven for an environment, and if that Will is not incarnated in man, and if the hero (of a novel or play or epoch or what you please) does not by the strength of his portion in that Will exorcise ghosts, sweep fathers into the chimney corner, and burn up all the rubbish within his reach with his torch before he hands it on to the next hero?

(Shaw to Henry James, 17 January 1909)

Man and Superman is sub-titled 'A Comedy and a Philosophy'. Shaw himself, in his discussion of the play and its antecedents in the Epistle Dedicatory addressed to A. B. Walkley, tends to encourage the notion that the comedy and philosophy are largely unrelated entities in the work. He refers to the Dream sequence as something 'totally extraneous' to the 'perfectly modern three-act play', and compares himself, in his offering Walkley a glimpse of the Mozartian Don Juan and his antagonist in the Dream, to 'the strolling theatrical manager who advertizes the pantomime of Sinbad the Sailor with a stock of second-hand picture posters designed for Ali Baba. He simply thrusts a few oil jars into the valley of diamonds, and so fulfils the promise held out by the hoardings to the public eye.'[1] But the dramatic artist at work in *Man and Superman* brings the play and the philosophical Dream into a much more closely integrated relation than this comparison suggests. The play and the Dream are mutually modifying and mutually illuminating, and the 'philosophy', that complex amalgam of views on politics, evolution, art, the relations of the sexes, and human nature in general, which emerges from the work, is partly defined in its import and directions by the shape and development of the comic action.

In his chapter on comedy in *Anatomy of Criticism*, Northrop Frye provides the following description of the characteristic structure and import of plays which belong to the Greek and Roman New Comedy:

> What normally happens [in these plays] is that a young man wants a young woman, that his desire is resisted by some opposition, usually paternal, and that near the end of the play some twist in the plot enables the hero to have his will. In this simple pattern there are several complex elements. In the first place, the movement of comedy is usually a movement from one kind of society to another. At the beginning of the play the obstructing characters are in charge of the play's society, and the audience recognizes that they are usurpers. At the end of the play the device in the plot that brings hero and heroine together causes a new society to crystallize around the hero.[2]

Elsewhere Frye summarizes this by characterizing the New Comedy as unfolding from 'what may be described as a comic Oedipus situation'.[3] The pattern is of course recognizable as being widely pervasive in the comedy of later periods, and its relevance to the structure of *Man and Superman* is immediately obvious. The play abounds in paternalistic figures: the deceased Mr Whitefield to whose authority Ann demurely and strategically appeals throughout Act I (Shaw's cue here is Doña Ana's overriding concern with the memory of her father in Mozart's *Don Giovanni*); Ramsden; Malone Senior; and behind the characters on the stage in Act I, portraits, busts and photographs of various figures of Ramsden's political and social philosophy. It is this array which 'Jack the Giant Killer' (to use Ann's nickname for Tanner in the play) must overcome, at least in effigy, for the comic resolution to be reached.

When the sub-plot is taken into account, *Man and Superman* can be seen to present us with two similar but contrasting patterns of action of the new Comedy type, the sub-plot being a negative and

decadent version of the main plot. In both main plot and sub-plot
we witness a complex and subtle manipulation of stock dramatic
materials. In addition, in the main plot we also see a radical re-
construction of the action of the Don Juan story as it is found in
the play's principal source, Mozart's *Don Giovanni*. The play
begins with, if not a reading of a deceased relative's will (a device
which Shaw himself refers to in the preface to *Three Plays for
Puritans* as a stock item in Victorian drama[4]), a problematical
solution brought about by the provisions of a will, namely the
appointment of the conservative Ramsden and the radical
Tanner as joint guardians of Ann. There are two potential
marriage partners for the heroine, and the development of the
plot brings about the rejection of one and capitulation to
marriage of the other. Paternalistic opposition to the marriage of
Ann and Tanner comes from Ramsden, who favours the
possibility of a match between Octavius and Ann, as did the
deceased Mr Whitefield. In the sub-plot the two lovers, Hector
Malone and Octavius's sister, Violet, have contracted a secret
marriage in order to circumvent the opposition of Malone
Senior. In the course of the play Violet gains the approval and
admiration of her father-in-law, and he becomes reconciled to
the marriage.

In Shaw's treatment of these materials the conventional and
relatively naturalistic surface of the social comedy is a veil
through which we catch progressively clearer glimpses of the
larger-than-life protagonists and universal conflicts which stand
more fully revealed in the Dream. An early indication of Shaw's
awareness of the way in which he is manipulating theatrical
conventions is provided in the stage direction describing
Octavius Robinson in Act I:

> *Mr Robinson is really an uncommonly nice looking young fellow. He
> must, one thinks, be the jeune premier; for it is not in reason to suppose
> that a second such attractive male figure should appear in one story.*

The description which follows shows that Shaw wanted Octavius
to appear as almost a parody of the pretty matinée idol, a
comically obvious object of audience sympathy:

> *The slim, shapely frame, the elegant suit of new mourning, the small*

head and regular features, the pretty little moustache, the frank clear
eyes, the wholesome bloom on the youthful complexion, the well brushed
glossy hair, not curly, but of fine texture and good dark color, the arch of
good nature in the eyebrows, the erect forehead and neatly pointed chin,
all announce the man who will love and suffer later on.

Only a few minutes after the entry of Octavius, John Tanner, a
second strong contender for the position of *jeune premier*, whose
'*Olympian*' appearance suggests '*Jupiter rather than Apollo*', arrives
on the scene and introduces a complicating factor in audience
expectations. This unsettling appearance of a rival *jeune premier*
forces us to attend closely to the comparison which is drawn
between the two figures; and it is a comparison which lies close to
the centre of the play's thematic concerns. In the larger allegory
of the play, Octavius is associated with sentimentality, debased
romanticism and the poetic idealization of woman. In the play he
is treated with good-humoured comedy. But in the Dream the
qualities he is associated with in the play are seen as forming part
of the condition of hell. Heaven, in Don Juan/Tanner's account
in the Dream, belongs to the 'masters of reality': it is a republic
from which eventually the poets must be banished. Conversely,
hell is partly defined in terms of certain literary forms and certain
aspects of the literary sensibility:

> [In hell] there are no hard facts to contradict you, no ironic
> contrast of your needs with your pretensions, no human
> comedy, nothing but a perpetual romance, a universal
> melodrama. As our German friend put it in his poem, 'the
> poetically nonsensical here is good sense; and the Eternal
> Feminine draws us ever upward and on' – without getting us a
> step farther.[5]

Up to a point, Tanner's argument in the Dream can be seen as
implying a defence of comedy as opposed to tragedy, melodrama
and romance. The play itself, as distinct from the Dream, forms
an analogy to Tanner's description of heaven in that in its human
comedy the pretensions of the philosopher are indeed upset by
the hard facts and ironies of experience. Perhaps the central point
to be grasped about the Dream is that it refers us to the human
comedy of the play as a typical arena in which the 'heavenly'

virtues can be realized and expressed. But in the final analysis no
analogy to heaven can be invoked, and metaphor has to be
discarded altogether: the heavenly condition is seen as a full,
direct and courageous engagement with life:

> DON JUAN: In Heaven, as I picture it . . . you live and work
> instead of playing and pretending. You face
> things as they are; you escape nothing but
> glamor; and your steadfastness and your peril
> are your glory. If the play still goes on here and
> on earth, and all the world is a stage, Heaven is at
> least behind the scenes. But Heaven cannot be
> described by metaphor.

Man and Superman thus includes in its comic pattern a self-
reflexive, critical contemplation of art, which arises out of and is
closely related to the dramatic action. In the conceptual
hierarchy which is established in the play, Art, although it is seen
as contributing to the contemplation of Reality, as offering a
means of extending human understanding and self-
consciousness, is subordinate to Reality. Sir Philip Sidney's
brazen world becomes here the golden world, and the
philosopher's vision is preferred to that of the artist. In the terms
of the stage direction describing Tanner, Apollo is firmly
relegated to the place he occupies in the Olympian hierarchy,
below Jupiter. There is an echo here of the challenging and
deliberate philistinism of *Caesar and Cleopatra*.

The death and the will which form the mainsprings of action in
the play are also relevant to its thematic concerns. The fact that
the action is initiated by a death is emphasized in the first few
moments of the play not only by Octavius's *'elegant suit of new
mourning'* but also by the stage business of Ramsden's face
dropping into an expression of *'decorous grief'* as the young man
enters. The progression from this death to the announcement of a
marriage at the end of the play gives the play a structural pattern
which recalls the analogy with primitive fertility ritual in the
structure of *You Never Can Tell*. This pattern has a special
significance in *Man and Superman*, in that it is closely paralleled by
the movement of the philosophical discussion in the Dream. The
argument which precipitates Don Juan/Tanner's departure from

Hell is the Devil's repudiation of the idea of a 'continual ascent by Man on the stepping stones of his dead selves to higher things', and his view of history as a cycle in which Man constantly regresses to degenerate and destructive behavioural patterns. Towards the end of the Dream the Devil invokes the biblical authority of his 'friend' Koheleth in support of his pessimistic argument, and exasperates Don Juan/Tanner by parroting the *vanitas vanitatum* theme of *Ecclesiastes*. In contrast, one of Don Juan's parting speeches is a declaration of his resolve to dedicate himself to the service of life and its evolutionary possibilities: 'at least I shall not be bored. The service of the Life Force has that advantage, at all events. So fare you well, Señor Satan.'

In her discussion of *Man and Superman* in *The Shavian Playground*, Margery Morgan questions whether the will which begins the action of the play is not Shaw's 'central, strategic pun'.[6] Certainly there is evidence of direct wordplay involving different senses of the term 'will' in the climactic scene between Tanner and Ann in Act IV:

TANNER:　. . . Your father's will appointed me your guardian, not your suitor. I shall be faithful to my trust.

ANN:　[*in low siren tones*] He asked me who I would have as my guardian before he made that will. I chose you!

TANNER:　The will is yours then! the trap was laid from the beginning.

ANN:　[*concentrating all her magic*] From the beginning – from our childhood – for both of us – by the Life Force.

TANNER:　I will not marry you. I will not marry you.

ANN:　Oh, you will, you will.

In a sense, of course, the end of the play can be seen as a victory of the will, both in the sense of the legal instrument and the volitional influence of the old society, and an ironic contradiction of Tanner's affirmation in the Dream of the potential of the individual human will to promote evolutionary change. (Miss Morgan, in fact, sees the play as embodying 'the smothering sense of security, comfort and complacency that can resist all change'.)[7] But the end of the play can be seen in a more positive light than this, especially if we take into account the meanings implicit in the action as a whole and the fuller substance of the debate in Hell.

One of the obvious functions of the sub-plot of *Man and Superman* is to extend the range of the play's critical and satirical reference. The Young Hector Malone has a good deal in common with the moralistic Hester Worsley in Wilde's *A Woman of No Importance*. He is described in a stage direction as a man of *'chivalrous manners to women, and . . . elevated moral sentiments'*, with a taste for improving rhetoric. He is an Eastern American, but, as Shaw facetiously informs us, *'English people of fashion . . . feel that he ought not to be made to suffer for what is clearly not his fault, and make a point of being specially kind to him'*. Not all of the stage direction description comes through in the play. One would scarcely gather from the dialogue, for instance, that *'Hector's culture is nothing but a state of saturation with our literary exports of thirty years ago'*. But his speeches do indicate clearly enough the monotonously conventional character of Hector's high-minded outlook and his alliance with Octavius as a sentimental believer in the ennobling power of woman.

Clearly the play holds out no hope that any profound social change will be wrought by either the old or the new generation in America, and the action of the sub-plot underlines this humorously adopted, but polemical, stance. The reason for Malone Senior's opposition to the marriage of Hector and Violet is that he wants Hector to marry into the English aristocracy. But when this opposition is overcome by the calculating commonsense of Violet, what crystallizes around the hero is not a new society but, for all Hector's good intentions, a consolidation of the old. In generally genial, but unmistakeable, terms, Malone and Violet are presented as embodiments of predatory, capitalistic forces. Louis Crompton draws attention to the dead bird in Violet's hat,[8] and we discover in the last act that Malone has financial interests in a firm called Mendoza Ltd, and is thus, as Tanner observes, a 'financier of brigands'. In presenting the comedy of love overcoming parental opposition in the sub-plot, Shaw skilfully adjusts the convention to his purposes, principally through his treatment of Violet, who is the reverse of the sort of young innocent we might expect in her dramatic situation. Violet remains a comic creation. Her Amazon-like behaviour at the end of Act I, and lines of dialogue such as 'Do you mean to work? Do you want to spoil our marriage?' ensure that. But the cold, narrowly authoritative, negotiating voice of Violet provides some of the more chilling notes in *Man and Superman*. It comes as a small shock in her Act II dialogue with Hector when she addresses him as 'dear'.

In contrast with the sub-plot, the main plot presents a positive and vital comic rhythm, a movement of action in which potentially regenerative forces win some ascendancy over those associated with moribund artistic, political and social ideals. How this is achieved can best be seen by contrasting Shaw's treatment of the Don Juan story with that of Mozart in *Don Giovanni*. In the opera, the main pivot of the plot is Don Giovanni's slaying of Doña Ana's father. This is alluded to in the Dream scene in *Man and Superman* when, to his surprise, Ramsden as Statue is introduced as not the guardian but the father of Ann:

> THE STATUE: [*puzzled*] My daughter? [*Recollecting*] Oh! the one you were taken with. Let me see: what was her name?
> DON JUAN: Ana.
> THE STATUE: To be sure: Ana. A goodlooking girl, if I recollect aright. Have you warned Whatshisname? her husband.
> DON JUAN: My friend Ottavio? No: I have not seen him since Ana arrived.
> *Ana comes indignantly to light.*
> ANA: What does this mean? Ottavio here and your friend! And you, father, have forgotten my name. You are indeed turned to stone.

The Dream thus temporarily restores the Mozartian relations between Tanner, Ann, Ramsden and Octavius. *Don Giovanni* ends with the triumph, in a superficial sense, of conservative forces. The ghost of Doña Ana's father returns in the form of a statue, and, after calling on Don Giovanni to repent and receiving his adamant refusal, takes him down to the fires of Hell. Ottavio is then assured, not altogether convincingly, that he will only have to wait another year for Ana to recover from the shock of all that has occurred and his hopes of blissful union will be fulfilled. Shaw himself underlines the comparatively superficial character of this moral ending in his remarks on the opera in the Epistle Dedicatory: 'Here you have freedom in love and in morality mocking exquisitely at slavery to them, and interesting you, attracting you, tempting you, inexplicably forcing you to range the hero with his enemy the statue on a transcendant plane, leaving the prudish daughter and her priggish lover on a crockery shelf below to live piously ever after.'9

Shaw's treatment of Tanner in the play is a natural extension of this comment. His most conspicuous alteration to the story is that of making the female the sexual pursuer instead of the male. But more significant in some ways is what happens to the triangular relations between Doña Ana, Ottavio and Don Giovanni. In the marriage stakes of the play, as we have observed, Octavius is the candidate of the paternalistic characters Whitefield and Ramsden. But by making Tanner a reluctant victor over this opposition, Shaw turns the Mozartian comic revenge plot into an entirely different structure, and produces a comic pattern which endorses the new values associated with the hero. The marriage is a defeat in the sense that it undermines all Tanner's previously held resolves and convictions on the subject of marriage. But seen in relation to the play as a whole it is a qualified victory, symbolizing as it does the planting of a revolutionary consciousness (however impaired this may be by Tanner's repeated failure of insight in practical matters) within the circle of the old society and the possible rescue of Ann from her Mozartian doom. Recognition, at the end of the play, of the strength of conservative forces does not negate the revolutionary thrust and critical energy of what has gone before.

In some respects, the comic methods of *Man and Superman* can be related to the political philosophies of Fabianism. On 6 February 1892, Shaw delivered a paper at a meeting of the Fabian Society entitled 'The Fabian Society: What It Has Done; and How It Has Done It'. This talk was in part a summary history of the Society, describing in particular the development of its relations with more militant socialist groups, such as the Social Democratic Federation and the Socialist League. It also provided an account of the evolution of the gradualist political philosophy of the Fabians and their methods of working towards the achievement of socialist aims by infiltration of ideas and propaganda into the established political parties. Beginning with aims which were virtually indistinguishable from those of anarchistic and insurrectionist groups, the Fabians came to accept the need to work, initially at least, through existing constitutional structures and political organizations. The 1887 Manifesto of the Society declared that 'the Fabian Parliamentary League is composed of Socialists who believe that Socialism may be most quickly and surely realized by utilizing the political power already possessed by the people. . . . Until a fitting opportunity arises for putting forward Socialist candidates to form the nucleus of a Socialist party in Parliament, it will confine itself to supporting those candidates who will go farthest in the direction of Socialism.'[10]

The strategy which had most success, according to Shaw, was what he called 'Permeating the Liberals', a subject to which a separate section of the paper was devoted: 'It is only necessary to compare the Nottingham program of the National Liberal Federation for 1887 with the Newcastle program for 1891, or to study the Liberal and Radical Union program for the 1892 London County Council election, to appreciate the extent to which the policy of permeating the party organizations with Socialism had succeeded. The official leaders of the Liberal party cannot now turn their followers back: they can only refuse to lead them and sit as tight as they can under the circumstances.'[11] Ideas such as this remained active in Shaw's political thinking throughout the 1890s. In 1896 he published an article in the *Contemporary Review* entitled 'Socialism for Millionaires', in which we find him offering friendly advice to misunderstood millionaires on how to 'unload' their surplus wealth for socially beneficial purposes. The article was republished as a Fabian Tract in July 1901, by which time Shaw had been working for about a year on the writing of *Man and Superman*.[12]

Certainly it would be a drastic oversimplification to interpret the play in its political aspects as simply an embodiment of Fabian principles. If by nothing else we should be warned against such a simplification by Tanner's 'Revolutionist's Handbook', where Fabianism is specifically referred to as one of the failed experiments in improving the human lot by political means. In this radically critical appendage to the Epistle Dedicatory (it contains some of Shaw's most acrimonious and pessimistic writing, and should strictly be called 'The Evolutionist's Handbook'), revolutionary political activity, whether it be violent or non-violent in method, is seen as being ultimately incapable of bringing about profound social change. But, despite this criticism, there are in the play itself some clear analogies to Shaw's description of Fabian strategy in the 1892 Tract. In the opening stage direction Shaw is at particular pains to identify Ramsden precisely as a representative of old-fashioned nineteenth-century Liberalism. He is described as a Unitarian, a Free Trader and a Darwinian Evolutionist. The works of art which adorn his study portray writers (Bright, Spencer, Cobden) who were major formative influences in the shaping of nineteenth-century Liberal philosophy. In the dialogue of Act I Ramsden boasts of his advanced, tolerant opinions, and of his stand for 'equality and liberty of conscience' in social and religious matters. A. H. Nethercot has suggested that Ramsden's first name, Roebuck, alludes to the nineteenth-century Liberal Independent MP, John Arthur Roebuck. The likelihood of this is confirmed by the fact that the historical Roebuck in the early part of his career professed himself to be a man of advanced political opinions, but became more and more reactionary and illiberal as time went on. Both aspects of his career are reflected in Shaw's portrayal of Ramsden.[13]

The relation between Tanner and Ramsden at the beginning of the play is one of pure hostility. Their appointment as joint guardians of Ann is seen by both as a disastrous misalliance. Tanner sees the appointment as the unfortunate consequence of a piece of advice about politics which he gave to Whitefield before the latter's death: 'I said the proper thing was to combine the experience of an old hand with the vitality of a young one. Hang me if he didnt take me at my word and alter his will . . . appointing me as joint guardian with you!' There is no indication of any substantial intellectual rapport between the two as the play develops, but their mutual hostility certainly declines, and Tanner's 'permeation' of Ramsden's world is both implicit in the action and explicit in the dialogue of the play. By the end of Act I the two reach a point of close accord on the question of Violet's assumed disgrace. Early in Act IV Ramsden introduces Tanner to Malone Senior as 'one of our circle'; and at the end of the play he steps forward to congratulate Tanner on his forthcoming marriage.

If we look at the end of the play for signs of a decisive and unequivocal victory of the new society over the old, we are, of course, disappointed. What we do see, however is a significant realignment of social forces and a phase in the possible evolution of a new society.

The opposition, in political, philosophical and religious terms, between the old and new societies embraced by the comedy is more fully explored in the Dream. The debate in the Dream ranges over a wide variety of topics, but two central areas of conflict can be isolated. On the one hand, there is the fundamental opposition between the Devil and Don Juan/Tanner, an opposition between life-denying and life-affirming viewpoints. The Devil and Don Juan disagree not so much in their views of the facts about human history and civilization as in the stances which they take towards them. The Devil is presented as both a sentimentalist and, at least in a shallow sense, a realist. He asserts that the power that governs the earth is not the power of Life but the power of Death, and that 'Man measures his strength by his destructiveness'. Progress is 'an infinite comedy of illusion'. The Devil sees man as the most predatory and destructive expression of life. In the face of this recognition the diabolonian resources are the pursuit of happiness, the cultivation of good taste, connoisseurship and romantic idealization of woman. What Shaw presents as Hell, in fact, is very close to the pleasures Mozart's Don Giovanni is enjoying before he goes to Hell. Shaw underlines this likeness by transferring to the Devil and the Statue during the Dream, Don Juan's famous exclamation in the opera:

> Vivan le femmine!
> Viva il buon vino! . . .
> Sostegno e gloria
> D'umanità.

The basis of the stance which Don Juan/Tanner presents in opposition is a belief in the possibility provided by man's creative and intellectual energies of achieving 'higher . . . organization and completer self-consciousness'. Like Milton, with whom he has a good deal in common, Shaw's Don Juan rejects the ethic of classical epic poetry: 'I sing, not arms and the hero, but the philosophic man: he who seeks in contemplation to discover the inner will of the world.'

In many respects the arguments of Don Juan and the Devil are closely aligned. Throughout the debate they vie with one another in presenting gloomy and unflattering descriptions of the human race. It is noteworthy that the Devil's comment on progress in the Dream is in fact an echo of one of the section headings in Tanner's 'Revolutionist's Handbook', 'Progress an Illusion'. But in the face of these recognitions Don Juan rejects the Devil's retreat into bon viveurism and art. Music, in this Mozartian Dream, is described as 'the brandy of the damned', and in one of his speeches Don Juan speaks of his discovery of romantic poetry as though it were the last phase in a spiritual Rake's Progress, because it led him to the worship of Woman.

The second major conflict presented in the Dream is the struggle between the male and female spirits. In describing his relations with women Don Juan tells us that whereas the philosopher had told him to say 'I think; therefore I am', woman had taught him to say 'I am; therefore I think'. In other words, woman brings him to recognize the primacy of existence itself over rational contemplation of existence. Because of her more profound involvement in the creation of life, woman is seen, in this rather reductive account, as at once more powerful, more fully embodying primary energies than man, and therefore as less concerned with the contemplation of life. Her concern is not with higher states of consciousness but with possession of the male for her own creative purposes. (In the play itself, of course – it is one of the many points of ironic contrast between play and Dream – Ann is seen as being far from merely the embodiment of primary creative forces. This fact is recognized in Tanner's despairing cry in the climactic scene of Act IV: 'Oh you are witty: at the supreme moment the Life Force endows you with every quality.') But Don Juan's quarrel is not with nature, with the procreative forces which drive woman in this role – he recognizes woman as being literally irresistible – but with the institutionalizing of these forces in marriage, the idea of man's being reduced to the role of a mere instrument of the Life Force in this narrower sense, rather than being enabled to pursue his own wider creative purpose of ennobling human life. Marriage, in the Dream, is described by Don Juan as a 'mantrap baited with simulated accomplishments and delusive idealizations'. In short, Don Juan differentiates between masculine and feminine forms of creativity, and sees them as essentially hostile to one another. This is why Ann's final wooing of Tanner is presented as a Titanic struggle of wills, echoing that between the Statue and Don Giovanni in *Don Giovanni*. But here again, Tanner's capitulation is not strictly a defeat. The social comedy of the play perhaps suggests that the marriage between Tanner and Ann may turn out to be a relatively conventional affair, at least by the standards of the contemporary intelligentsia. But behind the final scene of the play looms the Dream, and in the cosmic framework which this provides the marriage can be seen as a union of contemplative and primary forms of creativity, as defined by Don Juan/Tanner, and as an embodiment in the action of the play's positive affirmations.

Although the Dream is undoubtedly a daunting problem for producers, who, understandably enough, usually succumb to the temptation offered by Shaw of simply omitting it, it does nevertheless form an integral part of the whole and the play is the poorer without it. What the Dream does for the play is to brace its affirmative comedy with the profoundly sceptical diatribe against man with which Shaw arms the Devil. What the play does for the Dream is to subject its lofty idealism and philosophizing to the test of social realities, to place it in a context in which imposing concepts like the Life Force can be comically punctured (as by Ann's saying 'it sounds like the Life Guards'); or in which a Quixotic defence of unmarried motherhood can be upset by the discovery that the mother in question is in fact married. In such ways the play's comedy and philosophy are brought into a dynamic and mutually modifying relation.

The Dream is skilfully and imaginatively dovetailed into the main action, and is introduced by a scene which is one of the high points of the play's comedy. In his ambivalent position as advanced Socialist and wealthy Edwardian gentleman, Tanner leaves on his transcontinental flight for all the world like P. G. Wodehouse's Bertie Wooster, complete with car and chauffeur. The journey conveniently brings him to the Sierra Nevada, the home of the Don Juan legend, and it is here in the ensuing scene that the seeds of the Dream are sown. Preparing us for the universalizing debate of the Dream, the brigands are presented less as individuals than as political and racial types who together form a comically impressionistic picture of political ferment on a world scale and of stultifying, factious debate. With the marvellous freedom available in the world of Shavian comedy, the brigands are surprisingly discovered to be in their third day of debating the question 'Have Anarchists or Social-Democrats the most personal courage?' With Tanner's arrival melodramatic possibilities are immediately cancelled by the exchange of introductions between him and Mendoza:

> MENDOZA: . . . [*Posing loftily*] I am a brigand: I live by robbing the rich.
> TANNER: [*promptly*] I am a gentleman: I live by robbing the poor. Shake hands.[14]

As the scene develops, political discussion (during which Mendoza foreshadows his sceptical and ironic character as the Devil) gives way to romantic sentimentality with Mendoza's confession of his hopeless love for Louisa Straker. It is Mendoza's poem on this subject which finally sends everybody, including himself, to sleep.

With the eerie Mozartian strains which are heard in the deep silence following Mendoza's recitation, the Dream commences. Don Juan appears in the half-light and then a new strain of music is heard which announces the approach of Doña Ana. This tune is part of the melody of the aria which Doña Ana sings to Ottavio just before the commencement of the Statue scene in *Don Giovanni*, 'Crudele! Ah no! Mio bene.' The stage direction says that the clarinet turns this tune into '*infinite sadness*'. In the opera the aria is sung in response to Ottavio's bitter complaint at Ana's cruelty in delaying their union so long. Ana replies with magnificent indignation, 'Cruel, ah no my love', and goes on to sing her beautiful consolatory aria which looks forward to the final union of the two lovers. Shaw's use of this music is highly effective dramatically. The '*infinite sadness*' clearly relates to the rather surprising introduction of Ana as an old and lonely woman. For a short while at the beginning of the Dream scene, the play takes a decidedly un-comic turn. Here is the opening exchange:

THE OLD
    WOMAN: Excuse me; but I am so lonely; and this place is so
           awful.
DON JUAN: A new comer?
THE OLD
    WOMAN: Yes: I suppose I died this morning. I confessed; I
           had extreme unction; I was in bed with my
           family about me and my eyes fixed on the cross.
           Then it grew dark; and when the light came back
           it was this light by which I walk seeing nothing.
           I have wandered for hours in horrible loneli-
           ness.

This brief *memento mori* – one is reminded of Yeats's Crazy Jane:
'A lonely ghost the ghost is / That to God shall come' – puts the
duel of sex momentarily in a different perspective from the one in
which it is viewed in the play and prepares for the philosophical
contemplation of life and marriage in the Dream. But underlying
this there is also a certain romantic irony in Shaw's use of the 'O
crudele' theme in the presence not of Ottavio but of Don Juan/
Tanner. In this view it can be seen as pointing forward to the
conclusion of the play and to Tanner's cry, 'Oh, that clutch holds
and hurts'.[15] Shortly after the opening of the Dream, Ana is
rejuvenated and the play returns to its essentially comic
path.

Shaw produced in *Man and Superman* a play which is at once
deeply conventional – in one of his last comments on the so-called
drama of ideas, Shaw remarked that for his part he had been
'going back atavistically to Aristotle' in his dramatic methods[16] –
but which at the same time constantly turns conventions to his
own account to produce a highly original and quite distinctive
dramatic structure. No doubt the main reason for the extraordinarily long persistence of the comic form to which Frye
draws attention is that it is rooted in forms of human experience
which have remained essentially unaffected by social change: the
struggle for the securing of sexual partners and the conflict
between members of different generations which that struggle
commonly involves. The salient point of Shaw's adaptation of the
classic form to which *Man and Superman* is related, the centre of
the play's comic philosophy, lies in the uniqueness of its male

protagonist. Sexual attractiveness – and eventual dominance, in this oddly Darwinian comedy – is associated not with the sentimental and melancholy man of feeling in the Romantic tradition, nor with the rampant and insatiable seducer of the Don Juan legend, nor with the military hero, but with the politically alert, breezy, affable, vulnerable and humorous revolutionist.

NOTES

1. *Collected Plays*, vol. ii, p. 503.
2. Northrop Frye, *Anatomy of Criticism* (Princeton University Press, 1957) p. 163.
3. 'The Argument of Comedy', in *English Institute Essays*, ed. D. A. Robertson (New York: Columbia University Press, 1948) p. 58. My attention was drawn to Frye's earlier description of the New Comedy by A. N. Kaul's discussion in his *The Action of English Comedy: Studies in the Encounter of Abstraction and Experience from Shakespeare to Shaw* (New Haven and London: Yale University Press, 1970) p. 19.
4. Cf. p. 106 above. Bulwer Lytton's *Money* (1839) and Edmund Falconer's *Extremes; or, Men of the Day* (1858) provide Victorian examples of the conventional will-reading scene.
5. The last sentence of this passage is an ironic allusion to the end of Goethe's *Faust*.
6. Margery M. Morgan, *The Shavian Playground: An Exploration of the Art of George Bernard Shaw* (London: Methuen, 1972) p. 108.
7. Ibid., p. 115.
8. Louis Crompton, *Shaw the Dramatist* (Lincoln: University of Nebraska Press, 1969) p. 87.
9. *Collected Plays*, vol. ii, p. 499.
10. G. B. Shaw, *The Fabian Society: What It Has Done; and How It Has Done It*, Fabian Tract no. 41 (London: Fabian Society, Aug. 1892) p. 13.
11. Ibid., pp. 19–20.
12. Published as Fabian Tract no. 107.
13. See A. H. Nethercot, *Men and Supermen: The Shavian Portrait Gallery*, 2nd edn, corrected (New York: Benjamin Blom, 1966) p. 298, and *Dictionary of National Biography*, vol. 17, pp. 95–7.
14. Tanner's retort may have been borrowed from William Morris's story 'A King's Lesson':

> said the King . . . 'tell me what is thy craft and the craft of all these, whereby ye live as the potter by making pots, and so forth?' Said the captain: 'As the potter lives by making pots, so we live by robbing the poor.' (William Morris, *Stories in Prose, Stories in Verse, Shorter Poems, Lectures and Essays*, ed. G. D. H. Cole (London: Nonesuch Press; New York: Random House, 1974) p. 272)

15. Dr Jeremy Steele has suggested to me in a note that Tanner's cry may be an ironic allusion to the Commendatore's grasping of Giovanni's hand in *Don Giovanni*.
16. G. B. Shaw, 'The Play of Ideas', *The New Statesman and Nation*, vol. 39 (5 May 1950) p. 511.

10 Light in the Celtic Gloom: *John Bull's Other Island*

O Mr Bull, I look in that surly face of thine with a mixture of pity
and laughter, yet also with wonder and veneration.

(Carlyle, *Past and Present*)

In *Man and Superman* the dream is a device for slipping out of the
fictional time and space of the naturalistic action, for showing the
legendary archetypes of some of the characters in a new light, and
providing the scene for a philosophical exploration of the major
issues raised in the play proper. In *John Bull's Other Island* the
concept of the dream is put to a variety of different metaphorical
and non-metaphorical uses. In the most favourable light in which
it is presented in the play, the dream is coupled with the jest in
being seen as a hieroglyph of the future. It is by way of describing
his dream of Heaven that the former priest, Keegan, delivers his
oracular and utopian vision at the end of the play of a totally
unified organization of life in which all distinctions between the
divine and the human nature, between church and state, work
and play are dissolved. But if dreaming is associated with ecstatic,
visionary and ideal experience in the play, it also has its distinctly
pejorative senses. For Larry Doyle, Broadbent's partner in the
London firm of civil engineers, dreaming is the root cause of the
spiritual, political and economic paralysis of Ireland ('Oh, the
dreaming! the dreaming! the torturing, heart-scalding, never
satisfying dreaming') and he longs for a country where 'the
dreams are not unreal'. Then, also censoriously treated in the
play, is another kind of dream altogether, that of the materialist
culture of post-Renaissance civilization: 'For four wicked cen-

turies the world has dreamed this foolish dream of efficiency; and the end is not yet. But the end will come.'

John Bull's Other Island is, of course, a play about Ireland. But at several points in the play, Ireland becomes an arena for the treatment of conflicts which are by no means confined to Ireland: conflicts between different perceptions of reality, different understandings of sanity, different dreams. The intellectual roots of the play are grounded in the nineteenth century, and especially in the fulminations of Ruskin and Carlyle against the spirit of mechanistic utilitarianism. Yet although Ruskin and Carlyle are specifically mentioned in the play they are placed in a comic context which suggests that their rhetoric has become ineffectual. Broadbent's valedictory comment on Keegan as 'almost equal to Ruskin and Carlyle' is made in the indecorous context of his contemplation of Keegan as a potential tourist attraction at Rosscullen. Keegan will be the local eccentric.

Standing before the Sphinx in Act I of *Caesar and Cleopatra*, Caesar says 'Rome is a madman's dream: this is my Reality'. In *John Bull's Other Island* Keegan is presented as, like Caesar, a man displaced from the ordinary world. We recognize, of course, that Keegan is 'mad' only in superficial senses, and we are invited to speculate on the relative sanity and substance of his intangible values and the solid pragmatism of Broadbent and his world of 'real life and real work and real cares and real joys among real people: solid English life in London'. The play weighs in the balance Spirit, as represented by Keegan, Nora and 'holy' Ireland, and Matter as massively represented by Broadbent. It teases us with the question as to which constitutes the most potent force. Broadbent's solutions to disorders of the spirit, heartbreak, spiritual alienation, suffering and evil tend to be almost entirely physical in nature. He prescribes 'phosphorus pills' for Keegan's profound dissatisfaction with the world, offers a large silk handkerchief and the broad chest of a 'real man, a real friend' for the heartbreak of Nora, and prescribes the hotel and golf course and English capital as the remedies for the troubles of Ireland. But he has, he claims, read Shelley, and he gravitates towards the, to him, '*ethereal*' Nora for a marriage partner, contrasting his tastes in women with those of Larry Doyle who likes 'solid and bouncing' English girls.

Man and Superman, *John Bull's Other Island* and *Major Barbara* form a trilogy of plays which are concerned with the confrontation between, on the one hand, visionary idealism founded on a religious sense of life and, on the other, the stubborn materials of human nature in the here and now and the practical realities of economic power. Each play shows the need for spiritually enlightened idealists to come to terms with the fallen nature of man and with brute power. The metaphors of heaven and hell recur. In the first two plays, the states of heaven and hell are sharply distinguished, but in *Major Barbara* there is a clear movement towards dissolving this antinomy.

Of the three plays *John Bull's Other Island* is in some ways the most complex. Its range of themes and characters is immense and its structural organization, as F. P. W. McDowell has shown in an admirable essay, is remarkably intricate and skilful.[1] Apart from the structurally detachable Dream scene in *Man and Superman*, *John Bull's Other Island* was Shaw's boldest experiment up to that point in his career in the integrating of discussion of general issues with more specifically action-furthering dialogue. Yet to make that distinction is strictly misleading, since although we may recognize that a speech such as Larry Doyle's long analysis of the Irish character in Act I ('No, no; the climate is different . . . ') does not produce any immediate development of action, it is highly relevant to subsequent action, in that it helps to establish the context of feelings and attitudes in which later developments take place.

The portrayal of Ireland and its material and spiritual problems in *John Bull's Other Island* is both entertaining and perceptive. It is a portrait born out of love and hate, and executed with a fine, pugnacious wit. The first notes of the latter are heard in the opening lines of the play with Broadbent's grim instruction to his valet, Hodson, to pack his revolver, because 'I'm going to Ireland'. Although Shaw is always skilful in his selection and evocation of the locale of his plays, perhaps none other in the canon gives us such a strong sense of place as *John Bull's Other Island*. W. B. Yeats remarked of the play that it was the first of Shaw's to have a 'geographical conscience'.[2] The prosaic box set of Act I representing part of the office of Doyle and Broadbent's civil engineering firm in London effectively sets off the tranquil *'hillside of granite rock'*, the *'round tower'* and the *'great breadths of silken green in the Irish sky'* of the scene at sunset with which Act II begins. But this scene has been verbally anticipated in a speech of Doyle's in Act I in such a way as to place its soft, melancholy charm in a critical light. It is an indication of Shaw's dread of sentimentality that this passage, one of the very few of his writings where a landscape is so sharply and sensuously evoked, should be set in the context of a fierce denunciation of Ireland:

> But your wits cant thicken in that soft moist air, on those white springy roads, in those misty rushes and brown bogs, on those hillsides of granite rocks and magenta heather. Youve no such colors in the sky, no such lure in the distances, no such sadness in the evenings.

The stage directions in the play make demands of specificity unusual even for Shaw. Larry Doyle has to scream with laughter, at one point, '*in the falsetto Irish register unused for that purpose in England*'; the garden of Cornelius Doyle's should contain the remnant of a plaster statue of a Roman lady such as '*grow naturally in Irish gardens*'; the car which appears in Act II should be a Bianconi. Yeats's fears that the technical demands of the play might prove too great for the Abbey Theatre were possibly well-founded, though probably there were other reasons for not going ahead with production of the play.[3]

A foil for the play's later portrayal of the Irish characters is provided in Act I with the introduction of the scruffy, small-time confidence man, Tim Haffigan, a stage Irishman who is later discovered to be an impostor, born in Glasgow. With the help of Broadbent's magnificent gullibility, Haffigan brings out all the clichés which make up the popular image (in England) of the Irish. Wishing Broadbent 'the top of the mornin'' and any other such phrases he can work into his conversation, the actually grasping and alcoholic Haffigan presents himself to his genial victim as the epitome of the Irish character, 'rash and improvident but brave and goodnatured; not likely to succeed in business on your own account perhaps, but eloquent, humorous, a lover of freedom, and a true follower of that great Englishman Gladstone'.

Haffigan is also employed by Shaw to sound the first notes in later thematic developments in the play. The critique of English economic invasion and annexation of Ireland (the proprietorial, colonizing relation is, of course, suggested in the play's title) is anticipated by Haffigan's prompt translation of Broadbent's pompous phrase, 'the English plan', as 'Take all you can out of Ireland and spend it in England.' He innocently introduces the Dream of Heaven motif in the play with his ludicrously mistaken understanding of Broadbent's reference to the Garden City experiment of Ebenezer Howard as a reference to Heaven. And although he disappears from the play after the first scene of Act I, the audience is reminded of him when the completely unglamorous example of low Celtic stock appears in Act II in the form of Tim's irascible Rosscullen cousin, Matt.

In conformity with the generally antithetical development of the play's action, the stereotypes of Ireland and the Irish character which Haffigan conjures up are immediately undermined in Act I by Larry Doyle. Inevitably one is tempted to think of Doyle as in some measure a self-portrait of Shaw. Like Shaw as a young man, Doyle has left Ireland, and a father of little talent and less drive, for the larger horizons of London, to be 'made a man of' in contact with the 'world that belongs to the big Powers'. Doyle's embracing of this solid cosmopolitan ambience and rejection of Irish parochialism is certainly conveyed with a force that suggests close authorial involvement. Much of the play's most searching and trenchant criticism of Ireland and English attitudes towards Ireland comes from him. The picture Doyle gives Broadbent is one of Ireland as a squalid 'hell of littleness and monotony'. With a strongly critical glance (in the remarks on politics) at Yeats and the Irish Nationalist movement, Shaw has Doyle deliver the play's most fierce denunciation of the Irishman's religious and political character:

> He cant be religious. The inspired Churchman that teaches him the sanctity of life and the importance of conduct is sent away empty; while the poor village priest that gives him a miracle or a sentimental story of a saint, has cathedrals built for him out of the pennies of the poor. He cant be intelligently political: he dreams of what the Shan Van Vocht said in ninety-eight. If you want to interest him in Ireland youve got to call the unfortunate island Kathleen ni Hoolihan and pretend she's a little old woman. It saves thinking.

The most profound disgust in this speech is reserved for the 'horrible, senseless, mischievous laughter', the 'eternal derision' in Ireland, which Doyle speaks of as though revealing a guilty secret of the national character. This point in Doyle's Act 1 diatribe against his country is closely echoed in Shaw's Preface to *Immaturity*:[4] one can only guess at the kinds of experience in his Dublin days which gave Shaw such a profound and lasting impression of the destructive quality of its laughter. As the episode with Haffigan's pig suggests, this impression lies very close to the imaginative core of the play. *John Bull's Other Island* can be seen in one dimension as high comedy about Irish low comedy.

But if Doyle is in part an autobiographical creation, it is important to recognize that the portrait is also a highly critical one. Doyle may long for a country where 'the dreams are not unreal', but he is presented throughout the play as a rather negative, even callous, figure whose contribution to change would be unlikely to become more than that of a sideline critic. The morally authoritative, if also ineffectual, Keegan describes him late in the play as 'foolish in his cleverness', and holds him and his kind responsible for turning Ireland into 'a Land of Derision', thus making Doyle seem partly responsible for the very conditions he despises. In the skilfully written, demanding scene in Act IV in which he reveals to Nora the blankness of his feelings towards her, his insensitivity and detachment – the scene is echoed in Higgins's treatment of Eliza in *Pygmalion* – are in sharp contrast with the warmth and sympathy displayed immediately afterwards by Broadbent. At the end of the play, as the two go off to choose a site for Broadbent's hotel, Doyle seems to have become little more than an instrument in his partner's imposition of the 'foolish dream of efficiency' on Rosscullen.

In his presentation of the local inhabitants of Rosscullen, Shaw provides a deft, intimately knowledgeable, portrait in miniature of Irish village life. A far cry from the Irishmen and women of sentimental comedies such as *Finnucane's Rainbow* or *The Colleen Bawn* are Shaw's seedy ex-land agent Cornelius Doyle, the disgruntled and quarrelsome small-time landlord farmer, Matt Haffigan, the sturdy, but unimaginative and limited local Catholic priest, Father Dempsey, the superstition-ridden Patsy Farrell, the red-headed, loutish Doran, the commonsensical

Aunt Judy, and the wan, emotionally starved Nora. In the depressed economy caused by a combination of exploitative landlords, both local and absentee, inefficient farming and apathy, the village is ripe for takeover by the all-conquering Broadbent. Not even their perception of his ignorance and absurdity can prevent the locals from being drawn into the wake of his bustling energy.

Broadbent's political solutions to the problems of Rosscullen are based on the principles of Mr Gladstone. Gladstone's portrait is amongst those adorning the wall of Broadbent's study, and he is even provided with a Gladstone bag as part of the luggage to be taken to Ireland. Gladstone's views on Ireland are seen in the satirical perspective of Broadbent's sentimental political rhetoric and the old Liberal advocacy of Home Rule emerges in the play with all its ironies on its head: Home Rule for the Irish, under the direction of English money and English politicians.

The Irish vulnerability to English takeovers is revealed most sharply, perhaps, in the complex comedy surrounding the incident with Haffigan's pig, an incident which is associated with Broadbent's political ambitions. Barney Doran's narration of the series of accidents which occur when the pig escapes from the arms of Patsy Farrell in the back seat of Broadbent's car and, having jumped into the front seat, accidentally takes over the steering wheel is, of course, immediately funny.[5] There could be few audiences so solemn as to keep the same straight faces during this scene as do Keegan and, significantly, the two women. But as the laughter dies different perspectives on the incident do appear. It is an apt comic symbol of Broadbent's plans for Rosscullen that a pig (Shaw more than once makes the Carlylean association of the hog with greedy materialistic forces) should be driving a machine on a destructive path through a village; and one recalls of course that the primary cause of the accident is Broadbent's desire to impress the villagers with a vote-gaining act of generosity. Yet for all that, it is Broadbent who comes nearest to Keegan in taking a responsible view of the situation. Human life was endangered, an animal was killed and property damaged. Keegan's surly disgust at the laughter of his countrymen is the one of the two extremes of response towards which Broadbent is inclined. The sole reaction of Doran and the other locals is to rehearse the story over and over again and howl with laughter at it. The scene is constructed in such a way as to lead the audience into and out of a trap of insensitivity. Although one recognizes that Broadbent is being, throughout, a political opportunist, his attitude towards the accident shows a concern for the social weal which the guffaws of the local Irish do not.

The play presents Broadbent as, in the short term at least, an irresistible force. It is an indication of this that all the significant action in the play – the journey to Ireland, the engagement with Nora, the pre-selection for the Parliamentary seat, the laying of the tourist development plans for Rosscullen – depends on Broadbent for its motivation. Broadbent is foursquare, solid, persuasive. But, together with the recognition of Broadbent's power, there is expressed in the play a profound yearning for an Ireland, a human society, in which nobler and holier aspirations than those of Broadbent can be fulfilled. Broadbent is, of course, dimly aware of views of life which are radically different from his own. But his relation with the intellectual worlds of the writers whose names he drops in the play – Carlyle, Ruskin, Shelley – is aptly suggested in the comic play surrounding the lighting and smoking of his cigar in Act IV. At the beginning of his final scene with Keegan and Doyle, Broadbent's cigar is associated through a piece of stage business with poetry:

Theres poetry in everything, even [*looking absently into the cigar case*] in the most modern prosaic things, if you know how to extract it [*he extracts a cigar for himself and offers one to Larry who takes it*].

One senses the possibility of authorial assent here to the notion that poetry is discoverable in 'the most modern prosaic things'. But when the cigar comes into play again later in the scene, it becomes clear that in Broadbent's universe, in the long run, poetry and youthful idealism go the same way, and count for about as much, as the puffs of his smoke:

Dont sneer, Larry: I used to read a lot of Shelley years ago. Let us be faithful to the dreams of our youth [*he wafts a wreath of cigar smoke at large across the hill*].

The religious vision against which Broadbent's 'foolish dream of efficiency' is measured in the play is most fully, but not exclusively, embodied in the character and utterances of Keegan, a defrocked priest who nevertheless retains a priestlike, even saintly, authority for some of the inhabitants of Rosscullen. It is through Keegan's agency that we glimpse, whilst contemplating the relentless progress of Broadbent's dystopian folly, the possibility of a spiritual and political utopia, a truly unified human culture. The subject of Religion, the dominating, most important unifying theme in the play, is introduced in Doyle's speeches in Act I. Doyle and Keegan share a revulsion from parochial Christianity and subscribe to a larger, more cosmopolitan Catholicism: Shaw uses the word teasingly both in this play and in *Man and Superman* to suggest an all-encompassing religion, not confined to any institution. 'My Catholicism', says Doyle in Act I, 'is the Catholicism of Charlemagne or Dante, qualified by a great deal of modern science and folklore which Father Dempsey would call the ravings of an Atheist'. Even more eclectic (harsh critics would say amorphous), with its ingredients of medieval Catholicism, Hinduism and Comtean positivism, is the religious outlook with which Keegan is identified. In contrast, the village Catholicism presided over by Father Dempsey is associated with a narrow and essentially moribund culture, and the salmon which Patsy Farrell drops and breaks in half at Dempsey's mention of the 'early Church, pointing us all to God', seems more likely, in its immediate context at least, to be symbolic of the disintegrating religious traditions of Ireland than, as Margery Morgan suggests, a reference to Fintan, the salmon of knowledge.[6]

But if Father Dempsey Catholicism, sentimental miracle wonder and folk superstition are all critically viewed in the play, the framework of belief which Keegan provides might be seen not as diametrically opposed to those cults, but as finer weave from the same cloth. Keegan, in the final scene, reasserts the ancient religious traditions of Ireland, and provides the perspective on Broadbent's plans that they will be desecration of a sacred place. The ass of Mammon which comes to Ireland to serve such plans, 'comes to browse . . . without knowing that the soil his hoof touches is holy ground'. Throughout the play Keegan is presented as holding the ground and all that springs from it, its animals, insects and plants, as sacred. He chides Patsy Farrell for his childish superstitions about the grasshopper, but we recognize that there is, nevertheless, a bond of affinity between the two, as insightful characters who do not conform to conventional moulds of sanity. They are both in different degrees associated with the tradition of the divine fool.

The last scene is constructed in such a way as to bring the Broadbent and Keegan themes to their final point of development almost simultaneously. Keegan's account of his dream of heaven, delivered from a position upstage and above Doyle and Broadbent, forms part of a delicately constructed and highly effective coda to the last movement of discussion in Act iv. The elevated rhetoric of Keegan's dream – the speech has a strongly marked, liturgical rhythm – is prepared for in his arresting line as he turns to face the two below him, 'Every dream is a prophecy: every jest is an earnest in the womb of Time.' The tension created by this line is momentarily released by the conversational tone of the prose in Broadbent's next speech about his dream of heaven; but this provides a springboard for the measured, hieratic diction of:

> In my dreams it is a country where the State is the Church and the Church the people: three in one and one in three. It is a commonwealth in which work is play and play is life: three in one and one in three. It is a temple in which the priest is the worshipper and the worshipper the worshipped: three in one and one in three. It is a godhead in which all life is human and all humanity divine: three in one and one in three. It is, in short, the dream of a madman. [*He goes away across the hill*].

This vision, of a state in which the distinction between divine and human natures is dissolved; a society in which State and Church are identical institutions, embodied not in remote groups of politicians or priests, but in the whole population; a commonwealth in which work is play and play the business of life, harmonizes with Shaw's own outlook as expressed in non-dramatic contexts. Religious, political, cultural, economic pursuits should not, he believed, be regarded as stemming from distinct and separable human impulses and concerns. He once remarked to Hesketh Pearson: 'You are still a bit in the nineteenth-century in respect to arranging religion, politics, science, and art in braintight compartments, mostly incompatible and exclusive . . . They don't exist that way at all.'[7] But there is something of a paradox here since the nineteenth century offers some remarkably close parallels to Shaw's ideas in this regard. The notion that humanity itself should be an object of religious worship, for example, might well have been suggested to Shaw by the Positivist system of Auguste Comte.[8]

In one respect, Father Keegan's dream of Heaven is directly opposed to Comtean principles in that it was a major contention of Comte that spiritual and temporal power should be entirely separate. A country in which 'the State is the Church' is precisely what Comte strove to avoid. On the other hand, Comte would have found exactly in line with his own vision the notion of the Temple in which the worshipper becomes the worshipped, in which humanity is accorded divine status. In the final chapter of *A General View of Positivism*, entitled 'The Religion of Humanity', Comte declares that for Positivists Humanity is 'the only true Great Being' and it is towards this that 'we the conscious elements of whom she is composed' should direct every aspect of life.[9] Like Shaw's, Comte's conception of God is not of a perfect but of a perfectible being,[10] a notion coupled in his system with that of the identity of worshipper and worshipped. The 'new Deity' of Positivism is 'a Being whose nature is relative, modifiable and perfectible; a Being of whom her own worshippers form a part'.[11]

Closer at hand, as a possible influence on the ideas in Father Keegan's dream, was a work by William Morris. In Morris's prose tale *A Dream of John Ball*, the 'rascal hedge-priest'[12] John Ball, a rebel against established ecclesiastical authority, declares to the men of Kent his belief that 'earth and heaven are not two but one' and insists that they, the people, are the Church: 'in each one of you dwelleth the life of the Church, unless ye slay it'.[13] Shaw may well have had Morris in mind again when Father Keegan dreams of a society in which 'work is play'. Not only in the dream of *News from Nowhere*, but also in lectures and essays Morris again and again returns to the theme of 'the possibility and the urgent necessity that men should take pleasure in labour'.[14] But an equally possible influence here is Ruskin, whose insistence on the need for work to be pleasurable Morris himself found to be one of the central tenets of his teaching.[15]

Father Keegan's dream belongs in essence to a tradition

of romantic thought which M. H. Abrams, borrowing a phrase from Carlyle, has called 'natural supernaturalism'.[16] The notion of a state in which 'all humanity [is] divine' epitomizes the romantic quest for a religious faith centred not on concepts of the supernatural but on humanity and the natural world. T. E. Hulme's description of romanticism as 'spilt religion' is peculiarly appropriate to the vision of Father Keegan, a character whose position as a religious figure Shaw has deliberately surrounded with ambiguity. He is a priest but not a priest. His outlook is religious but not ecclesiastical. Patsy Farrell has trouble with his name as a result: 'Arra, hwat am I to call you? Fadher Dempsey sez youre not a priest; n we all know youre not a man: n how do we know what ud happen to us if we shewed any disrespect to you?'

Keegan's dream is cast in a deeply ironic light by Broadbent's remarks on him at the end of Act IV. Of course, we realize that Keegan's utopian dream has been dreamed before and that Broadbent's twentieth-century 'progressive' bustle will almost certainly keep it firmly in its place as a dream. Keegan is echoing the lost causes of the previous century. But if in one way the comic anticlimax here works against Keegan, reducing him, in the debasing perspective of Broadbent's business eye, to a mere tourist attraction, it is clear that Broadbent is victorious in only limited senses. Keegan's attitude towards Ireland as a place sanctified by its ancient religious traditions, and his lofty utopian dream, give us the measure against which to place Broadbent's schemes, and his declaration about dreams as prophecy, with its reminder of the evolutionary thought of *Man and Superman*, to some degree balances the more sceptical aspects of the end of the play.

NOTES

1. F. P. W. McDowell, 'Politics, Comedy, Character, and Dialectic: the Shavian World of *John Bull's Other Island*', *PMLA*, vol. LXXXII, no. 2 (1967) p. 546.
2. Cited by M. J. Sidnell, '*John Bull's Other Island* – Yeats and Shaw', *Modern Drama*, vol. XI, no. 3 (Dec. 1968) p. 248.
3. See my article, 'Yeats, Shaw and Unity of Culture', *Southern Review*, vol. VI, no. 3 (Sept. 1973) pp. 194–5.
4. Shaw wrote 'A certain flippant futile derision and belittlement that confuses the noble and serious with the base and ludicrous seems to me

peculiar to Dublin' (*The Complete Prefaces of Bernard Shaw* (London: Paul Hamlyn, 1965) p. 673).

5. Vivian Mercier writes that in this scene Shaw 'reveals the sadistic nature of a certain kind of Irish humour, while at the same time disapproving of it through the mouths of several of his characters' (*The Irish Comic Tradition* (Oxford: Clarendon Press, 1962) p. 67).

6. Margery M. Morgan, *The Shavian Playground: An Exploration of the Art of George Bernard Shaw* (London: Methuen, 1972) p. 127.

7. Hesketh Pearson, *G. B. S.: A Postscript* (New York: Harper, 1950) p. 61; cited by Alan P. Barr, *Victorian Stage Pulpiteer* (University of Georgia Press, 1973) pp. 60–1.

8. Shaw would have become familiar with Comte's philosophy in his early London days through his friendship with fellow Fabian and student of Comte, Sydney Olivier:

> I first met Sydney Olivier when we were both in our twenties, and had from different directions embraced Socialism as our creed. I had come by the way of Henry George and Karl Marx. He had begun with the Positivist philosophy of Auguste Comte, and was as far as I know, the only Fabian who came in through that gate' ('Some Impressions by Bernard Shaw', in *Sydney Olivier: Letters and Selected Writings*, ed. Margaret Olivier (London: Allen & Unwin, 1948) p. 9)

9. Auguste Comte, *A General View of Positivism*, trans. J. H. Bridges (New York: R. Speller, 1957) p. 365.

10. The red-headed Irishman who marries the heroine at the end of Shaw's story, *The Adventures of the Black Girl in her Search for God* (London: Constable, 1932), and whose views on religion somewhat resemble those of the auburn-headed author, says of God:

> My own belief is that he's not all that he sets up to be. He's not properly made and finished yet. There's somethin in us that's dhrivin at him, and somethin out of us that's dhrivin at him: that's certain; and the only other thing that's certain is that the somethin makes plenty of mistakes in thryin to get there. (Standard Edition, London: Constable, 1934, p. 69)

11. Comte, A. *General View of Positivism*, p. 391.

12. William Morris, *Stories in Prose, Stories in Verse, Shorter Poems, Lectures and Essays*, ed. G. D. H. Cole (London: Nonesuch, 1974; New York: Random House, 1974) p. 215.

13. Ibid., p. 212.

14. Preface to John Ruskin, *The Nature of Gothic: A Chapter from the Stones of Venice* (London: George Allen, 1899) p. ix.

15. Ibid., pp. viii–x.

16. M. H. Abrams, *Natural Supernaturalism: Tradition and Revolution in Romantic Literature* (London: Oxford University Press, 1971).

11 Action and Meaning in *Major Barbara*

> Men are not Materialists. I have never seen the logic of the dynamiter refuted, nor that of the vivisectionist. But this is a *reductio ad absurdum* of logic regarded as a prime motor, not a justification of dynamite or vivisection.
>
> (Shaw to E. C. Chapman, 29 July 1891)

First performed in 1905, *Major Barbara* was one of the most notable plays written for the Royal Court Theatre under the Vedrenne–Barker management of 1904 7. It has remained a deservedly popular, and frequently performed, play. Intellectually, it is a robust, challenging play which decisively and memorably defines the dilemmas which perennially confront reforming idealists when they come to grips with the realities of power in society. But Shaw achieves in *Major Barbara* a happy marriage of intellectually sophisticated and broadly popular ingredients. Like many of Shaw's characters, the romantic heroine cum Salvation Army Major, Barbara, epitomizes a type, and has become part of the folk mythology of the twentieth century.[1] Her successors in real life joined the Aldermaston rallies, or protested against the Vietnam war and apartheid in Africa, or left upper middle class homes to serve in organizations for the relief of suffering in the Third World. Equally impressive and enduring as a dramatic image is Shaw's portrait of the munitions maker, Undershaft. No other writer of the twentieth century has so authoritatively portrayed the type of the unrepentantly successful, engaging but ruthless business tycoon as does Shaw in this work. *Major Barbara* is a play which, once read or seen, permanently affects the landscape of the mind.

Theatrical invention and thematic development are skilfully

and closely integrated in *Major Barbara*, and crucial contributions to the play's meaning are made by non-verbal events in the stage action. The changing *mise en scène* and narrative lines are an essential (as opposed to merely vehicular) part of the play's unfolding argument. The movement in scene, from the library of Lady Britomart's elegant home in Wilton Crescent to the wretched East End Salvation Army shelter to the model town and munitions factory of Undershaft's Perivale St Andrews, expresses in bold visual signs the play's gradually deepening engagement with the social, moral and spiritual issues which are raised by Undershaft's profession and attitudes. Within the play two related strands of narrative are developed, the one concerning the romance of Barbara and Cusins, the other a family reunion. In basic outline the romance plot is a conventional one, in which obstacles in the way of the lovers' union are introduced and overcome. The match earns the initial disapproval of Lady Britomart. Barbara herself falls temporarily out of sympathy with Cusins at the end of Act II, when he joins the march-off with Undershaft. But the two are reunited at the end, and Cusins is able, through a lucky turn in the plot, to combine his success in love with an inheritance and a new job. In the family reunion plot, the renegade husband, Undershaft, reaches a point of entente with his estranged wife, and a new understanding and accord with his children. The two plots form the basis of a delicately traced allegory of power in its relations with religion and culture.

The fundamental movement of theme and action in *Major Barbara* is towards the bringing about of a union between different kinds of energy. In some respects the forms of energy which are presented in the play seem diametrically opposed to one another. The Salvation Army shelter and the munitions factory rest upon apparently irreconcilable philosophies; the love, forgiveness and peace preached in the one standing in stark contrast to the destructiveness and nakedly Darwinian premises ('Thou shalt starve ere I starve') of the other. But one feature of the play's development is the discovery of a kind of *discordia concors* in the relation between salvationism and munitions-making in themselves, as well as in the relations between the principal characters.

The hidden links between munitions-making and salvationism

are first suggested in Undershaft's remark in Act I: 'I am rather interested in the Salvation Army. Its motto might be my own: Blood and Fire.' The remark balances on a knife edge between black joke and serious statement: Charles Lomax's exclamation 'But not your sort of blood and fire, you know' can draw a laugh in the theatre. But Undershaft's jest calls to mind the advice of the He-Ancient in *Back To Methuselah*: 'When a thing is funny, search it for a hidden truth.' Both munitions-making and Salvationism express energies which cannot be contained within ordinary rational or moral frameworks. Both belong to Dionysian rather than Apollonian aspects of human nature. The god Dionysos is, of course, referred to in the play itself, and to understand Shaw's use of this motif it is helpful to go outside the play and examine one of the major influences on its writing.

Major Barbara bears strong imprints of Shaw's association with the Australian-born Professor of Greek and translator of Euripides, Gilbert Murray, upon whom the character of Cusins is modelled. The two, whose friendship began some five years before the writing of *Major Barbara*, were both among the authors represented in the Vedrenne–Barker season, and correspondence between them on the subject of Shaw's play survives. There is clear evidence that Shaw adopted, with modifications, some suggestions for dialogue in Act III which Murray had sent in a letter of 2 October 1905.[2] Murray's comments and suggestions touch on a subject of central importance in the play, the final relations between Undershaft, Cusins and Barbara. But first it is necessary to consider another aspect of his influence on the play.

Murray's translation of Euripides' *The Bacchae*,[3] from which Cusins recites in the discussion with Undershaft in Act II of *Major Barbara*, was published in 1902, and Shaw was clearly deeply impressed by this work. In *The Bacchae* the god Dionysos has taken human form and, having wandered through various lands teaching the rites and dances and mysteries of his cult, has arrived at Thebes, the birthplace of his mother, Semele, and home of her father, Cadmus, formerly king of Thebes. When the play opens, Dionysos has already succeeded in planting his religion amongst the Thebans and induced many of the women of the city to engage in his secret rituals in the surrounding hills. But implacably opposed to the cult is the present king of Thebes, Pentheus, Cadmus's grandson. Despite the pleadings and advice of the elders, Teiresias and Cadmus, both of whom have been converted to Dionysos worship, Pentheus orders the god to be captured, bound and thrown into prison. Dionysos easily escapes and exacts terrible vengeance upon Pentheus by exposing him to the fury of his devotees, the Maenads, one of whom is Pentheus's mother, Agave. The Maenads put Pentheus to death and tear him limb from limb. In her frenzy Agave is deluded into imagining that what they are sacrificing is a lion. Still under this delusion she returns to Thebes triumphantly bearing Pentheus' head. As the play moves to its close she gradually recovers her senses and discovers the truth.

The primary attribute of the Dionysian religious experience is joy. As the god of wine, Dionysos releases the energies of music, dance, erotic desire, ecstasy and frenzy, and he inspires prophecy. The chorus of Maenads express their religion in both verbal and non-verbal ways. They appear with ivy-bound hair and carrying timbrels, pipes and other instruments, some bearing the sacred thyrsus or wand. Their songs celebrate natural beauty, simplicity of life and joyous communion with the natural world. Ranged against the Dionysian principles in the play are the forces (epitomized in the character of Pentheus) of puritanical morality, thought ('dream not thought is wisdom', Teiresias warns Pentheus),[4] worldly wisdom and tyrannical power, especially the kind of physical power with which Pentheus seeks to bind Dionysos. Pentheus fails in his attempt to bind the god physically. But Dionysos, in his counter-action is able, by exerting hypnotic will, to persuade Pentheus to go to the place where he is to meet his death.

Major Barbara draws upon and parodies *The Bacchae* in several ways. When Cusins declares before the march-off at the end of Act II of Shaw's play that 'Dionysos Undershaft has descended' he makes explicit a comparison which has far more than momentary significance. Cusin's declaration forges a brilliant imaginative link. Just as Dionysos converts his followers to his religion of beautiful and terrible energies, so Undershaft can be seen here to have triumphantly insinuated his religion of 'money and gun powder' into the Salvation Army and become the cause of a jubilant march, which, with its accompaniment of tambourine and drum and trombone, comically echoes a Dionysian revel. By the end of Act II Undershaft has, in a sense, succeeded in

achieving what a little earlier he has accused Cusins of attempt-
ing, 'the conversion of the Salvation Army to the worship of
Dionysos'. But Cusins has already drawn attention to the
connections which naturally exist between the two religions. The
Salvation Army is,

> the army of joy, of love, of courage . . . it marches to fight the
> devil with trumpet and drum, with music and dancing. . . . It
> takes the poor professor of Greek, the most artificial and self-
> suppressed of human creatures, from his meal of roots, and lets
> loose the rhapsodist in him; reveals the true worship of
> Dionysos to him; sends him down the public street drumming
> dithyrambs.

The comparison with Dionysos is the most potent of the allusions
Shaw employs to help create the character of Undershaft. (He is
also likened to Satan, Machiavelli, Mephistopheles, and
Marlowe's Barabbas.) The play of allusion associating
Undershaft with Dionysos begins near the end of the scene of his
first appearance, when he declares himself to be 'particularly
fond of music', and, rejecting Lady Britomart's instructions for a
more subdued prayer meeting, joins the younger people in
rendering 'Onward Christian Soldiers' on the concertina and
tambourine in the drawing room. The comparison is again
recalled in Act III when Cusins reports his drinking bout with
Undershaft and his (temporary) possession by Undershaft's
ideas. The episode later in Act III when Undershaft looks
hypnotically into Barbara's eyes also recalls the role of Dionysos
in *The Bacchae*, when he mesmerizes Pentheus. But, as will be
shown, Shaw introduces a significant point of difference in this
episode.

It is important to see that it is not only the character of
Dionysos that Undershaft recalls. Shaw also associates him, in
critical ways, with the antagonist of the god, Pentheus. The first
of the choruses which Cusins recites to Undershaft is one that in
its context in *The Bacchae* is implicitly critical of Pentheus, as a
man who attempts to rely for his authority on mere physical
force. Earlier in the play, Teiresias has warned Pentheus of this
flaw, with the injunction 'dream not thou that force is power'.[5]
The verses from *The Bacchae* which Cusins recites in Act II contain

a similar warning for Undershaft, serving as they do to underline the limitations of his relentless materialism, *his* confusion of force with power:

> One and another
> In money and guns may outpass his brother . . . [6]
> But whoe'er can know
> As the long days go
> That to live is happy, has found his heaven.

Undershaft is certainly a magnificently impressive character in the play. His wit and irony, the brilliance of his rhetoric, qualities balanced by the disarming modesty of his demeanour with Lady Britomart, guarantee him a great deal of audience sympathy. His jokes succeed, not only because of their arresting novelty, but also because they contain truthful and penetrating insights. Audiences find it easy to acquiesce in Undershaft's audacities, which succinctly describe some of the central problems of twentieth-century democratic societies:

> When I want anything to keep my dividends up, you will discover that my want is a national need. When other people want something to keep my dividends down, you will call out the police and military. And in return you shall have the support and applause of my newspapers, and the delight of imagining that you are a great statesman. Government of your country! Be off with you, my boy, and play with your caucuses and leading articles and historic parties and great leaders and burning questions and the rest of your toys. *I* am going back to my counting-house to pay the piper and call the tune.

But Undershaft's hauteur, clarity of insight and rhetorical brilliance do not conceal the serious flaws in his moral armour. Although he may argue that physical force is an essential weapon in the struggle for human dignity, and the ground, so to speak, of the virtues, he can hardly be said to be a strong spokesman for civilized values. Primarily, he is presented in the play as an exponent of anarchic, acquisitive and destructive social Darwinism. Ultimately, he is not able to escape from Barbara's accusation that there is 'bad blood' on his hands, nor from the truth that 'nothing but good blood can cleanse them'. There is a fundamental distinction to be preserved between Undershaft's 'blood and fire' and that of the Salvationists. Undershaft is a Pentheus-like apostle of physical force, and his power is seen in the end as limited by that fact. In spite of all the attractions of Perivale St Andrews, the model village founded on munitions factory wealth, it remains, as Barbara recognizes, only an environment for, not a creator of, spiritual values. Perivale St Andrews is not Utopia; its inhabitants are 'full-fed, quarrelsome, snobbish, uppish creatures, all standing on their little rights and dignities'. They need spiritualizing, salvation from themselves.

In October 1905, Murray sent to Shaw some brief passages of dialogue which he had himself written for Undershaft, Cusins and Barbara, in order to illustrate his view that the two younger members of this trinity should emerge more strongly in the dénouement of the play. In explaining his views, Murray wrote:

> [What I am driving at, is to get the real dénouement of the play, after Act II. And I think that something like what I suggest *is* the real dénouement. It makes Cusens [sic] come out much stronger; but I think that rather an advantage. Otherwise you get a simple defeat of the Barbara principles by the Undershaft principles, which is neither what one wants, nor so interesting as the (as it seems to me) right way out: viz. that the Barbara principles should, after their first crushing defeat, turn upon the U[ndershaft] principles, and embrace them with a view of destroying or subduing them, for the B[arbara] P[rinciple]'s own ends. It is a gamble, and the issue uncertain.[7]]

Shaw might well have retorted that in fact Murray was simply saying what the end of the play is about. But it is nevertheless true that Murray was drawing attention to a sensitive and rather vulnerable point in the construction of the play, especially with regard to the portrayal of Cusins in his relation with Undershaft. Cusins's too easy capitulation to Undershaft's logic is a weakness in the otherwise tight argument of the play, which G. K. Chesterton,[8] as well as Gilbert Murray, observed; and it is a problem not completely remedied by Shaw's adoption of some of Murray's hints.

Gilbert Murray's letter to Shaw assumes too readily that we

know what 'the Barbara principles' are. Barbara's character in
the play in fact shares some of the ambiguous qualities of
Undershaft's. Overridingly, the impression she creates is radiant,
vital and attractive. She is a woman of character and spirit who,
in her active engagement with society's ills, contrasts in a
favourable way with the utterly rigid Stephen and her female
foil, the '*slender, bored and mundane*' Sarah. There is no doubt that
Barbara is a centre of moral and emotional sympathy in the play.
In the tightly written closing movements of Act II her integrity
and courage are stressed, even to the point where the audience is
invited to make comparisons with the betrayal and death of
Christ. This latter notion is introduced when Barbara alludes to
Judas and the thirty pieces of silver in rejecting her father's offer
to cap Bill Walker's offer of a one pound donation to the Army
with another of ninety-nine pounds. The comparison is later
made more explicit (after the ironically joyous march-off of
Undershaft, Cusins and the easily bought Salvationists near the
conclusion of Act II) when Barbara utters the words of Christ
from the cross: 'My God: why hast thou forsaken me?'

There is a further development of the Barbara-as-Christ image
in the metaphors of her final speeches in the play. Having
suffered utter defeat in Act II, she undergoes a kind of resurrection
in Act III, and her work in turn is to be work of restoration of life
and the raising of man to God from the 'hell' of Undershaft's
factory:

CUSINS: Then the way of life lies through the factory of
            death?
BARBARA: Yes, through the raising of hell to heaven and of
            man to God, through the unveiling of an eternal
            light in the Valley of The Shadow.

In the last moments of the play Cusins's remark humorously
suggests that Barbara herself has experienced a kind of Ascension:
'She has gone right up into the skies.' But if such a comparison
represents the pinnacle of Barbara's moral and spiritual authority in the play, it is important to recognize that she is at times seen
in a rather less favourable light. She is, for instance, presented in
her treatment of Bill Walker as, like her father, a distinctly bossy
and coercive person. There is a nagging quality about her

attempts to convert Walker;[9] and although we may feel that Walker gets his just deserts in being kneeled upon and prayed over by the music-hall wrestler cum Salvationist, Sergeant Todger Fairmile, Barbara's exultation over, and her association, by implication, with Fairmile's brute force methods of conversion (which are like those of the giant Ferrovius in *Androcles and the Lion*), rather diminish her stature. She is, inevitably, involved in the critical aspects of the play's examination of Salvationism.

The view of Salvationism which is presented in the play is as ambivalent as the portrayal of the major characters. On the one hand, it is an 'army of joy' and a promoter of the virtues of tolerance and humane altruism. But on the other hand, the Army is also presented as being seriously flawed as an instrument of social and spiritual reform. Through the dialogue between the two down-and-out characters, Snobby Price and Rummy Mitchens, at the beginning of Act II, a very sceptical view of the workings of the Army is immediately conveyed. Christian conscience is something that can be glibly turned on by these two in exchange for bread and milk. In the final analysis, the Army is seen as being thoroughly subjected to the power of those forces in society which it exists to combat. It is saved from collapse by the proceeds from Bodger's whisky and Undershaft's munitions. Undershaft himself sees the activities of the Army as 'most convenient and gratifying to all large employers of labor', his implication being that they function as a dampener on political and industrial unrest. Despite its concern with the problems of the downtrodden and oppressed members of society, the Army emerges from the play as essentially a reactionary force. That is why Barbara needs lessons from Peter Shirley, in Tom Paine's books, and Bradlaugh's lectures.[10]

Barbara does not capitulate to Undershaft. Rather, she comes to a gradual recognition of the need to come to terms with the realities of his power. The moral imperatives on which the Army is based, and which Stephen in his different way espouses, are inadequate for dealing with the world as it is. Both Barbara and Cusins arrive at essentially the same recognition at the end of the play, that forces of evil must be not shunned but re-directed. Cusins's remark that 'you cannot have power for good without having power for evil too', is in tune with the insights which Barbara is given a little further on in their final dialogue:

BARBARA:	Turning our backs on Bodger and Undershaft is turning our backs on life.
CUSINS:	I thought you were determined to turn your back on the wicked side of life.
BARBARA:	There is no wicked side: life is all one.

Shaw's play presents a parallel in this last scene with the well-known passage in Milton's *Areopagitica* beginning with the words 'I cannot praise a fugitive and cloistered virtue', and arguing that 'the knowledge and survey of vice is in this world . . . necessary to the constituting of human virtue'.

Shaw's choice of a professor of Greek as the third member of the triumvirate of characters in *Major Barbara* provided him with a means of extending the compass of the play's social allegory in several important directions. Just as the representatives of religion must come to terms with power in society, the play leads us to see, so must those who stand for intelligence and culture. Cusins is presented as a man of mature intelligence and cultivated tastes. In his argument with Undershaft he becomes a spokesman for the generally accepted values of Western democratic societies, for 'honour, justice, truth, love, mercy, and so forth'. His views are very much in line with the small 'l' liberalism for which Gilbert Murray himself was such a deeply committed spokesman. By drawing him into the pact which is reached at the end of the play – Shaw playfully makes the Undershaft–Cusins relation remind us of Mephistopheles tempting Faust–Undershaft is bringing into being his version of Plato's idea of the Philosopher–King: 'Plato says, my friend, that society cannot be saved until either the Professors of Greek take to making gunpowder, or else the makers of gunpowder become Professors of Greek.'[11]

Shaw's handling of the differences of outlook which remain between Undershaft, Cusins and Barbara as their alliance is forming at the end of the play deserves close examination. The key word in the closing movements of the play is 'power'. Cusins's strongest moments in the play come in the tautly written passage of dialogue following Undershaft's admonition to him near the end of Act III: 'Dont come here lusting for power, young man':

| CUSINS: | If power were my aim I should not come here for it. You have no power. |

UNDERSHAFT:	None of my own, certainly.
CUSINS:	I have more power than you, more will. You do not drive this place: it drives you. And what drives the place?
UNDERSHAFT:	[*enigmatically*] A will of which I am a part.
BARBARA:	[*startled*] Father! Do you know what you are saying; or are you laying a snare for my soul?
CUSINS:	Dont listen to his metaphysics, Barbara. The place is driven by the most rascally part of society, the money hunters, the pleasure hunters, the military promotion hunters; and he is their slave.

Undershaft's 'metaphysics' here have a distinct ring of the Life Force ideas in *Man and Superman*; and perhaps Shaw was thinking too of the related Schopenhauerian concept of the 'world will'.[12] Barbara sees that Undershaft's idea of the 'will of which he is a part' comes dangerously close to a religion by which she could be trapped. But Cusins provides – his repeated metaphor of 'hunters' underlines the common factor of predatoriness in all the activities referred to – a clear-sighted and forthright moral judgement of the forces which sustain Perivale St Andrews, a judgement not effectively countered by Undershaft's taunt, in the following speech, about 'morality mongering'.

Barbara's distancing of herself from Undershaft in these crucial moments of Act III occurs in a less verbally articulated way. The most important indication of the independence of her power from that of Undershaft comes, not in the dialogue, but in a piece of action which takes place on the stage. After delivering his taunt to Cusins, Undershaft turns to Barbara, taking her hands in his and looking into her eyes.:

UNDERSHAFT:	. . . Tell him, my love, what power really means.
BARBARA:	[*hypnotized*] Before I joined the Salvation Army, I was in my own power; and the consequence was that I never knew what to do with myself. When I joined it, I had not time enough for all the things I had to do.
UNDERSHAFT:	[*approvingly*] Just so. And why was that, do you suppose?

BARBARA: Yesterday I should have said, because I was
in the power of God.
[*She resumes her self-possession, withdrawing her
hands from his with a power equal to his own*].

Undershaft's failure to hold Barbara in hypnotic sway shows
that, unlike Dionysos in *The Bacchae*, he is not the wielder of
ultimate power. By her withdrawal of her hands from him,
Barbara shows that she is not the servant of Undershaft's will.
There are fairly clear, if muted, sexual undercurrents in
Undershaft's relationship with Barbara. Earlier in the play
Cusins tells him that 'a father's love for a grown-up daughter is
the most dangerous of all infatuations'. Underlying the exchange
about power between the three characters in Act III is a struggle
for possession of Barbara; and her withdrawal of her hands from
Undershaft's marks the beginning of the re-establishment of her
allegiance to Cusins, as well as an assertion of her independence
from Undershaft.

It is true that in the remainder of Act III Undershaft scores
some convincing victories in argument. His speech on the 'crime'
of poverty, for example, is one of the most powerful in the play.
But his victories are not spiritual or psychological victories.
Within the triumvirate, Barbara and Cusins become, in some
important ways, allies against Undershaft. The alliance of the
three is one of spiritually autonomous powers.

At the end of the play another power struggle, which has been
in progress since near the end of Act I, between Undershaft and
Lady Britomart for control over the children, is brought to a
close, and it is. not Undershaft who is the victor. In the final
moments of the play Lady Britomart, who has previously been
moved to tears by the children's apparent rejection of her, claims
their overwhelming affection. Barbara, in particular, is moved to
clutch at her mother's skirt '*like a baby*'.[13] This reassertion of Lady
Britomart's authority is a significant part of the emotional and
thematic pattern of the play's close. Undershaft has had
innumerable intellectual victories in the course of the play, and
in that respect Lady Britomart is clearly no match for him. But
Shaw's handling of the last scene of the play allows full weight to
be given to Lady Britomart's strength of character, a strength
which includes pragmatic and instinctive judgements about

Undershaft to which it is impossible not to assent.

Lady Britomart is a formidable figure in the play, and a vital component of its comic spirit and thematic structure. As a comic creation she is comparable in stature with Wilde's Lady Bracknell, and the comedy surrounding her, especially in the opening scene with Stephen, has a strongly Wildean flavour: 'Not break the law! He is always breaking the law. He broke the law when he was born: his parents were not married.' Shaw arms Lady Britomart with an unfailing rhetorical assurance, and great alacrity in seizing on the right moment for making discomforting remarks about personal mannerisms and disorderly dress. Her name recalls Spenser's female knight of chastity, and carries its later associations with militant, British female rectitude. She is presented as a domineering character, but also as, at times, emotionally vulnerable. Together with Stephen, she expresses a view of morality which is quite different from Undershaft's – one in which the categories of right and wrong are indisputably clear and forever defined:

> STEPHEN: . . . Right is right; and wrong is wrong; and if a man cannot distinguish them properly, he is either a fool or a rascal: thats all.
>
> LADY
> BRITOMART: [*touched*] Thats my own boy [*she pats his cheek*]!

Absurdly simple as Lady Britomart's and Stephen's pronouncements are, such uncomplicated judgements of Undershaft's 'wickedness' are not without force in the intellectual and emotional dynamics of the play. Lady Britomart's role as deflator of Undershaft's rhetoric ('Stop making speeches, Andrew') is not unlike that of Ann Whitefield's in relation to Tanner. Undershaft is another of Shaw's revolutionary figures who are firmly placed in the world of social and personal realities, and not allowed easy victories.

It is possible that Shaw did not rationalize the end of the play to such an extent. But the focussing on Lady Britomart at the end adds a significant dimension of meaning. The closing moments of the play suggest that, despite their comical rigidity and openness to satire, the English national character and the Britomart qualities will remain powerful forces to be reckoned with, for all the heady potency of Undershaft's logic.

The core of the meanings which are embodied in the play's action, characterization and dialogue is contained in Cusins's remark to Barbara: 'I think all power is spiritual'. Undershaft can create weapons of power, but the weapons themselves, as Cusins points out, have to be triggered by a human hand, acting according to the dictates of human will. Perivale St Andrews may furnish the necessary material foundations of the good society; but the good society does not develop consequentially from those foundations. The munitions factory needs a patron saint, not as an ornament, but as an essential promoter of the proper use of power. As has been pointed out elsewhere Shaw seems to have chosen the name of his heroine with that ultimate development of her role in mind.[14]

NOTES

1. Desmond MacCarthy comments on the 'peculiar quality' of Shaw's characters 'which makes them stay in the memory, and enables them to pass, like the types of Dickens, into conversation. . . . Once seen on the stage they become types in the spectators' imagination, approximations to which he is constantly meeting in real life' (*The Court Theatre, 1904–7: A Commentary and Criticism* (London: A. H. Bullen, 1907) pp. 47–8).

2. For a full discussion, with transcripts of the documents in the Humanities Research Centre, University of Texas at Austin, and the British Library, see Sidney P. Albert, '"In More Ways Than One": *Major Barbara*'s Debt to Gilbert Murray', *Educational Theatre Journal*, vol. xx, no. 2 (May 1968) pp. 123–40.

3. Gilbert Murray, *The Bacchae*, in *The Athenian Drama*, 3 vols (London: George Allen, 1900–2) vol. iii. I am indebted in the following discussion of *Major Barbara* and *The Bacchae* to Louis Crompton's chapter on Shaw's play in his *Shaw the Dramatist* (Lincoln: University of Nebraska Press, 1969). But the present essay draws attention to some essential points in the relations between the two plays which are overlooked in Crompton's account.

4. *The Bacchae*, p. 93.

5. Ibid., p. 93.

6. In order to point the quotation more directly at Undershaft, Shaw has altered the first part of this line. Murray's translation has 'In gold and power' (ibid., p. 126).

7. MS in Humanities Research Centre, University of Texas at Austin. Shaw borrowed quite substantially from Murray's two pages of suggested dialogue. Undershaft's reference to Plato and Cusins's speeches about the rascality of the social forces underlying the munitions factory and Undershaft's essential powerlessness are closely based on Murray's suggestions.

8. Chesterton censures Shaw for 'the incredibly weak fight which [Cusins] makes in the play in answer to the elephantine sophistries of Undershaft' – (see G. K. Chesterton, *George Bernard Shaw* (London: John Lane, 1909) pp. 171–2).

9. Barbara's attempt to convert Walker by a kind of hypnotic exertion of will is closely paralleled by Undershaft's unsuccessful attempt to dominate Barbara's own will in Act III.

10. Charles Bradlaugh's teaching would underline Undershaft's perception of the connection between religion and social oppression. In the first number of *The National Reformer* (8 April 1860) Bradlaugh said: 'the Bible is the great cord with which the people are bound; cut this, and the mass will be more free to appreciate facts instead of faiths' (quoted by Hypatia Bradlaugh Bonner in her *Charles Bradlaugh: A Record of his Life*, 2 vols (London: T. Fisher Unwin, 1894) vol. I, p. 123).

11. Undershaft adapts the words of Socrates in Book v of *The Republic*:

    unless . . . philosophers bear kingly rule in cities, or those who are now called kings and princes become genuine and adequate philosophers, and political power and philosophy are brought together . . . there will be no respite from evil. (*The Republic of Plato*, trans. A. D. Lindsay (London: J. M. Dent, 1935) p. 166)

12. Another possible meaning of the term 'will' in Undershaft's speech is that it refers to the Dionysian energies which he and his munitions trade embody.

13. Mrs Pat Marshall has suggested to me in conversation that Shaw may have had in mind here the biblical text: 'Except ye be converted, and become as little children, ye shall not enter into the kingdom of heaven' (Matt. 18:3).

14. J. D. Schuchter points out that Saint Barbara is the patron saint of fusiliers and protector of artillery-men, and that she is often represented with a cannon, as the symbol of her sphere of tutelage: see Schuchter, 'Shaw's *Major Barbara*', *The Explicator*, vol. XXVIII, no. 9 (May 1970) Item 74.

12 The End of *Pygmalion*

Quas quia Pygmalion aevum per crimen agentis viderat, offensus vitiis, quae plurima menti femineae natura dedit, sine coniuge, caelebs vivebat thalamique diu consorte carebat.[1]

(Ovid, *Metamorphoses*, Bk x)

Galatea never does quite like Pygmalion: his relation to her is too godlike to be altogether agreeable.

(*Pygmalion*, Epilogue)

The original version of *Pygmalion* – as distinct from the film version, the revised text of 1941 and the musical comedy based on the play[2] – ends in the following way:

MRS
HIGGINS: I'm afraid youve spoilt that girl, Henry. But never mind, dear: I'll buy you the tie and gloves.

HIGGINS: [*sunnily*] Oh, dont bother. She'll buy em all right enough. Goodbye.

They kiss, Mrs Higgins runs out. Higgins, left alone, rattles his cash in his pocket; chuckles; and disports himself in a highly self-satisfied manner.

Higgins has a persistent habit of rattling the contents of his pockets as he does in this final moment of the play. Shaw employs this piece of stage business on two other occasions in the play, and draws audience attention to it on the first occasion in the surrounding dialogue. The first two occasions have in common the fact that they are each associated with revelations about certain failings in Higgins's relations with women. On each occasion he is shown to be avoiding close engagement with subjects or questions which threaten his own emotional tranquillity. He uses his nonchalance as a means of insulating himself from emotional demands. The cash rattling is a small but significant indicator of Shaw's conception of Higgins's character, and the closing use of the device, it can be argued, helps to establish the meaning of the end of the play.

Shaw's first explicit use of the device occurs near the beginning of Act III during Higgins's dialogue with his mother, before Eliza's first launching in society. The more obvious reason for Higgins's 'fidgeting' in this scene is his apprehension about the first test of his experiment. But his speech to his mother, on the subject of young women, suggests a more deep-seated reason for unease:

> HIGGINS: Oh, I cant be bothered with young women. My idea of a lovable woman is something as like you as possible. I shall never get into the way of seriously liking young women; some habits lie too deep to be changed. [*Rising abruptly and walking about, jingling his money and his keys in his trouser pockets*] Besides, theyre all idiots.

With an appropriately classical term ('idiots') Higgins recalls his Ovidian prototype's contempt for the female mind, a contempt which is expressed in various ways in the play. To this, Shaw adds the notion that the female ideal for Pygmalion/Higgins is his mother, a sexually unchallenging figure who looks after him and buys him his ties and gloves, and for whom he has found a counterpart in Mrs Pearce, his housekeeper.

The most searching challenges in the play to Higgins's responses as a man and to his responsibility as a creator come at the beginning of Act IV, when he returns with Pickering and Eliza after the success of the experiment. Infuriated by Higgins's failure to express any sympathy with her ordeal or congratulations on her success, Eliza demands to know from her creator what is to become of her. Higgins's blankness in response to this plea is the most striking instance in the play of his failure to recognize the humanity of his creation:

> LIZA: . . . What am I fit for? What have you left me fit for? Where am I to go? What am I to do? What's to become of me?

HIGGINS: [*enlightened, but not at all impressed*] Oh, thats whats
             worrying you is it? [*He thrusts his hands into his
             pockets, and walks about in his usual manner, rattling
             the contents of his pockets, as if condescending to a trivial
             subject out of pure kindness*]. I shouldnt bother
             about it if I were you. I should imagine you wont
             have much difficulty in settling yourself some-
             where or other, though I hadnt quite realized
             that you were going away.

The dialogue in the final scene turns not only on the question of
Eliza's need for friendly concern, but also on her new economic
plight as a 'lady'. In the Pygmalion story as recounted by Ovid,
Pygmalion is described as having a profound aversion to the
female sex, and it is explained that this arises from his disgust at
the behaviour of the propoetides, women of Amathus who were,
so the myth has it, the first women to become prostitutes. The
implication of Ovid's tale is that it is his desire for a woman
beyond the imperfection of those around him which inspires
Pygmalion to create Galatea. Shaw subtly reverses this theme in
Pygmalion. As a flower girl in Tottenham Court Road Eliza sold
flowers. As a 'lady' she is threatened with the prospect of having
nothing to sell but herself ('Now youve made a lady of me I'm not
fit to sell anything else'). The analogy between Eliza's situation
and that of a prostitute has been lightly insinuated from very near
the beginning of her progress towards becoming a lady, when
Higgins 'buys' her from her father, Doolittle, for five pounds.
Until the last scene of the play Eliza is in a position of economic,
as well as emotional and intellectual, dependence on Higgins.
She is a kept woman; and Higgins's rattling of the money and
keys in his pocket may thus be seen to have a further dimension of
meaning, in addition to its significance as one of the signals
of failure in his understanding of, and response to, 'young
women'.

On the whole, Higgins is presented in the play as a likeable and
entertaining eccentric. But the critical notes in Shaw's portrayal
of his character are clear. He has certain qualities in common
with a later Pygmalion in Shavian drama, who appears in the
final play of the *Back to Methuselah* cycle. The Pygmalion of *As Far
As Thought Can Reach* is a scientist enthusiastically and intensely

absorbed in his creations, but failing to take account of the consequences. As the irresponsible creator of living beings, he is very similar to Victor Frankenstein in Mary Shelley's story. By the time he came to write *As Far As Thought Can Reach*, the Pygmalion and Frankenstein legends had clearly become very closely identified with one another in Shaw's mind.[3] The Pygmalion of *As Far As Thought Can Reach* plays dangerous games with the creation of live 'dolls' (the term is also used of Eliza in *Pygmalion*) who turn upon their creator in revengeful, destructive spirit. His first creation is an abortion, 'a dreadful mixture of horror and absurdity' (a type of Yahoo or primitive man) who threatens to kill Pygmalion and perishes 'in torments, howling' after indiscriminately devouring a variety of chemicals in the laboratory. The Female Figure and the Male Figure (later identified as Cleopatra and Ozymandias respectively) who appear on stage are successful as physical creations, but equally dangerous. In the scene which follows their appearance, Pygmalion dies as the result of a bite given to him in a struggle with the Female Figure. His death is a judgement. The He-Ancient and She-Ancient who arrive on the scene after Pygmalion's death express severe disapproval of his game of making live dolls: 'Let it be a lesson to you all to be content with lifeless toys, and not attempt to make living ones.' The limits of legitimate experimentations with the moulding of life are suggested in the He-Ancient's advice to the young man, Acis, that 'you can create nothing but yourself'.

Suggestions of a Frankenstein-like relation between creator and creature are also present in *Pygmalion*. In one of their meetings in *Frankenstein*, the monster passionately complains to his creator about his callous lack of concern for the consequences of his experiment: 'Unfeeling, heartless creator! you had endowed me with perceptions and passions, and then cast me abroad an object for the scorn and horror of mankind.'[4] Like Victor Frankenstein, Higgins is a scientist absorbed in the process of his creativity. But he is equally unconcerned about its end, about what Mrs Higgins calls 'the problem of what is to be done with [Eliza] afterwards'.

A gloss on Shaw's thinking about the subject of experimentation with human life as its material is provided by some remarks in the Preface to *Misalliance* published in 1914, a year after the

first production of *Pygmalion*. In that Preface, under the heading,
'What is a child?', Shaw wrote in answer:

> An experiment. A fresh attempt to produce the just man
> made perfect: that is, to make humanity divine. And you will
> vitiate the experiment if you make the slightest attempt to
> abort it into some fancy figure of your own: for example, your
> notion of a good man or a womanly woman.[5]

Elsewhere in the same Preface he counsels 'schoolmaster ab-
ortionists'[6] to leave experiments with life to the Life Force. A
similarly critical attitude towards such experimentation is hinted
at in *Pygmalion*. In the first scene in Higgins's studio-laboratory,
Pickering twice uses the term 'experiment' in reference to the
project of transforming Eliza, without qualm. But in Act v the
word becomes a source of embarrassment to him:

> LIZA: . . . Will you drop me altogether now that the
>   experiment is over, Colonel Pickering?
> PICKERING: Oh dont. You mustnt think of it as an
>   experiment. It shocks me somehow.

But Higgins's project clearly is an experiment, and one which is
carried out without regard to its human implications and
consequences.
    Understandably, because of its generic connections with
Cinderella romance, *Pygmalion* has always held out strong
temptations to producers and authors of musical comedy to make
the work conform to conventional sentimental moulds. We know
from Shaw's Epilogue and from his correspondence about the
play that he himself did not intend the ending of the play to imply
a future marriage between Higgins and Eliza. But in writing the
last act he was working against the grain of a powerful tradition
of romantic fiction in which love overcomes the barriers of class.
The trouble began with the very first production of the play in
which Sir Herbert Tree played Higgins to Stella Campbell's
Eliza. Shaw had the utmost difficulty in converting these two to
his own views about the play, and complained especially of the
'raving absurdity'[7] of Tree's acting of Higgins. His exasperation
is understandable when we learn that, during the run, Tree

introduced a piece of theatrical business, whereby between his speech and the curtain, Higgins casts a rose to the departing Eliza, thus leaving no doubt in the audience's mind as to the likely outcome of their relations.

Since the meanings of a play have effective existence only in the occasional transactions which occur between readers and the signs of verbal and non-verbal expression in the text, or between performers and audiences, it is inevitable that several suppositional endings to the plot of *Pygmalion* will always exist in potential. Some passages in the play's dialogue undeniably tend to encourage the presumption of an eventual marriage between Higgins and Eliza. We learn that Higgins bought Eliza a ring on a visit to Brighton. He has grown 'accustomed' to her voice and face. She performs little services for him around the house. But there are compelling reasons for saying that the ingredients of Cinderella romance are a foil to a tougher and more interesting line of narrative in the play which concludes decisively with Eliza's final words to Higgins: 'Buy them yourself'. In this view, *Pygmalion* is a play not about the growth of love between master and pupil, but about the pupil's regaining, through struggle, of her identity and independence. Her movement upwards in the social scale has involved not an increase but a diminution of freedom. In that respect her career is like that of Doolittle, whose social ascent leads to unwelcome imprisonment: 'Who asked him to make a gentleman of me? I was happy, I was free', he complains. In Eliza's case it is not so much the imprisonment of class, but imprisonment by her 'creator' from which she needs to escape. But her words closely echo Doolittle's: 'Why did you take my independence from me? Why did I give it up? I'm a slave now, for all my fine clothes.'

Despite Higgins's expressions of fondness for Eliza in the final scene between the two, what emerges most clearly is the fundamental incompatibility of their views of life. In saying to Eliza that he wastes the 'treasures of [his] Miltonic mind' on her, Higgins reminds us of the poet who made slaves of his daughters whilst producing a poem which distinguishes between an Adam who pursues 'thoughts abstruse' and an Eve who has a more immediate knowledge of feelings and things ('Not Words alone pleas'd her').[8] As a codifier of language and manners, Higgins is interested in generalities and principles. Eliza's complaint is not only that he neglects her feelings but also that he fails to individuate her as a person from the human species ('I care for life, for humanity; and you are a part of it that has come my way'). Eliza's attitude is, of course, seen sympathetically in the play; but its less appealing aspects are also discernible. She is presented as an intensely subjective person, whose outlook is inimical to thought because she tends to reduce all general issues to a personal level: 'I dont notice things like that. I notice that you dont notice me.'

Shaw allows Higgins the recognition that 'making life means making trouble'. But it is also clear that there are strict limits on the extent to which Higgins is prepared to engage with the 'trouble' of life. In one of his Act v speeches, after being confronted with the question of Eliza's future prospects, he callously tells her that she should 'go back to the gutter', where life is 'real', 'warm' and 'violent'. For the newly-educated Eliza this is hardly a feasible plan; but at least the warmth and vitality of the life of the gutter may be preferable to the coldness of Higgins. In the same speech in Act v, Higgins presents the prospect of a future marriage for Eliza in terms which, whilst presenting another impossible choice for her, also suggest a squeamishness in his attitude to sexual relations which sorts ill with the idea of his marrying Eliza himself: 'Marry some sentimental hog or other with lots of money, and a thick pair of lips to kiss you with and a thick pair of boots to kick you with.' Higgins does not lose his will to possess Eliza. He reacts sharply to challenges to his ownership of her from Freddy and Doolittle, and shows at the end of the play that his confidence in his ownership of her is still intact. But the relationship which he offers her is that of forming part of a sexless alliance, with himself and Pickering, as one of 'three old bachelors'.

As the richly funny, but intensely hostile, final clash between Higgins and Eliza draws to its conclusion, the exasperated creator (momentarily descending to the behaviour of 'the gutter' himself) lays violent hands on his creation. As his next speech makes clear this laying on of hands is Pygmalion/Higgins's final and decisive creative act in the play, an act which simultaneously brings his work of art to life and secures for both the artist himself and his creation their complete freedom from one another. The Pygmalion legend comes brilliantly to the surface at this point in the play, charged with meanings which give a new direction to the Ovidian tale. Shaw's Pygmalion does indeed create (or re-create) a woman. But the essential sign of her coming to life is that she is no longer a doll-like projection of her creator's will. She has gained self-ownership and freedom of choice ('I'm not afraid of you, and can do without you'). Her defiance of Higgins elicits from him the wondering comments: 'By George, Eliza, I said I'd make a woman of you; and I have. . . . Five minutes ago you were like a millstone round my neck. Now youre a tower of strength: a consort battleship.'

Shaw provides Higgins with at least these insights into what making 'a woman' of Eliza means. But he withholds from his character a full understanding of the completeness of the success of his experiment. Left alone on the stage at the end of the play, chuckling to himself and rattling his cash in his pockets in expectation of Eliza's compliance with his wishes, Higgins reaches the zenith of his capacity for imperceptiveness and misplaced confidence, and stands before us as a figure of engaging but doomed comic hubris.

NOTES

1. 'Pygmalion had seen these women spending their lives in shame, and, disgusted with the faults which in such full measure nature had given the female mind, he lived unmarried and long was without a partner of his couch' (Ovid, *Metamorphoses*, trans. F. J. Miller, Loeb Classics, 2 vols (London: Heinemann, 1916; New York: G. T. Putnam's Sons, 1916) vol. II, pp. 81–3).

2. The discussion in this chapter is concerned with the original stage version of *Pygmalion*, as represented in the text included in Bernard Shaw, *Androcles and the Lion, Overruled, Pygmalion* (London: Constable, 1916) and in the various editions of *The Complete Plays of Bernard Shaw*, of which that published by Constable in 1931 was the first. The Standard Edition (London: Constable, 1931) incorporates revised sequences from the film scenario. As Eric Bentley observes, the film version of *Pygmalion* is structurally inferior to the original stage version, an objection which also applies to the revised text of 1941. In particular, the inclusion of the Ambassador's reception scene weakens the impact of the true climax of the play, which is contained in the final encounter between Eliza and Higgins – see Eric Bentley, *Bernard Shaw*, 2nd British edn (London: Methuen, 1967) p. 85. In the Standard Edition, Shaw evidently attempted to clear up the ambiguity of the original ending by altering Higgins's last speech as follows:

HIGGINS: Pickering! Nonsense: shes going to marry Freddy. Ha ha! Freddy! Freddy! Ha ha ha ha ha!!!!!
[*He roars with laughter as the play ends*].

Alan J. Lerner and Fritz Loewe's *My Fair Lady* has an obviously romantic close, suggesting clearly that Higgins and Eliza will marry. In the final scene of *My Fair Lady*, Eliza softly enters Higgins's study as he is listening to a recording of her voice. After watching him for a moment, she turns off the machine, and the following dialogue ensues:

ELIZA: [*Gently*] I washed my face and hands before I come, I did.
Higgins straightens up. If he could but let himself, his face would radiate unmistakeable relief and joy. If he could but let himself, he would run to her. Instead, he leans back with a contented sigh pushing his hat forward till it almost covers his face.
HIGGINS: [*Softly*] Eliza? Where the devil are my slippers?
[*There are tears in Eliza's eyes. She understands*]
The curtain falls slowly

(Alan J. Lerner, *My Fair Lady: A Musical Play in Two Acts, Based on 'Pygmalion' by Bernard Shaw* (London: Max Reinhardt & Constable, 1956) pp. 155–6)

3. This connection is also observed by Margery M. Morgan in her article 'Edwardian Feminism and the Drama: Shaw and Granville Barker', *Cahiers Victoriens & Edouardiens: Studies in Edwardian and Anglo-Irish Drama (Montpellier)* no. 9/10 (Oct. 1979) p. 78. Miss Morgan's discussion of *Pygmalion* in that article came to my notice too late to be taken into account in this chapter.
4. Mary Shelley, *Frankenstein, or the Modern Prometheus*, ed. M. K. Joseph (London: Oxford University Press, 1969) p. 139.
5. *Collected Plays*, vol. IV, p. 20.
6. Ibid., p. 70.
7. See Martin Meisel, *Shaw and the Nineteenth-Century Theater* (Princeton University Press, 1963; Oxford University Press, 1963) p. 177.
8. *Paradise Lost*, VIII, 39–57.

13 The Tragi-comic Vision of *Heartbreak House*

Make a note that wishes for the destruction of the human race, however rational and sincere, are contrary to human nature.
(Smilash-Trefusis in *An Unsocial Socialist*)

Old men are dangerous: it doesn't matter to them what is going to happen to the world.
(Captain Shotover)

Despite the oscillations of its critical fortunes in the past, *Heartbreak House* has come to be regarded by many critics as Shaw's greatest play. In the second half of the twentieth century there has been a steadily emerging recognition of its outstanding quality, in relation both to Shaw's other work and to twentieth-century English drama in general. It is a play of great imaginative power and intellectual range, and its portrait of 'cultured, leisured Europe before the war'[1] includes some of Shaw's most astringent and uncompromising social criticism. The methods of the play are frequently comic, even farcical, in character, but the comedy and farce form an integral part of Shaw's searching analysis of the predicament of contemporary society. Of all his plays, *Heartbreak House* shows least evidence of such salving balms of the Shavian universe as Creative Evolution, or Fabian Socialism or feminine wisdom and vitality. The play confronts darkness and violence and the shattering of illusions in an unflinching, exhilarated mood. Although some positive affirmations are discernible in its overall vision, they appear in a context of fiercely negative and destructive feeling. The play is unquestionably one of the most complex of all Shaw's works, and existing critical discussion is often disappointing in its failure to do justice to the complexity, and to come to grips with the meaning of the play's central metaphors.

Like Eliot's *The Waste Land* and Yeats's 'The Second Coming', *Heartbreak House* is a work which clearly reflects the new dimensions of disorder and violence which were brought into being by the First World War. The biographical background to Shaw's play has been well examined by Stanley Weintraub in his *Bernard Shaw 1914–1918*. Shaw was enraged at and disgusted by the war from the outset: 'You and I at war, can absurdity go further?' he asked of his German translator, Siegfried Trebitsch in 1914.[2] By November 1914 Shaw had completed his hard-hitting and penetrating essay *Common Sense About The War*, in which he strongly attacked the spirit of jingoistic and sentimental patriotism which attended Britain's entry into the war, and in which he analysed the war itself as a struggle between avaricious imperial powers. Such views were hardly calculated to win Shaw popularity in the England of 1914 and 1915, and he was condemned and ostracized by wide sections of the public, including many former friends and fellow writers. Later, Shaw had at least become persuaded that Britain, having entered the war, should win it, and had returned sufficiently to favour in official quarters to be invited to the front in France to see allied troops in action. But the war clearly had a profound influence on the themes and atmosphere of *Heartbreak House*. During the writing of the play, events such as the sinking of the *Lusitania* (1915) and the first of the Zeppelin raids on England (1916) were bringing his fiction into sharp contact with reality. The war must also have helped to produce the strong undercurrent of anger which continually makes its presence felt in the play, as well as contributing to the emotional pattern and major theatrical effects of the tumultuous last scene.

In some respects – though it does not do as a summary of the themes of the play – *Heartbreak House* can be interpreted as a warning to the contemporary cultured élite of the dangers inherent in their isolation of themselves from the sources of power in society. A link between the society portrayed in the play and the Bloomsbury circle is suggested in a letter from Shaw to Virginia Woolf in 1940, in which he wrote:

There is a play of mine called *Heartbreak House* which I

always connect with you because I conceived it in that house somewhere in Sussex where I first met you, and, of course, fell in love with you. I suppose every man did.[3]

The play presents us with a deeply ambivalent view of the inhabitants of the house. To Hector's despairing description of them in Act III as 'all heartbroken imbeciles', Mazzini Dunn replies:

Oh no. Surely, if I may say so, rather a favourable specimen of what is best in our English culture. You are very charming people, most advanced, unprejudiced, frank, humane, unconventional, democratic , free-thinking, and everything that is delightful to thoughtful people.

We are offered no resolution of such conflicting views of the characters in the play. As a group, the women in the play are attractive, sensitive and intelligent. But indications of their demoniacal and destructive qualities are present throughout the course of the play's action. They bear strong resemblances to the *femmes fatales* of Romantic and post-Romantic literature and art. Even a minor character, the loyal and apparently kindly Nurse Guiness, becomes, in the final scene of the play, a wrathful harpy, screeching imprecations on the head of her burglar husband as he goes to meet his death in the gravel pit. Similarly, the principal male characters in the play are viewed in constantly changing lights of sympathy and condemnation.

Heartbreak House is sub-titled 'A Fantasia in the Russian Manner on English Themes', and the Preface indicates that Shaw was particularly acknowledging, as previous explorations of aimlessness and despair, the plays of Chekhov and Tolstoy's 'ferociously contemptuous' indictment of contemporary cultured society in 'The Fruits of Enlightenment'.[4] Though he does not say so, Shaw may also have had in mind whilst writing this play Tolstoy's Lear-like relations with his daughters. Certainly Shakespeare's *King Lear* itself is an important component of the many-sided intellectual and imaginative background to the play. In the puppet play, *Shakes versus Shav*, which Shaw wrote in 1949, Shav responds to a challenge from Shakes by conjuring up a tableau of *'Captain Shotover seated, as in Millais' picture called North-*

West passage, with a young woman of virginal beauty', exclaiming as he does so: 'Behold my Lear'.[5] Chekhov's influence is apparent both in details and in the general structure of *Heartbreak House*, a structure which in some ways echoes *The Cherry Orchard* and which can also be seen as a development of the methods pursued in Shaw's own earlier works, *Getting Married* and *Misalliance*. Borrowing from the models of Chekhov and his own earlier plays, Shaw employs a slight and relatively simple central situation as the axis of a complex pattern of fitful meetings and proposals, flirtations and discussions, which progressively reveal the attitudes, convictions and delusions of the characters and the society they represent. It is true that there are important differences in theme and mood between Shaw's play and *The Cherry Orchard*. But there are also close parallels. Trofimov, in Chekhov's play, makes articulate the general social issues involved in the Ranevsky microcosm ('All Russia is our garden') in a way which is closely paralleled in speeches by Shotover and Hector. Both plays deal with themes of illusion and reality; both use their settings as central images associated with the impending disintegration of a social order. In both plays sounds are heard in the air which seem to warn of far-reaching catastrophe.

One of the principal problems of interpretation which *Heartbreak House* presents is the question as to what attitudes we are to adopt towards the commonplace businessman, Boss Mangan, on the one hand, and his antagonist, the eccentric retired naval officer and inventor, Captain Shotover, on the other. But before turning to this question it is necessary to take a more general view of the play's themes and development and its patterns of imagery.

If the greater part of the action of the play revolves around the question as to whom the young woman, Ellie Dunn, is to marry, with the flirtations between Hesione and Mangan, and between Ariadne, Hector and Randall forming fragmentary sub-plots, the thematic and imaginative centre of the play lies in the image of the house itself. The house has been built to resemble a ship, an idea which Shaw based on Lena Ashwell's account of a sailing ship which had been converted into a house by her father, Captain Pocock. As in Dickens's similarly named *Bleak House*, the place becomes a flexible metaphor for a social condition. The set, the stage properties and dialogue combine to keep the ship image before us, without its becoming over-insistent. The house is a ship full of souls, voyaging through the nightmare of contemporary history, a nightmare the voyagers themselves have helped to create. The last act of the play, which begins with quiet conversation in the garden of the house, threatened only by Hesione's report of hearing a 'sort of splendid drumming in the sky', ends with the roar of enemy bombers overhead and the sound of shattering explosions nearby. The house is called Heartbreak House not only because of the broken love affairs it witnesses, but also because of the larger social dilemma which it symbolizes. However attractive, witty and delightfully candid the occupants of the house may be, in their absorption with private feeling, and living 'foolish lives of romance and sentiment and snobbery', they have insulated themselves from the tragic realities of the public world. Even Captain Shotover, who of all the characters in the play engages most closely with the problem of power, does so in a desperate and isolated manner, with his half comical, rum-assisted search for 'the seventh degree of concentration' and his sinister quest for weapons of immense destructive capacity. The ambiguous feelings which the house arouses, and something of the unusual atmosphere of the play, are well conveyed in a speech by Ellie in Act III, in which she gives the house its name:

ELLIE: [*musically*] Yes: This silly house, this strangely happy house, this agonizing house, this house without foundations. I shall call it heartbreak house.

In the dialogue, the ship image is employed to describe both private and social predicaments. In Act II the play's title is drawn into relation with its key image in a usage which relates to the inner vessel of the spirit: 'when your heart is broken, your boats are burned: nothing matters any more. It is the end of happiness and the beginning of peace.' But in the final scene of the play the metaphor is expanded to embrace the whole condition of England:

HECTOR: And this ship that we are all in? This soul's prison we call England?

It is also employed here to express Shotover's, and perhaps

Shaw's, deepest dread, the dread of drifting, trusting to Providence.⁶ In the context of the final scene, and coming as it does just before the first *'dull distant explosion'* which heralds the arrival of the bombers, Shotover's terse answer to Hector's question about his business as an Englishman has peculiar resonance and power:

HECTOR: And what may my business as an
                           Englishman be pray?
CAPTAIN SHOTOVER: Navigation. Learn it and live; or leave
                           it and be damned.

In this scene the queer humour of Shotover's nautical language is turned to effective allegory, whilst still retaining its comic edge. The destruction of the nearby rectory produces a grim joke about the Church's lack of realism and courage: the Church is 'on the rocks, breaking up' because of its failure to head out for 'God's open sea'.

Ellie Dunn's progress through the play, on the other hand, might be described, as a voyage towards 'God's open sea' out of the shelter of her illusions. It is a voyage from innocence to experience, in the tragi-comic course of which she penetrates all the secrets of Heartbreak House. Ellie's experience of heartbreak in the play is part of a process in which she is enabled not only to see through her own illusions but also, more positively, to see the inadequacy of the cynical, materialist stance she adopts when her romance has been shattered. Like other key Shavian characters, she renounces the quest for happiness in favour of a quest for reality. But reality becomes defined for her in the play in terms other than those of security and acquisition. Eventually Ellie progresses beyond heartbreak to a state, at once tranquil and alert, which recalls the condition described in T. S. Eliot's 'Burnt Norton' as 'the inner freedom from the practical desire'. In a scene with Shotover in Act II Ellie says 'I feel now as if there was nothing I could not do, because I want nothing.'

Through Shotover and Ellie we see – it is one of the many ways in which the play recalls *King Lear* – that heartbreak may be the beginning of wisdom. Ellie has come to the house on a visit to Hesione, one of Shotover's two daughters. Near the beginning of the play we learn that she has 'drifted' into an understanding with Mangan, a middle-aged industrialist and business associate of Ellie's father, the mild mannered liberal idealist, Mazzini Dunn. Meanwhile, however, she has fallen deeply in love with a glamorous, 'rather dignified' gentleman calling himself Marcus Darnley, who, Othello-like, has been captivating her with tales of strange exploits. (Ellie has been brought up on Shakespeare, and she develops in the play from an innocent Desdemona to an experienced, ambiguous Cordelia). Ironically, Mr Darnley turns out to be Hesione's husband, Hector, who is a courageous man, but who enjoys creating fictions, including the fiction that he is unmarried. Far from objecting to Hector's behaviour, Hesione assists him in his flirtations, this being part of the continual game she plays of arranging and manipulating romantic affairs. Under her influence, Hector loses his resolve as an idealist and potential reformer and is reduced to impotent Byronism and love-in-idleness. Left alone on the stage near the end of Act 1, Hector performs a farcical charade of imaginary sword-fighting and imaginary embraces which epitomizes his character as a frustrated hero. Although Hector is not an unsympathetically treated character, it is Ellie's disillusionment with his 'Marcus Darnley' persona which constitutes the first experience of heartbreak in the play, and which marks the beginning of her progress towards maturity.

Hesione, in this most allusive and poetic of Shaw's plays, calls up more than one literary association. As Shotover's two 'demon daughters', she and Ariadne have obvious affinities with Goneril and Regan. Both Shotover and Hector stress the diabolical character of these two sirens in the play in terms reminiscent of Lear's 'anatomies' of his daughters. Hesione's namesake in classical legend was a Trojan woman whose abduction to Greece by Telamon eventually led to the downfall of Troy, a fact which supports other suggestions in the play that Hector's name is probably intended to recall the classical hero. Beneath the literary disguises, Hesione is probably also Stella Campbell, whose statuesque beauty, unreliability and charm are all reflected in the part.

In some respects, the progressively deepening relation between Ellie and the inhabitants of Heartbreak House, and particularly with Hesione and Shotover, presents itself as the development of a marriage of good and evil, of powers of light and of darkness.

After her disillusionment with Hector, and as she grows out of her role as protégée to Hesione, Ellie begins to match the Shotover daughters in their capacity for destructive behaviour towards men, as we see in her bullying treatment of Mangan. Her gradual acquaintance with darkness is brought out in one of the play's image-motifs. Early in the play a pointed contrast is drawn between the beautiful black hair of Hesione (mentioned several times in the play) and the fair hair of Ellie. In their quarrel in Act II Hesione contemptuously calls Ellie 'Goldylocks' and invites her to pull her own hair to show its strength. At the end of the play we see a symbolic climax of their relationship, when the fair and dark beauties embrace as they listen ecstatically to the Beethoven music of the bombers. Shotover, who succeeds in wresting Ellie away from Mangan, entering into a spiritual marriage with her himself, is also associated with dark powers. In the present he is preoccupied with the invention of destructive weapons, and has his stock-pile of dynamite 'to kill fellows like Mangan'. In the past he has pretended to sell his soul to the devil in Zanzibar, the better to deal with degraded and corrupt underlings. He has also, sometime in the past, dissolved traditional oppositions by happily marrying a black wife in Jamaica. It is significant that before her initiation into experience in the play, Ellie's ideal Othello is 'of course, white'.

The pattern of Ellie's development is thus clear: she progresses from the delusions of the affair with 'Marcus Darnley' through the Undershaft-like temptation to marry Mangan, in order, as she puts it 'to save my soul from the poverty that is damning me by inches', to the experienced realism and daring of her final outlook. Ellie's radiant excitement at the end of the play as she listens to the bombers needs to be understood in relation to her marriage with Shotover, and in the light of his very positive attitude towards danger. Mangan and the burglar, 'the two practical men of business', have gone in search of safety to the gravel pit and been killed. The implication is that facing up to reality, rather than sheltering, offers the best hope of survival. In an earlier scene, when Ellie is still at the stage of contemplating marriage with Mangan, Shotover says to her: 'At your age I looked for hardship, danger, horror, and death, that I might feel the life in me more intensely'; and later, as the bombers arrive, he shouts: 'Courage will not save you; but it will show that your souls are still alive.' In welcoming the bombers, then, Ellie can be seen to be living out the philosophy of her 'spiritual husband', Shotover, and at the same time coming into line with earlier Shavian characters, such as Lina Szczepanowska and Margaret Knox, as exponents of living dangerously, in order to live fully, and with Don Juan/Tanner and Lavinia as seekers of reality. Thus it is difficult to accept Robert Brustein's view that Ellie's final speech of welcome to the bombers represents a moment of absolute negation and revolt on Shaw's part.[7] Viewed in context, Ellie's final stance may be seen to represent not negation, but a daring and disturbing affirmation. At the end of the play – to return to the language of its central metaphor – the ship of Heartbreak House is heading with all its lights on towards the open sea, inviting danger and possible destruction, but moving in the only direction of life.

Even Hector, whose earlier expressions of frustration and self-disgust may lead us to think that his action in rushing around the house turning lights on to guide the bombers in arises from self-destructive impulses, has declared just before he does so: 'I still have the will to live'. When he returns to the stage, Ellie, urging him to set fire to the house, calls him by the old pseudonym, Marcus, suggesting that in her eyes at least he has regained his earlier heroic character. It seems highly likely that Shaw is alluding in the last scene of the play to the end of the legend of Troy, as related by Homer and Virgil: the quixotic self-sacrifice of the Trojan, Hector, the burning of the city, the catastrophic destruction of one civilization leading to the birth of another.[8]

The lighting effects which Shaw employs in the play form a symbolic pattern which is directly related to its central themes. At the end of Act I, as Captain Shotover sits down to ponder the invention of some new instrument of destruction, he rejects Hector's offer to turn up the lights, with the words: 'No. Give me deeper darkness. Money is not made in the light.' At the beginning of Act II the lights are up, but when Ellie leaves the stage after putting Mangan into an hypnotic trance, she turns out the lights, leaving Mangan alone in his darkness. Act III opens with the light from a single arc lamp cutting into the darkness of a moonless night. This effect is a prelude to the full 'marriage' of darkness and light at the end as the fully lit house voyages into the night, to the sardonic accompaniment of Randall's final success with the tune of the old war-time song 'Keep the home fires burning'.

The lighting at the end of the play provides an effective symbolic counter of the final development of the play's tragi-comic vision, in which we see that the only prospects of life and regeneration lie in a journey of deliberately courted danger and in a union of the forces of light and darkness. This echoes in visual terms Ellie's Act III announcement that she has become Shotover's 'white' wife. The final thematic development of *Heartbreak House* recalls the conclusion in *Major Barbara* that 'the way of life lies through the factory of death'.[9] But the later play is much more open-ended and pessimistic. In the writing of *Heartbreak House* Shaw brought his tragi-comic muse to its most intense pitch of expression, and there is more than a slight suggestion of *schadenfreude* about the end of the play. In the bold theatrical device of having the play end with Randall's tune, Shaw compresses into a few moments an expression of his profound loathing of sentimental patriotism and a joyful salute to the twin prospects of destruction and new life. The mood of the end of the play is reminiscent of Yeats's image of the Chinese sages looking out over scenes of devastation in the poem 'Lapis Lazuli': 'Their ancient glittering eyes are gay.'

It would certainly simplify our view of the play if we could regard Ellie's two principal 'suitors', Shotover and Mangan, as, respectively, its hero and its villain. It is true that this is a conclusion encouraged by the Preface to *Heartbreak House* which Shaw wrote in 1919, three years after completing the play itself. In that essay he launched a two-fold attack, directed on the one hand against cultivated pleasure-seekers who wish to realize not 'Utopia for the common people' but 'their favourite fictions and poems in their own lives',[10] and, on the other, against the 'practical business men', the hogs of self-interest, who are also, Shaw maintains, politically incompetent.[11] The Preface is also concerned with the theme of the separation of culture from power: the idea of a Cusins – Undershaft alliance has clearly failed. In some way the enlightened élite must acquire power unilaterally. These ideas are reflected in the play, and it is at least understandable that critics should equate Shotover with Shaw, and see Mangan as the enemy. Thus Fred Mayne, for example, employs the phrase 'Shotover – Shaw', calling Shotover an 'impersonation of the author' and Mangan 'the deepest damned of all the characters'.[12] Brustein describes Mangan as 'one of the most unredeemable characters that Shaw ever created', and refers to Shotover as an 'author's surrogate', with qualifications which do not cover the vital issue of Shotover's callous destructiveness.[13] Very similar views of the two characters are presented by Eric Bentley and Louis Crompton.[14] There are, however, serious difficulties in the way of accepting these assumptions without extensive qualification. Shaw was remaining true in this play to an old principle of his that 'there are no heroes and no villains'; and he presents Mangan much more sympathetically and Shotover much more critically than the accounts of many of the play's critics suggest.

In the middle of Act II there is a scene between Ellie, Hesione and Mangan which is rarely mentioned in critical discussion of the play, but which makes a strong impression in the theatre. The situation contains strong elements of farce; but the comedy of the scene is offset by the viciousness of the two women in their treatment of Mangan and by the subsequent shame of Hesione. After a quarrel between them, Mangan has been put into a sort of hypnotic trance by Ellie, in which he gives every appearance of being asleep, but is actually conscious. Hesione and Ellie conduct a callous discussion about him in which they refer to him by such titles as 'the object' and 'that creature'. When Ellie wakes him at length he delivers a furious protest to the two women, ending by bitterly reproaching Hesione for making a fool of him by flirting with him in the garden. Her action, he says, was 'like a man hitting a woman in the breast'. This is the one moment in the play when Hesione loses her poise: 'I was ashamed for the first time in my life', she confesses. It is also a moment in which it is discovered that even Mangan has a heart which can be broken. Hesione's incredulity at this idea is countered by his Parolles-like plea: 'I'm a man, ain't I?', to which she responds adroitly: '[*half coaxing, half rallying, altogether tenderly*] Oh no: not what I call a man. Only a Boss: just that and nothing else. What business has a Boss with a heart?' But Hesione's next discovery is that he is not just 'Boss' Mangan, a type, but a person, with a name which, in a nice comic moment he reluctantly reveals is Alfred. Hesione's delighted response makes recognition of his identity as an individual complete:

> It comes to me suddenly that you are a real
> person: that you had a mother like anyone else.
> [*Putting her hands on his shoulders and surveying him*]
> Little Alf!
> MANGAN: Well, you have a nerve.
> MRS
> HUSHABYE: And you have a heart, Alfy, a whimpering little
> heart, but a real one.

Dangerous as this scene may be to the consistency of Shaw's social criticism in the play, it does serve to illustrate the integrity of his vision as a comic dramatist. Mangan is revealed by Shaw to be an individual, capable of suffering, just as Higgins finds in *Pygmalion* that Eliza Doolittle is not merely an experiment, but a person capable of feeling. However much Shaw may write in terms of classes and types in the Prefaces to his plays, the plays themselves present individualized personae whose humanity complicates and deepens the vision which the works embody.

It seems possible that, in naming Mangan, Shaw had in mind the celebrated nineteenth-century Irish poet, James Clarence Mangan, one of whose best-known poems is called 'The Nameless One'. Some of the misfortunes of the Nameless One in the poem fit those of Shaw's Mangan very closely: he is condemned to 'herd with demons'; he is 'Betray'd in friendship, befool'd in love, / With spirit shipwreck'd'; and now that he is 'Old and hoary / At thirty nine', the readers ('ye pitying noble') are asked to grant him a grave in their bosoms. But the scene in the play makes its point without this association, and the point is underlined later in such moments as that when Hector rebukes Hesione for calling Mangan a fool: 'Do not scorn the man: we are all fools.'

The sympathy aroused by Mangan is not confined to the 'naming' scene. Shaw must have been aware of the laugh Mangan would get in the theatre when he complains in a later scene that 'The very burglars cant behave naturally in this house.' Mangan also voices a powerful criticism of the 'spiritual striptease' (to borrow Brustein's apt phrase)[15] which entertains the inhabitants of Heartbreak House, when he asks: 'How are we to have any self-respect if we don't keep it up that we're better than we really are?' When Mangan is destroyed with the other, un-licensed, burglar at the end of the play, the pity of Mazzini Dunn is balanced against the callousness of Shotover.

Shotover provides an outlet for destructive feelings which are certainly part of the play's meaning and impact, but which cannot be identified as the whole of its meaning. With his eccentricities, his forthright rudeness of manner, his abrupt entrances and exits, his sly confusions of identity, Shotover has a kind of fool's licence which makes him an excellent vehicle for the play's more radical social criticism. His outrageous description of the mild but inadequate Mazzini Dunn, whose name recalls the struggles for liberation of nineteenth-century Europe, as 'a thief, a pirate, and a murderer', perhaps contains a sub-logical half-truth. But producers who have Shotover made up to look like Shaw himself fail to do justice to the distancing effect of some aspects of Shotover's characterization in the play. In the scene in which Shotover tells Hector of his ambition to 'kill fellows like Mangan' in order to get power into the right hands, Hector points out that Mangan's son may be a Plato, and reminds Shotover of the fundamental social contract: 'We are members one of another'. Although Shotover's destructive impulses are deployed in the play as a powerful expression of contempt for and frustration at contemporary society, they are themselves viewed critically. Even Shotover himself, more than once in the play, reminds us that his views are those of an old man who no longer cares so much what happens to the world. Shaw's Lear can often be blind as well as wise.

It might be contended that the ambivalence of Shaw's treatment of Mangan and Shotover blunts the edge of the play's attack on society. The portrayal of Shotover in the play occasionally brings to mind D. H. Lawrence's remark that 'sometimes it is even honourable, and necessary, to hate society, as Swift did, or to hate mankind altogether, as often Voltaire did'.[16] But there is a strong case for saying that the ambivalence of *Heartbreak House* is an essential part of its strength. The flexibility of the treatment of Shotover and Mangan is typical of the methods of characterization in the play, and it is that flexibility, Shaw's refusal to be unfaithful to the human materials of the play, which gives *Heartbreak House* its impressive inclusiveness of vision, and which makes it a great work of dramatic art, and not a diatribe.

NOTES

1. *Collected Plays*, vol. v, p. 12.
2. From a cable in the Albert A. Berg Collection, New York Public Library.
3. Letter to Virginia Woolf, 10 May 1940, Albert A. Berg Collection, New York Public Library. In her reply to this letter (15 May 1940, British Library, MS Add. 50522), Virginia Woolf wrote, in a postscript: '*Heartbreak House*, by the way, is my favourite of all your works.'
4. *Collected Plays*, vol. v, p. 12.
5. Millais' painting has considerable relevance to *Heartbreak House*. It shows an old rum-drinking sailor living over his past exploits in his mind as he listens to the log-book accounts of them which are being read to him by the young woman sitting at his feet, and, as one commentator puts it, 'yearns once more to battle with the hardships which must be faced by the traveller in the frozen north' (A. Lys Baldry, *Millais* (London: T. C. & E. C. Jack, 1909) p. 69). The tag which is always associated with the picture, 'it might be done, and England ought to do it', is perhaps echoed in the play's concern with the responsibilities of Englishmen.
6. In the Dream scene in *Man and Superman* Don Juan declares 'to be in hell is to drift: to be in heaven is to steer'.
7. Robert Brustein, *The Theatre of Revolt* (London: Methuen, 1965) p. 227.
8. There are thematic parallels with the end of *Heartbreak House* in Yeats's late poem 'The Gyres', as well as in 'Lapis Lazuli'. Cf., for example, the lines from 'The Gyres':

> Hector is dead and there's a light in Troy;
> We that look on but laugh in tragic joy.
> (*The Collected Poems of W. B. Yeats*, 2nd
> edn (London: Macmillan, 1950) p. 337)

9. Cf. also the imagery of light and darkness at the end of *Major Barbara*: 'the unveiling of an eternal light in the Valley of the Shadow'.
10. *Collected Plays*, vol. v, p. 13.
11. Ibid., p. 38.
12. Fred Mayne, *The Wit and Satire of Bernard Shaw* (London: Edward Arnold, 1967) pp. 110, 116, 136.
13. Brustein, *The Theatre of Revolt*, pp. 224, 225.
14. See Eric Bentley, *Bernard Shaw*, 2nd edn (London: Methuen, 1967) pp. 96 and 140, and Louis Crompton, *Shaw the Dramatist* (Lincoln: University of Nebraska Press, 1969) pp. 155 and 163.
15. Brustein, *The Theatre of Revolt*, p. 226.
16. D. H. Lawrence, *Selected Literary Criticism*, ed. A. Beal (London: Heinemann, 1955) p. 270.

14 The Failure of Politics

Man is a failure as a political animal.
(*Geneva*)

Were there any hopes to outlive vice, or a point to be super-annuated from sin, it were worthy our knees to implore the dayes of *Methuselah*. But age doth not rectifie, but incurvate our natures, turning bad dispositions into worser habits.

(Sir Thomas Browne, *Religio Medici*)

I

Shaw's political stance has always had the reputation of being difficult to pin down. Critics of the left say both that he is insufficiently rigorous as a Socialist – Lenin described him as 'a good man fallen among Fabians'[1] – and that the Socialist in Shaw is constantly betrayed by the playwright. As Fabianism poses problems for hardline Socialists, so the plays pose problems for anyone wanting to read them as the expression simply of a Socialist political philosophy. Such difficulties are compounded by the fact that in some moods, and increasingly in the late political plays, Shaw comes close to a position of complete despair about man as a political animal. Hovering in the background of most of the late writings is the spirit of the King of Brobdingnag in *Gulliver's Travels* who, to quote Shaw's words at the opening of *Everybody's Political What's What*, found mankind 'incorrigibly villainous'.[2]

If we consider the non-dramatic writings on their own, a reasonably consistent picture of Shaw's political outlook can be seen to emerge. In the non-dramatic writings he remained fairly steadily on the paths which he and his fellow Fabians had mapped out in the last two decades of the nineteenth century. Although they cannot be precisely equated, since the later book

includes some significant shifts in argument, Shaw's two major
political works of the twentieth century, *The Intelligent Woman's
Guide to Socialism and Capitalism* (1928)[3] and *Everybody's Political
What's What* (1944) show clear threads of continuity with what
Shaw was saying in the earlier Fabian essays and speeches. Both
books are a development of Shaw's earlier criticisms of the
Capitalist system and its social consequences, and both argue in
favour of the socialization of the state by gradual and constitutional means.

The arguments in *The Intelligent Woman's Guide* are conducted
with exemplary good humour and fair-mindedness. The teaching of Fabian Socialism is offered as an *opinion* as to how wealth
should be distributed 'in a respectable civilized country'.[4] Shaw's
method is to open the subject up and to invite his readers to join
him in exploring it. His diagnosis of the ills of Capitalism is
incisive, and not at all easy to refute. As in the plays, so here, he
adopts the strategy of giving the devil his due.[5] Capitalism, he
argues, may be thoroughly benevolent, even visionary, in
intention. But the major problem of Capitalism is that there is no
way of *guaranteeing* that its motives will be altruistic. In two
masterly chapters at the centre of the book ('Capitalism in
Perpetual Motion' and 'The Runaway Car of Capitalism') Shaw
describes the ungovernable forces of Capitalism in terms which
still have a clear ring of truth:

> Capitalism leads us into enterprises of all sorts, at home and
> abroad, over which we have no control, and for which we have
> no desire. The enterprises are not necessarily bad: some of
> them have turned out well; but the point is that Capitalism
> does not care whether they turn out well or ill for us provided
> they promise to bring in money to the shareholders. We never
> know what Capitalism will be up to next; and we never can
> believe a word its newspapers tell us about its doings when the
> truth seems likely to be unpopular.[6]

Apart from its creation of social divisiveness and alienation, one
of the chief moral flaws in the Capitalist system, Shaw argues, is
that it destroys belief in 'any effective power but that of self-
interest backed by force'.[7]

Shaw arrives at what he describes as the central tenet of

Socialism in *The Intelligent Woman's Guide* after a careful analysis of various plans for the distribution of wealth. Formulae such as 'To Each What She Produces', 'To Each What She Deserves', 'To Each What She Can Grab', are shown to contain serious pitfalls and insoluble problems of equity. The 'true diagnostic' of Socialism, as distinct from other ideologies, radical, philanthropic, liberal or syndicalist, which might seem to have similar aims, is equality of income. To achieve this aim the government must become 'the national landlord, the national financier, and the national employer'.[8]

The question of Shaw's attitude towards the use of violence in the revolutionary process is well analysed in a valuable essay by Martin Meisel.[9] But Meisel's account of Shaw's attitudes needs modification in one important matter of emphasis. It is true that Shaw of course acknowledged that violence is one instrument by which the power of opponents of Socialism may be broken. But this is different from saying, as Meisel has done, that Shaw argues in *The Intelligent Woman's Guide* that 'the transfer of political power *need* not be bloody' and that 'he makes the peaceful acceptance of the parliamentary way to socialism seem exceedingly unlikely'.[10] Shaw is much less equivocal about violence than this might suggest. In the chapter on revolutions in *The Intelligent Woman's Guide* he clearly argues against the use of violence: 'Socialists who understand their business are always against bloodshed'.[11] Violence does not create Socialism. It only creates waste, and leaves the basic work of constitutional and economic planning still to be done. It is necessary to be aware of the possibility of violent revolution. But after violent revolutions the problems remain to be solved, and the bloodshed might just as well not have occurred:

> In the long run (which nowadays is a very short run) you must have your parliament and your settled constitution back again; and the risings and *coups d'état*, with all their bloodshed and burnings and executions, might as well have been cut out as far as the positive constructive work of Socialism is concerned.[12]

In *Everybody's Political What's What*, the term Shaw employs for the creed he advances is 'democratic Socialism'.[13]

Despite its great length, *The Intelligent Woman's Guide* is an extraordinarily well co-ordinated book, a healthy and playful giant. *Everybody's Political What's What*, diverging as it often does from its more strictly political themes into general sociological and cultural topics, is more diffuse. In its treatment of political themes it does show some significant changes of emphasis. Shaw does not withdraw from the principle that incomes need to be levelled up. But, referring to the Russian experience that even in a Communist society some men (bureaucrats and professionals) need to be more equal than others, he argues here that equality of income should be attained 'virtually if not mathematically'.[14] He also concedes, in the chapter on 'Equality', that in the USSR it was found to be impossible to increase or even maintain production 'until piece-work and payment by results was established'.[15] Shaw was treading on very delicate ground in this chapter, and it could be argued that the formula 'To Each What She Produces', having been thrown out of the door with a pitchfork in *The Intelligent Woman's Guide*, returns through the window in *Everybody's Political What's What*. Yet, in the main, Shaw does not desert the principles of the earlier work.

The opening chapter of *Everybody's Political What's What* well illustrates the peculiar (and by no means facile, as Walter Stein asserts[16]) amalgam of optimism and despair which characterizes so much of Shaw's later writing. The chapter is entitled 'Is Human Nature Incurably Depraved?' As he wrote, a second World War was being waged, and many of the gross inequalities against which Shaw had fought for a lifetime were still deeply entrenched in the English social system. Perhaps it would be better, Shaw sardonically advises the reader, to take up a detective story or 'some pleasant classic', and enjoy for the time being the felicity of being well deceived:

For though the book is in a sense a detective story inasmuch as it is an attempt to track down some of the mistakes that have landed us in a gross misdistribution of domestic income and in two world wars in twenty five years, yet if we have neither the political capacity nor the goodwill to remedy them, we had better not torment ourselves uselessly by making ourselves conscious of them. Better cling to our delusions and keep our hope and selfrespect, making the most of our vices and follies before they destroy us.[17]

Shaw readily allows that there is a strong case for the Brobdingnagian view of mankind. But he goes on to say that Swift 'did not know the whole truth of the condition of mankind', nor, he adds, did Goldsmith, 'though his Deserted Village shews how he concluded that "honour sinks where commerce long prevails" '.[18] Shaw clings precariously to the hope that there may be ways of correcting the 'mistakes' and goes on to write a constructive if (as he admits) necessarily inconclusive book. In the late political plays, however, such positive notes are very much more difficult to discover.

II

In the late political plays Shaw's creative energies are clearly more fully engaged with satirical exposure of the weaknesses of existing political institutions and experiments than with any advocacy, either directly or by implication, of programmes for reform. Two of these plays, *The Apple Cart* (1929) and *On the Rocks* (1933), are concerned with the problems of parliamentary democracy in England. *Geneva* (1938) deals with international politics, and particularly with the rise of Fascism in Germany, Italy and Spain.

The Apple Cart is a virtuoso piece in the discussion play form. In this work, as in most of the late plays, Shaw takes jester's licence to dispense almost completely with conventional plot material. The structure of the play resembles that of a musical composition, falling somewhere between symphony and light opera in character. An elegant, obliquely relevant overture[19] introduces the first of two main movements. The two movements are separated by an Interlude, which has something of the character of an operatic duet, between the king and his mistress; and the play concludes with a coda-like passage of dialogue in which the king declares the final situation to be 'a farce that younger men must finish'. As if to underline the musical analogies Shaw has one of his characters, Bill Boanerges, burst briefly into song towards the end of Act I, and the same character leads the cabinet in a short-lived rendition of 'For he's a jolly good fellow' in Act II. A constitutional crisis arising from the clash between the king and his cabinet, the king's relations with his exotic mistress and plain

wife, and the American Ambassador's proposal for the amalgam-
ation of the British Empire with the United States provide the
slender – too slender for some tastes – narrative props upon which
the debates of the play are mounted.

The major crisis of the play develops from the fact that
Magnus, an intelligent, polite constitutional monarch, with a
finely developed sense of irony, refuses to accept the role of being
a mere indiarubber stamp. Magnus's outspoken comments to the
press about the importance of the king's veto as a 'defence of the
people against corrupt legislation' bring him into conflict with a
fractious, unruly cabinet, tenuously commanded by the Prime
Minister, Proteus, whose cunning shifts of position in the interests
of political expediency recall the behaviour of his namesake in
classical legend. Out of the clashes between king and cabinet
there emerges a picture of democracy in total disarray. Far from
being a representative form of government, democracy is seen in
the play to be in the grip of organizations such as the
multinational Pentland Forth Syndicate, devoted to exploitation
of power resources in Scotland, and Breakages Ltd, a large
monopolistic industry committed to planned obsolescence.
England's economy rests on exports (headed by chocolate
creams) for which the overseas markets are entirely unstable.
Politics, the king declares in a long, magisterial speech, has lost
all its dignity as a profession:

> Our work is no longer even respected. . . . Politics, once the
> centre of attraction for ability, public spirit, and ambition, has
> now become the refuge of a few fanciers of public speaking and
> party intrigue who find all the other avenues to distinction
> closed to them.

The overture, a conversation between the king's secretaries,
subtly provides the opening notes of the play's concerns. In
discussion of Sempronius's father two significant thematic motifs
are sounded. His father is described by Sempronius as having
been a 'Die Hard Ritualist'. By profession, he was an organizer of
public pageants, of coronations, military tattoos and the like,
which, Sempronius perceives, represented for his father a form of
stable reality. In essence the pageants are meaningless shows; but
their description in Act I provides an image of one kind of social

cohesiveness and order against which the chaos of democracy is later to be measured.

The discussion of Sempronius's father also occasions some reflections on solitude. Pamphilius declaims the lines from Byron's *Childe Harold* in praise of solitary communion with nature, beginning

> To sit on rocks; to muse o'er flood and fell;
> To slowly trace the forest's shady scene
> Where things that own not man's dominion dwell.

This provides, at the beginning of the play, another image which contrasts with the raucous disorder of democracy. The temptations to be private, to turn one's back, like Shakespeare's Henry VI, on the turbulent world of politics and to find consolation in nature, is a theme introduced early in the play, to be taken up in a different key in the Interlude. But Sempronius's father, we learn, died of solitude. Sempronius's musing on the subject of his father's terror of solitude serves as a reminder of man's essentially social nature and, by implication, of his fundamental need to create some kind of social order. Byron's 'flock that never needs a fold' is not man. Later in the play, the king describes political science as 'the science by which civilization must live or die'.

The Interlude is a stormy meeting between the king and his beautiful but demanding mistress, Orinthia, in her bedroom in the palace. The scene (founded, Shaw says, on an actual encounter between himself and Stella Campbell) ends hilariously with the two rolling locked in combat on the floor as a result of Magnus's attempts to extricate himself from Orinthia's embraces in order to go and deal with the cabinet crisis. The scene is sometimes described as extraneous and F. P. W. McDowell's explanation that Orinthia is a parallel figure to the father of Sempronius, as a person deficient in spiritual reserves, is not satisfactory.[20] In depicting the quarrel between Orinthia and the king, Shaw was returning to a major theme of *Heartbreak House*. The Interlude is a further exploration of the problem of the dissociation of cultivated, intelligent people from the realities of political power. It is that concern which constitutes the major link between the Interlude and the rest of the play. The quarrel in the Interlude picks up and develops Magnus's Act I complaint about the decline of politics as a profession. The principal cause of the quarrel is Orinthia's discontent with Magnus's interest in and concern for the grey world of politics, instead of devoting himself to the 'higher' life of beauty and love: 'Why do you surround yourself with political bores and frumps and dowdy busybodies who can talk?'

Like Hesione in *Heartbreak House*, Orinthia prefers the enjoyment of a private world of refinement and romance to vulgar concern with the ship of state. Female politicians such as Amanda and Lysistrata are classed by her as 'creatures whose idea of romance is a minister in love with a department, and whose bedside books are blue books'. Thus the Interlude presents the play's concern with political life and responsibility in a new light. Magnus is as keenly aware as Orinthia of the bores and frumps of politics, but the crucial difference between them lies in their attitudes, respectively, of commitment and dissociation. Orinthia, without winning the argument, pushes it to a fine point in the speech in which she asks Magnus: 'Has all the tedious public work you have done made you any the better?' But eventually the demands of this witty Pilgrim of Love must give way to those of dull *Respublica*.

When *The Apple Cart* was first performed, it seemed to many people to represent a complete volte-face in Shaw's political attitude. Shaw himself was aware that the play could be misinterpreted as an argument in favour of autocratic government. In the page proofs of the edition published in 1930, he took pains to remove this impression by adding to one of Magnus's speeches the lines:

> Do not misunderstand me: I do not want the old governing class back. It governed so selfishly that the people would have perished if democracy had not swept it out of politics. But evil as it was in many ways it stood above the tyranny of popular ignorance and popular poverty. Today only the King stands above that tyranny.[21]

This is perhaps insufficient to cancel the impression that Shaw, in one part of his mind at least, was attracted towards the idea of intelligent and far-sighted autocracy as one possible road out of the morass of democracy. But Magnus does not argue in the play for his own appointment as dictator, and it is clear that his principal role in the play's political argument is that of critic of democracy rather than advocate of absolute or even limited monarchy. Light is thrown on Shaw's intentions in the creation of Magnus by a letter to his German translator, Siegfried Trebitsch, in which he describes the play as 'a warning to those who are still dreaming the old dream and listening to the old speeches':

> When King Magnus says that democracy [has] destroyed responsible government and given the political leadership to neither king nor minister as such, but to the strong men and the adroit humbugs, without giving them any real power over the organized might of private capital, sensible Germans will ask themselves whether this is happening or not instead of wasting time discussing whether I have changed my mind or not.[22]

III

Written at the time when England was moving towards the worst period of the Great Depression, *On the Rocks* reflects contemporary politics in what is fundamentally a much grimmer mood than *The Apple Cart*. The opening speeches of the later play refer to streets becoming impassable with crowds of the unemployed and reports of violence in the streets. A new urgency is given to the political debates of this play by the strong, recurrent images of social anarchy and of violent confrontation on the brink of large-scale conflict. The milder image of an apple cart upturned has given way to one (already foreshadowed in *Heartbreak House*) of shipwreck. The play remains what its subtitle declares it to be: 'A Political Comedy' but the realities of social disorder are brought into focus in peculiarly graphic ways in this play.

On the Rocks begins in Shaw's most extravagant satirical vein. The Prime Minister (initially a 'walking anachronism' of the kind that Shaw describes most Prime Ministers to be in *Everybody's Political What's What*[23]), Sir Arthur Chavender, is on the verge of mental collapse. Following an unsatisfactory interview with his Chief of Police, the mildly mannered Sir Broadfoot Basham, about the violence in the streets, he sets to work dictating a speech on the Family as the Foundation of Civilization and the Empire. Having repeatedly lost the thread of his thoughts on this speech, he is interrupted by members of his own family in the throes of a violent quarrel. Left alone after an interview with a deputation from the Isle of Cats, the Prime Minister is finally visited by a mysterious lady in grey robes, who describes herself as 'a ghost from the future'. The lady turns out to be the proprietor of a retreat, equipped with meditation parlours, in the Welsh mountains. She diagnoses Chavender's complaint as 'an acute want of mental exercise . . . a bad case of frivolity, possibly incurable'. Sir Arthur accepts the lady's invitation, and departs, taking with him all the works of a writer he describes in his unenlightened state as 'a revolutionary German Jew named Harry Marks'. He returns, and immediately puts into practice an alarming and far-reaching programme of 'boiling socialism' which rapidly comes to grief through the implacable opposition from opponents on all sides of the political spectrum.

Even in a synoptic account of the play it is possible to see signs that Shaw's pessimism is not absolute. But at the end of the play the faint notes of hope in Sir Arthur Chavender's speeches are virtually annihilated by the relentless 'live documentary' of what is actually happening in the streets outside his windows:

HILDA: The unemployed have broken into Downing Street; and theyre breaking the windows of the Colonial Office. . . . cant the police let them run away without breaking their heads? Oh look: that policeman has just clubbed a quite old man.

SIR ARTHUR: Come away: it's not a nice sight. [*He draws her away, placing himself between her and the window*].

HILDA: It's all right when you only read about it in the papers; but when you actually see it you want to throw stones at the police.

Defiant singing through the tumult.

LADY
CHAVENDER: [*looking out*] Some one has opened the side gate and let them through into the Horse Guards Parade. They are trying to sing.

SIR ARTHUR: What are they singing? The Red Flag?

LADY CHAVENDER:	No. I dont know the tune. I caught the first two words. "England, arise".
HILDA:	[*suddenly hysterical*] Oh, my God! I will go out and join them [*she rushes out through the main door*].
LADY CHAVENDER:	Hilda! Hilda!
SIR ARTHUR:	Never mind, dear: the police all know her: she'll come to no harm. She'll be back for tea. But what she felt just now other girls and boys may feel tomorrow. And just suppose – !
LADY CHAVENDER:	What?
SIR ARTHUR:	Suppose England really did arise! *Unemployed England, however, can do nothing but continue to sing, as best it can to a percussion accompaniment of baton thwacks, Edward Carpenter's verses.*

England, arise! the long, long night is over,
Faint in the east behold the dawn appear;
Out of your evil dream of toil and sorrow –
Arise, O England, for the day is here;
From your fields and hills, Hark! the answer swells –
Arise, O England, for the day is here!

The word 'arise', in the closing scene of *On the Rocks*, is charged with threatening, ironic ambiguity, as to whether England will arise to the dawn of a new dispensation, or in violent revolution.

The most strident critic of democracy in *On the Rocks* is the old revolutionary Socialist, Hipney. Hipney might have been referring to a later phase of democracy, across the Atlantic, when he refers in the play to contemporary politicians as 'windbags and movie stars and soldiers and rich swankers and lawyers on the make'. Through Hipney, Shaw offers a sharp glimpse of the dangerously narrow gulf which separates revolutionary socialism from Fascism. The word 'dictator' holds out no fears for Hipney because, as he explains, he and his confrères of the working class have been used to being dictated to all their lives by 'swine that have nothing but a snout for money'. The 'answer' of dictatorship is present as an imminent possibility in the spectrum of thematic motifs in *On the Rocks*. Five years and several plays later, Shaw returned to this theme in *Geneva*.

IV

A reviewer of the first English production of *Geneva*, at Malvern in 1938, described the play correctly as 'untidy, garrulous and ingenious', but added, with equal truth, that its eccentricities are 'still the eccentricities of genius'.[24] *Geneva* is most memorable for its daring last act, in which figures representing the major European dictators of the 1930s obligingly agree to present themselves for trial at an international Court of Justice at the Hague. In the rambling narrative which leads up to this scene, Begonia Brown, a pert cockney secretary of the International Committee for Intellectual Co-operation, has brought about a European crisis by referring to the Court a number of accusations addressed to the Committee by various aggrieved parties.

The trial at the Hague presents a panoramic view of the conflicting ideologies of Europe in the 1930s. Hitler and Mussolini appear in the guise of Ernest Battler and Signor Bombardone (dressed respectively in the first production as Lohengrin and Julius Caesar). Battler and Bombardone are later joined by their Spanish counterpart, General Flanco de Fortinbras. Others included in this assembly are a British Foreign Secretary, Sir Orpheus Midlander (modelled on the elder Chamberlain[25]); a Jew; a Creole widow bent on the revengeful settlement of a blood feud; an English Deaconess, calling on all to follow the Master; and Begonia Brown, now a Dame of the British Empire and Conservative MP for Camberwell.

Like Milton's Satan, the dictators are defiant, resolute and impressively articulate. Bombardone – the suggestions in the name of bombardment and bombast are both appropriate – speaks with powerful rhetoric about the failings of Liberalism and Democracy, and delivers nonsensical opinions about the necessity of war, in crushingly authoritarian tones. The sinister flaw in Bombardone's arguments is brought out in the resounding pun on the word 'execution' in his exchange with an anonymous Newcomer:

B. B. D. E.: Out of the Liberal democratic chaos comes form, purpose, order and rapid execution.

NEWCOMER: Yes, the executions come along all right. We know what dictators are.

B. B. D. E.: Yes: the triflers and twaddlers are swept away.

Battler, in a rival display of rhetoric to Bombardone's, sees himself as part of a 'mighty movement in the history of the world' in which the legacies of Roman law and Hebraistic religion will be discarded. Flanco, for his part, candidly declares himself to stand for 'government by gentlemen against government by cads'.

Striking an apocalyptic note which is heard more than once in the late plays, Shaw brings the trial to a close by the device of a false report from Greenwich of the imminent approach of a new Ice Age. This threat has the effect of a trick of perspective. The clash of ideologies is diminished in significance, and the towering figures of the dictators are reduced to absurdity. Battler breaks down in sobs at the thought of his 'little doggie', Blonda, being frozen to death. Bombardone promises that his people will die in an orderly, stoical fashion and remain 'to all eternity in cold storage'. Flanco dashes off to organize a mass absolution for the people of Spain. But before this reduction to absurdity occurs, a more serious judgement of the assembled company at the Hague has been delivered by the presiding Dutch Judge. Nowhere in the late plays are echoes of Swift more clearly heard than in the Judge's elaboration of his view that the 'black depth of scoundrelism' which the behaviour of the company confronts him with, calls for their immediate execution:

Your objective is domination: your weapons fire and poison, starvation and ruin, extermination by every means known to science. You have reduced one another to such a condition of terror that no atrocity makes you recoil and say that you will die rather than commit it. You call this patriotism, courage, glory. There are a thousand good things to be done in your countries. They remain undone for hundreds of years; but the fire and the poison are always up to date. If this be not scoundrelism what is scoundrelism? I give you up as hopeless. Man is a failure as a political animal. The creative forces which produce him must produce something better.

Obviously we cannot make a simple equation between the pronouncements of the Judge here and Shaw's own outlook. What the Judge says in this speech is tempered by his final speech in the play when he corrects the Secretary's view that the trial was a 'farce',[26] and by other features of the play, such as the fact that one leader who escapes relatively unscathed from the trial is the Russian Commissar. But it is difficult to avoid the impression that the Judge's summing up in the speech just quoted carries a large measure of authorial endorsement. The Judge's speech in *Geneva* reveals a vein of pessimism which can be traced back in Shaw's writings at least as far as 'The Revolutionist's Handbook' in *Man and Superman* (1903). In the section of 'The Revolutionist's Handbook' entitled 'Progress an Illusion' Shaw gave vent to thoughts which are very closely echoed in the Judge's speech in *Geneva*. In the present state of human evolution, Shaw maintained in the earlier work, the 'ifs and ans' of reformers, progressives and meliorists never become 'pots and pans':

> Whilst Man remains what he is, there can be no progress beyond the point already attained and fallen headlong from at every attempt at civilization; and since even that point is but a pinnacle to which a few people cling in giddy terror above an abyss of squalor, mere progress should no longer charm.[27]

There is clearly a very strong connection between Shaw's sense of the failure of politics and his thinking on the subject of evolution. In sum, he says that if man is a failure as a political animal he must, if he is to survive, evolve into a different kind of animal: that strain of thought becomes particularly strong in the late plays.

Closely associated with the same complex of ideas in the late writings is Shaw's increasing interest in non-European races and cultural traditions. His spiritual journeys eastward in the later period of his career, and his playful experimentation with ideas for marriages, of various sorts, between Western and Eastern cultures, are the main subjects of the next chapter.

NOTES

1. In a letter to *The Times* of 31 Aug. 1950 (p. 5, col. 5) Shaw made a retrospective comment on Lenin's remark, as follows:

Lenin, recognized as a great statesman by me and Mr. Churchill when everyone else was denouncing him as a bloodthirsty bandit, began by kindly excusing me as 'a good man fallen among Fabians'. When he had to govern and administer instead of theorizing, experience soon brought him to his senses; and he proclaimed his New Economic Policy, the first instalment of Russian Fabianism.

2. *Everybody's Political What's What* (London: Constable, 1944) p. 1.
3. Shaw produced a revised and expanded edition of this work, taking account of developments in Russia and the rise of Fascism. The full title of the revised work is *The Intelligent Woman's Guide to Socialism, Capitalism, Sovietism and Fascism*, 2 vols (London: Penguin, 1937). All references in this chapter are to the Constable Standard Edition (1949).
4. Ibid., p. 1.
5. See, for example, *The Intelligent Woman's Guide*, p. 492, and cf.: 'Capitalism is not an orgy of human villainy: it is a Utopia that has dazzled and misled very amiable and public spirited men, from Turgot and Adam Smith to Cobden and Bright. The upholders of Capitalism are dreamers and visionaries who, instead of doing good with evil intentions like Mephistopheles, do evil with the best intentions' (*Everybody's Political What's What*, p. 2).
6. *The Intelligent Woman's Guide*, pp. 313–14.
7. Ibid., p. 214.
8. Ibid., p. 97.
9. Martin Meisel, 'Shaw and Revolution: the Politics of the Plays', in Norman Rosenblood (ed.), *Shaw: Seven Critical Essays* (University of Toronto Press, 1971) pp. 106–34.
10. Ibid., p. 132.
11. *The Intelligent Woman's Guide*, p. 377. Shaw's position should not be identified with that of his character Undershaft, an apostle of force who says that 'the ballot paper that really governs is the paper that has a bullet wrapped up in it'.
12. Ibid., p. 379.
13. 'When democratic Socialism has achieved sufficiency of means, equality of opportunity, and national intermarriageability for everybody, with production kept in its natural order from necessities to luxuries, and the courts of justice unbiased by mercenary barristers, its work will be done' (*Everybody's Political What's What*, p. 57).
14. Ibid., p. 56.
15. Ibid., p. 57.
16. In his essay on 'Drama' in C. B. Cox and A. E. Dyson (eds), *The Twentieth-Century Mind*, vol. II: *1918–1945* (Oxford University Press, 1972) p. 421.
17. *Everybody's Political What's What*, p. 1.
18. Ibid.
19. Shaw employs this term for the opening scene in a letter to Siegfried Trebitsch. He describes the opening as:

> my little overture for Sempronius, which at once establishes the tone of the palace as refined and quiet, and gives the utmost relief and effect to

the violent intrusion of Boanerges. (Shaw to Trebitsch, 23 Apr. 1930, Albert A. Berg Collection, New York Public Library)

20. F. P. W. McDowell, ' "The Eternal against the Expedient": Structure and Theme in Shaw's *The Apple Cart*', *Modern Drama*, vol. II, no. 2 (Sep. 1959) pp. 99–113.
21. The page proofs of the play showing this addition are held in the Humanities Research Centre, University of Texas at Austin.
22. Shaw to Trebitsch, 29 Nov. 1929, Albert A. Berg Collection, New York Public Library.
23. *Everybody's Political What's What*, p. 3.
24. *Evening News*, London (2 Aug. 1938). An interesting collection of 1938 reviews of the play is included amongst the Archibald Henderson papers in the Library of the University of North Carolina, Chapel Hill.
25. 'The play is a lampoon with Hitler and Mussolini unmistakably on the stage, and a thinly disguised Austen Chamberlain as the British Foreign Secretary' (Shaw to H. K. Ayliff, 10 May 1938, Burgunder Collection, Cornell University Library, New York).
26. Shaw may have been recalling here, and modifying, the judgement of the king at the end of *The Apple Cart*.
27. *Collected Plays*, vol. II, pp. 764–5.

15 Journeys Eastward

I, too, have found in the east a quality of religion which is lacking
in these islands.
(Shaw to Sir Francis Younghusband, 1934)[1]

One of the most distinctive features of the later writings of Shaw is
the interest they show in non-European races and cultures. The
action of the later plays frequently involves a journey away from
England to exotic settings in localities which include the Middle
East, the Pacific, and, finally, the place where the twain of East
and West do meet, Panama. Negroes, Chinese, Indians and
island natives perform major roles in the plays' narrative and
thematic developments. In the final act of Shaw's last full-length
play, *Buoyant Billions: A Comedy of No Manners* (1947), the journey
comes full cycle, and the drawing room of English comedy
undergoes a radical transformation. The setting for Act III of
Buoyant Billions is '*a drawing room in Belgrave Square, London,
converted into a Chinese temple on a domestic scale*'.

The coloured characters in Shaw's later works are usually
physically beautiful, and endowed with qualities of dignity and
grace which are generally in strong contrast with the qualities of
the white characters. Assumptions about the superiority of white
races and of Western standards of civilization are continually
undermined in the late plays. The behaviour of Sir Jafna
Pandranath, the elderly Sinhalese plutocrat in *On the Rocks* is an
exception to the usually unruffled bearing of the coloured people
in the late plays. But Sir Jafna's parting speech in Act II is one of
the most eloquent and impassioned denunciations of Western
pretensions and prejudices in all of Shaw's works:

[*finding his tongue*] I am despised. I am called nigger by this
dirty faced barbarian whose forefathers were naked savages

worshipping acorns and mistletoe in the woods whilst my
people were spreading the highest enlightenment yet reached
by the human race from the temples of Brahma the thousand-
fold who is all the gods in one. This primitive savage dares to
accuse me of imitating him: me, with the blood in my veins of
conquerors who have swept through continents vaster than a
million dogholes like this island of yours. They founded a
civilization compared to which your little kingdom is no better
than a concentration camp. What you have of religion came
from the east; yet no Hindu, no Parsee, no Jain, would stoop to
its crudities. Is there a mirror here? Look at your faces and look
at the faces of my people in Ceylon, the cradle of the human
race. There you see Man as he came from the hand of God,
who has left on every feature the unmistakeable stamp of the
great original creative artist. There you see Woman with eyes
in her head that mirror the universe instead of little peepholes
filled with faded pebbles. Set those features, those eyes, those
burning colors beside the miserable smudged lumps of half
baked dough, the cheap commercial copies of a far away
gallery of masterpieces that you call western humanity, and
tell me, if you dare, that you are the original and I the
imitation.

Sir Jafna's speech is from a play about the failure of the English to
govern themselves properly. In the England of 2170 AD which is
projected in Part III of *Back to Methuselah*, government has at last
been taken out of the hands of the incompetent English, and
successfully entrusted to educated negresses and Chinese.

Marriage between white and coloured people recurs as a
thematic motif, with varying significances, in the late works.
Captain Shotover, in *Heartbreak House*, initiates this theme with
his announcement that he has 'a wife somewhere in Jamaica: a
black one'.[2] In the prose tale, *The Adventures of the Black Girl in her
Search for God* (1932), the nubile heroine, 'a fine creature, whose
satin skin and shining muscles made the white missionary folk
seem like ashen ghosts by contrast',[3] reaches the end of her
unsuccessful search for God in a garden owned by an old
gentleman (who is clearly Voltaire). There she meets and marries
a redhaired Irish socialist, who, in John Farleigh's authorized
engraving, closely resembles Shaw, and who believes God to be

'an eternal but as yet unfulfilled purpose'. The black girl and the Irishman settle down in tranquil and fruitful domesticity, raising coffee-coloured children and tending their garden, and finding their divinity in the here and now. In *The Millionairess* (1936) the formidable and compulsive capitalist, Epifania, seizes as her marriage partner a gentle, un-grasping Muhammadan doctor from India. Her successor Clemmy, in *Buoyant Billions*, migrates to Panama, where she lives in a state of primitive simplicity, charming serpents and alligators with her saxophone playing, and becoming one of the 'hundred earthly brides' of the local god, Hoochlipoochli.

Running through the farcical comedy of these late fantasies and fables of Shaw is a strong sense of disgust at Western arrogance and white assumptions of superiority. 'Pink trash' is the phrase used for whites by the lordly Native in *Buoyant Billions*. The coloured personages, often priestly in character, fulfil a function like that of the rural characters in pastoral literature. They provide moral and spiritual norms against which the decadence of 'civilized' white society is measured. The plays do not espouse any particular Eastern religious doctrines. But characters such as Pra and Prola in *The Simpleton of the Unexpected Isles*, the Doctor in *The Millionairess*, the Native and the Chinese Priest in *Buoyant Billions*, share qualities of spiritual authority and integrity which are in marked contrast with the generally irreligious or pseudo-religious character of the whites.

The most complex of all Shaw's Eastern fables is *The Simpleton of the Unexpected Isles*. 'G.B.S.'s Queer New Play on Judgement Day'[4] was the heading of one of the several puzzled newspaper reviews of the opening performance at Malvern in 1935. In this bizarre (but fundamentally coherent and meaningful) satirical and allegorical fantasy, Shaw presents his most extensive treatment in the plays of the theme of racial intermarriage. But here that theme is intricately interwoven with a strongly critical treatment of Western, and especially British, imperialism, and capped with the arrival of an angel announcing a selective Day of Judgement.

Recalling the opening of *Too True to be Good* (1932), *The Simpleton* begins with a series of metaphors of the spiritual bankruptcy and decadence of the West. Act 1 of *Too True to be Good* is set in an expensively furnished bedroom in a suburban villa in one of the richest cities of England. A young woman, of *'unhealthy complexion'* and suffering from measles, is asleep in the bed. The action is presided over by a monster microbe of disease. From a scene of fever and ennui, the Patient embarks with a party of burglars and others on a journey of adventure to a place somewhere in the Middle East, where the characters set about the task of revitalizing their existence. *The Simpleton* is set on a tropical island belonging to the British Empire in the Pacific. The play begins with a Prologue, comprising three brief sketches of events on the island twenty years before the commencement of the main action. The first sketch, in a harbourside office, introduces an Emigration Officer, *'an unsatisfactory young man of unhealthy habits'*, his clerk, Wilks, dressed in *'a shabby dark lounge suit'*, and a young woman. The two men are in a state of degradation and despair; and Wilks, after a rambling speech in which he describes himself as a failed Empire builder, takes a swig of brandy, sings 'Rule Britannia' and shoots himself dead. In the second sketch, the Emigration officer also attempts suicide, but this attempt is foiled by a handsome young native Priest of Life, Pra, who practises a trick on the would-be suicide like that employed by Edgar with his father, Gloucester, in *King Lear*. The Emigration Officer suffers only a dousing in the sea, and returns to the stage in the third sketch dressed in a white robe and *'regenerated'*.

Apart from presenting a rapid, impressionistic survey of Western degeneracy and the seamier sides of British imperialism, the main function of the Prologue is to assemble six characters – Pra and his equally handsome female counterpart, Prola, and four whites – who become engaged in a 'eugenic experiment'. The object of the experiment (the word carries its usual critical edge in Shaw) is to 'try out the result of a biological blend of the flesh and spirit of the west with the flesh and spirit of the east'. The Prologue might seem to contain a forecast of success. But a complicating feature of the work as a whole is that the redemptive possibilities which are suggested by the rescue of the Western Emigration Officer by the Eastern Priest are in some ways contradicted by the development of the main action.

At the beginning of Act I, the Simpleton, an intellectually feeble, but endearingly honest and friendly, English clergyman named Iddy Hammingtap arrives on the island. His account of his kidnapping from the Church at Weston-super-Mare by a gang of men he describes as 'crooks, racketeers, smugglers, pirates, anything that paid them', is not, as it might seem at first glance, mere whimsy. In the context of the play's account of imperialism, the identity of the entrepreneurs of Iddy's naively told story is clear, and the audience is able to supply its own perspective on the clergyman's role in their schemes. Shaw creates a fine moment of comic Sophoclean irony when Iddy reports his kidnappers' cry at the time of his capture: ' "You look so innocent and respectable" they said. "Just what we want!" ' As the soft front of the pirates' activities, Iddy has been taken all over the world, 'where I couldn't speak the language and couldn't explain'. Eventually the pirates tire of their sport of making Iddy preach sermons so as to make themselves ill with laughter, and they put him ashore on the island.

The eugenic experiment on the island results in the creation of four beautiful but brainless children, two girls, Maya and Vashti, and two boys, Janga and Kanchin. The allegorical significance of these characters is not fully revealed until very near the end of the play. When Iddy first meets them, the girls are alluringly amorous and the boys threatening and admonitory. This meeting is probably intended to suggest the first stages of colonialism. Iddy falls desperately in love with Maya; but it is explained to him that, on the island, being in love with only one woman is not permitted. At the end of Act I, his conscience overcome, Iddy succumbs to the advances of the two girls, in a scene which, with its hypnotic verbal patterning, resembles an erotic rite:

VASHTI: And Maya? You love Maya. You would die a million times for Maya?
IDDY: Yes, yes, I would die for either, for both: for one, for the other—
MAYA: For Vashti Maya?
IDDY: For Vashti Maya, for Maya Vashti.
VASHTI: Your lives and ours are one life.
MAYA: [*sitting down beside him*] And this is the Kingdom of love.
          The three embrace with interlaced arms and vanish in black darkness.

In the second of the play's two acts, the four children

mysteriously disappear, like the beautiful child of the eponymous hero and Helen in Goethe's *Faust*. It is only after their disappearance that Iddy utters the true names of the children, as Love, Pride, Heroism and Empire. They thus become finally identified as the abstract, moribund ideals upon which the power-hungry, acquisitive expansion of the West is based. Western imperialism is implicitly likened to a Faustian quest for power, ending in empty, ephemeral abstractions. As they approach their judgement, the four children become an increasingly sinister presence in the play. The 'Antiphonal Quartet', as Iddy calls them, produces a chanting fantasia of senseless obeisance (of masochistic dimensions: 'Oh, what ecstasy to be beaten by Prola!') and jingoistic aggression:[5]

> JANGA: For our flag and for our Empress.
> VASHTI: For our country, right or wrong.
> MAYA: Let there be sex appeal. Let the women make the men brave.
> KANCHIN: We must defend our homes.
> JANGA: Our women.
> VASHTI: Our native soil.
> MAYA: It is sweet to die for one's country.
> VASHTI: It is glorious to outface death.
> ALL FOUR: Yes. Death! death! Glory! glory!

The failure of the scheme of founding 'a millennial world culture' is seen in the play as, in part, a reflection of the inadequacy of love as a unifying force and a human ideal. 'Nothing is lovelier than love, up to a point', says Iddy in one of his speeches in Act II. But, like music, he argues, it can pall in excess. His love for the children of the island eventually produces not reciprocal love, but contempt and hatred on their part, and a desire to be rid of him. It is this situation which prompts Iddy's thoughtful plan for a sermon on the subject of eternity and love:

> You couldnt go on playing the harp for ever; and if you sang "Worthy is the Lamb" for ever you would drive the Lamb mad. The notion is that you cant have too much of a good thing; but you can; you can bear hardship much longer than you could bear heaven. Love is like music. Music is very nice:

the organist says that when the wickedness of mankind tempts him to despair he comforts himself by remembering that the human race produced Mozart; but a woman who plays the piano all day is a curse. A woman who makes love to you all day is much worse.

This critical view of love is recalled in *Geneva*, when the international assembly, asked by the Judge whether they are prepared to love one another, responds with a resounding 'No!', and the British Foreign Secretary chimes in with 'Not indiscriminately'.

The major theatrical sensation of Act II is the arrival, by air, of the Angel of Judgement. The angel's arrival initiates a vast expansion of the range of the play's satirical reference. The Judgement he has come to announce is to be not a single, apocalyptic event, the end of the world, but a selective process in which 'the useless people, the mischievous people, the selfish somebodies and the noisy nobodies' are to be dissolved. After the Angel's departure, reports come in from all over the world of mysterious disappearances. Sir Ruthless Bonehead, Egregious Professor of Mechanistic Biology to the Rockefeller Foundation, disappears as he opens his mouth to address a large audience on the subject 'Whither have they gone?' Happy husbands and fathers vanish together with the soup from the family dinner. Over a million people disappear 'in the act of reading novels'.

Near the end of *The Simpleton*, the spirit of Voltaire makes a fleeting appearance, in Sir Charles Hyering's remark that 'gardening is the only unquestionably useful job'.[6] But the final words and actions are given to the Eastern characters, Pra and Prola. The concluding affirmations of the play involve a rejection of millennial dreams and Utopian schemes, and of security, routine and system. 'Plans are only jigsaw puzzles' Prola declares, and 'We are not here to fulfil prophecies and fit ourselves into puzzles, but to wrestle with life as it comes.' It is to the miracle of life itself, to its infinite prospects of change, surprise and wonder that Pra and Prola dedicate themselves. Unexpectedness, from being the principle of the play's artistic design, finally becomes its thematic core. The ritualistic close of Act II echoes, but contrasts with, the end of Act I:

PRA: All hail, then, the life to come!
PROLA: All hail. Let it come.[7]
         They pat hands, eastern fashion.

One reviewer of the 1935 production of *The Simpleton* expressed the view that the play signalled a significant change in Shaw's outlook. This writer began his account of the play with the comments that

> The common difficulty experienced by Shavians in keeping up with Mr Shaw has been traced to the combination of a life-long positiveness and finality of assertion with a life-long capacity for growth and change of mind . . . he continues to change his mind and now attaches more importance to the faculties of surprise and wonder than to the intellectual virtues of the omniscient Ancients of the Metabiological Pentateuch.[8]

Certainly the emphases in *The Simpleton* are very different from those of *Back to Methuselah*, with its concluding vision, expressed by Lilith, of 'the vortex freed from matter . . . the whirlpool in pure intelligence' as the final goal of evolution. But in essence the final speeches of Pra and Prola refer us back to familiar Shavian themes. The waiter addressing Valentine at the end of *You Never Can Tell*, the heroine reporting the unlikely Cambridge motto 'The ice of life is slippery' in *Fanny's First Play*, Lina Szczepanowska stirring the other characters out of middle-class inertia in *Misalliance*, the characters embracing danger and the threat of disaster at the end of *Heartbreak House*, are all, in different ways, Shavian forerunners of Pra and Prola. What is new about *The Simpleton* is that the principal custodians of the Life Force are dwellers not in the West but in the East.

NOTES

1. Burgunder Collection, Cornell University Library, New York. Shaw's interest in Eastern religions would have been fostered in friendships such as those with Annie Besant and Florence Farr, the actress and theatre manager, with whom he associated in the 1890s, and who later became headmistress of a Hindu School in Ceylon. Shaw was not greatly impressed by Florence's book, *Egyptian Magic*, describing it as 'exoteric Egyptology'

(*Bernard Shaw: Collected Letters 1874–1897*, ed. Dan H. Laurence (London: Max Reinhardt, 1965) p. 674), but his correspondence with her after her move to Ceylon reveals his keen interest in her accounts of Hindu religious beliefs and practices (see British Library, MS Add. 50535). Shaw's wife, Charlotte, also had a deep and knowledgeable interest in the East. The Shaw library at Ayot St Lawrence contains numerous books on Eastern religion, including such works as Charles Johnston (trans.), *The Great Upanishads*, Nur ud-din Jami, *Lawa ih: A Treatise of Sufism*, S. Vivekananda, *Jnana Yoga*, and Swami Sivanandra, *Brahma Sutra*.

2. For an account of the way in which this is related to the images and themes of *Heartbreak House*, see above (pp. 183–4).

3. *The Black Girl in Search of God and Some Lesser Tales* (London: Constable, 1934) p. 22. (The title of *The Black Girl* tale was altered, as shown, in the 1934 Standard Edition.)

4. *Daily Mirror*, London, 30 July 1935.

5. Shaw's reflections in this play on English colonial countries as places of beautiful inanity and mindless reverence for authority recall D. H. Lawrence's portrayal of Australia, a decade earlier in *Kangaroo*.

6. Other echoes of *Candide* in *The Simpleton* are noted by Margery M. Morgan, *The Shavian Playground: An Exploration of the Art of George Bernard Shaw* (London: Methuen, 1972) pp. 288–90, 295–6.

7. The closing words of the play pick up the refrain of the Young Woman in the Prologue, 'Let life come'.

8. *The Times*, London, 30 July 1935.

16 Epilogue: Shaw and Suffering

> Sympathy with pain there will always be. It is one of the first instincts of man. . . . But it must be remembered that while sympathy with joy intensifies the sum of joy in the world, sympathy with pain does not really diminish the amount of pain.
>
> (Wilde, *The Soul of Man under Socialism*)

Discussing Shaw in an essay on modern drama, Walter Stein wrote:

> Whatever the ultimate verdict on Shaw as a focal consciousness of human dilemmas should be, we only need to recall such works as *Arms and the Man, You Never Can Tell, The Devil's Disciple, Captain Brassbound's Conversion, Pygmalion, Too True to be Good, Village Wooing*, and, supremely perhaps, *Man and Superman*, to acknowledge a comic creativeness that will always enrich men with sheer, celebratory high spirits – a subtly renewed capacity for 'these childish games – this dancing, and singing and mating'.[1]

The latter part of this statement is certainly high, and surely deserved, praise. But for Stein, as for other commentators, a major question about Shaw's claim to be regarded as 'a focal consciousness of human dilemmas' arises in connection with the treatment in his plays of human suffering. Referring to the play in which the question is perhaps most sharply raised, *Heartbreak House*, Stein remarks that 'the essential point' was made by Desmond MacCarthy when he said, in reviewing a 1921 production of the play, that 'Mr Shaw does not know what heartbreak is'.[2]

To approach Shaw's work (as do both the critics just mentioned) in search of Chekhovian qualities of compassion for individual suffering is a quest that is, in general, likely to result in disappointment. But Shaw's aim was not to outdo Chekhov in that field of mastery.[3] *Heartbreak House* is a play which, whilst borrowing (as we have seen in an earlier chapter of this study) some Chekhovian techniques,[4] offers a perspective on the theme of private heartbreak which is quite different from that found in Chekhov's major plays. In Shaw's play, heartbreak is presented – the theme is defined in several speeches by Ellie Dunn–not as a 'maiming misery',[5] but as a state from which new growth and wisdom develop. In what is admittedly a rather severe (but not heartless) vision, Shaw identifies the experience of heartbreak as part of that absorption in private worlds of 'romance and sentiment' which contributes to the larger cultural malaise which is explored in *Heartbreak House*. Shaw's treatment of suffering in the play has its own profundity, interest and firmness of grasp.

The character of Shaw's attitude to suffering is partly attributable to his reaction to the conventions of the Victorian theatre. 'Scenes of suffering nobly endured and sacrifice willingly rendered', to borrow the words of the Victorian theatre critic in *The Philanderer*, are not generally the stock-in-trade of Shavian drama.[6] In Shaw's plays, suffering is usually treated either with zestful dispatch (as in the cases of Spintho in *Androcles and the Lion* and Wilks in *The Simpleton of the Unexpected Isles*) or as a state from which the characters concerned emerge, as does the Emigration Officer in *The Simpleton*, 'regenerated'. A model of the way in which the comic spirit overrules the tragic in Shaw is provided in the scene of the death of the artist, Dubedat, in *The Doctor's Dilemma*, where the largely solemn mood of the opening disintegrates under the influence of the congenitally erroneous Newspaper Man (who finds '*voluptuousness in languor and drama in death*') and is finally converted into an exquisite blend of comedy and pathos in Bloomfield Bonington's well-meant, but hopelessly confused, recitation of famous lines from Shakespeare's tragedies and *The Tempest*. The comic resolution of the scene as a whole is made complete by Jennifer Dubedat's splendid reappearance, not in a conventional costume of mourning, but '*wonderfully and beautifully dressed, and radiant, carrying a great piece of purple silk, handsomely embroidered, over her arm*'.

Shaw's treatment of the theme of suffering in the plays reflects an outlook which, whilst not being shallowly optimistic, remained remarkably and tenaciously affirmative. Shaw was not unsympathetic in his attitude to the sufferings of his fellow beings; and he spent the greater part of his adult life in combat with forces in human society which he saw as contributing to the sum of suffering. Few, if any, writers of the twentieth-century could be claimed to have waged such a wide-ranging, courageous and subtle attack on the enemies in society of what Ellie Dunn calls 'life with a blessing', as does Shaw in his plays and other writings.[7] But Shaw refused to be led, by his own insights, into a fatalistic acceptance of human vice and folly. The Shavian forms of comedy and tragi-comedy celebrate life, and the recurring miracle of its self-renewal. In the vision of life which is expressed in his plays, things that are funny belong to the essence of truth, and extended commiseration with sorrow is out of place. Shaw provides a memorable defence of that stand in his reply to Leo Tolstoy's criticism of the comedy in *Man and Superman*:

> You said that my manner in that book was not serious enough – that I made people laugh in my most earnest moments. But why should laughter and humour be excommunicated? Suppose the world were only one of God's jokes, would you work any the less to make it a good joke instead of a bad one?[8]

NOTES

1. Walter Stein, 'Drama', in C. B. Cox and A. E. Dyson (eds), *The Twentieth-Century Mind*, vol. II: *1918–1945* (Oxford University Press, 1972) p. 424.
2. This remark was made in the first of two largely favourable reviews by MacCarthy of productions of *Heartbreak House*. See Desmond MacCarthy, *Shaw* (London: MacGibbon & Kee, 1952) p. 144.
3. Such an assumption is revealed, for example, in Stein's remark that 'Lady [*sic*] Hushaby [*sic*] . . . is perhaps the only truly Chekhovian re-creation within Shaw's play' (Walter Stein, 'Drama', p. 420).
4. See above, pp. 179–80.
5. MacCarthy's phrase (*Shaw*, p. 144).
6. There are exceptions to this generalization, in *The Devil's Disciple, The Doctor's Dilemma* and *Saint Joan*.
7. Cf. W. B. Yeats's comments on Shaw: 'He could hit my enemies and the enemies of all I loved, as I could never hit, as no living author that was dear to me could ever hit' (*Autobiographies* (London: Macmillan, 1955) p. 283).
8. *Bernard Shaw: Collected Letters 1898–1910*, ed. Dan H. Laurence (London: Max Reinhardt, 1972) p. 902.

Index

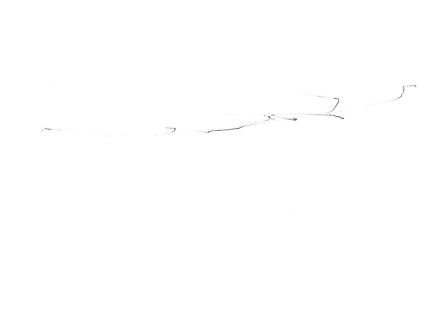